教育部基础学科拔尖学生培养计划 2.0 项目(20212060)
山东省高等教育本科教学改革研究重点项目(Z2022113)
拔尖创新人才英语系列教材

中华文化传播(下)

Introducing Traditional Chinese Culture

丛书主编　周小兰
主　　编　孙路平　周小兰
副 主 编　左　宁　李　红　陈登峰
编　　者　薛冠琳　董艳灵　赵　鹏
　　　　　李钧秀　曹文润

山东大学出版社
SHANDONG UNIVERSITY PRESS
·济南·

图书在版编目(CIP)数据

中华文化传播. 下:汉文、英文 / 孙路平，周小兰主编. —济南:山东大学出版社,2023.7

ISBN 978-7-5607-7849-5

Ⅰ. ①中… Ⅱ. ①孙… ②周… Ⅲ. ①中华文化—文化传播—汉、英 Ⅳ. ①G125

中国国家版本馆 CIP 数据核字(2023)第 087984 号

责任编辑 孙艳凤
封面设计 牛 钧

中华文化传播(下)
ZHONGHUA WENHUA CHUANBO(XIA)

出版发行 山东大学出版社
社 址 山东省济南市山大南路 20 号
邮政编码 250100
发行热线 (0531)88363008
经 销 新华书店
印 刷 济南乾丰云印刷科技有限公司
规 格 787 毫米×1092 毫米 1/16
12.25 印张 270 千字
版 次 2023 年 7 月第 1 版
印 次 2023 年 7 月第 1 次印刷
定 价 48.00 元

Contents

Unit 1 Traditional Chinese Medicine

Part A Herbal Medicine

A1. Introduction

Chinese Herbalism

The use of plants for healing purposes predates recorded history and forms the origin of much of modern medicine. Many conventional drugs originate from plant sources: a century ago, most of the few effective drugs were plant-based. Examples include aspirin (from willow bark), digoxin (from foxglove), quinine (from cinchona bark), and morphine (from the opium poppy). The development of drugs from plants continues, with drug companies engaged in large-scale pharmacologic screening of herbs.

What is Chinese herbalism?

Chinese herbalism is one of the most prevalent of the ancient herbal traditions currently practiced. It is based on concepts of yin and yang and of qi energy. Chinese herbs are ascribed qualities such as "cooling" (yin) or "stimulating" (yang) and are often used in combination, according to the deficiencies or excesses of these qualities in the patient. "The biggest difference between Western and traditional Chinese herbalism is that herbalists don't treat symptoms or diseases. They treat entire human beings, including their patterns of symptoms," says Galina Roofener, certified and licensed Chinese herbalist located in L.A. Chinese herbal medicine has thousands of years of data to back it up. "Throughout history, Chinese emperors worked to preserve and multiply the knowledge of the previous ages. That means today we have almost 2,000 years of clearly written records about how herbs and herb combinations work in different people."

Differences from conventional drug use

Although superficially similar, herbal medicine and conventional pharmacotherapy have important differences.

- **Use of whole plants**: Practitioners of herbal medicine generally use unpurified plant extracts containing several different constituents. Typically, they claim that these can work together synergistically so that the effect of the whole herb is greater than the total of the effects of its components. They also claim that toxicity is reduced when whole herbs are used instead of isolated active ingredients ("buffering"). Although two samples of a particular herbal drug may contain constituent compounds in different proportions, practitioners claim that this does not generally cause clinical problems. Some experiments have yielded evidence of synergy and buffering in certain whole plant preparations, but how far this is generalizable to all herbal products is unknown.
- **Herb combining**: Several different herbs are often used together. Practitioners say that the principles of synergy and buffering apply to combinations of plants and claim that combining herbs improves efficacy and reduces adverse effects. Herb combining contrasts with conventional practice, in which polypharmacy is generally avoided whenever possible.
- **Diagnosis**: Herbal practitioners use diagnostic principles that differ from those used by conventional practitioners. For example, when treating arthritis, herbal practitioners might observe "the under-functioning of a patient's systems of elimination" and decide that the arthritis results from "an accumulation of metabolic waste products". A diuretic, choleretic, or laxative combination of herbs might then be prescribed alongside herbs with anti-inflammatory properties.

The formulations in Traditional Chinese Medicine (TCM)

Medicinal herbs are typically dispensed to patients in one of five forms:

- **Chinese Herbal Decoctions**: These tea-like mixtures often have a strong taste and smell and involve lengthy preparation times, making them less popular to use among Western practitioners of TCM.
- **Herbal Powders**: When mixed with water to brew a tea, these herbal formulations typically have a less intense taste and smell than decoctions, making them a more popular option in the west.
- **Chinese Patent Formulas**: These popular and frequently-used formulations come in the form of a pill or tablet.

- **Syrups**: Perfect for soothing coughs and sore throats, herbs that come in the form of a syrup also make a great option for getting children to take TCM.
- **Liniments, Salves, Compresses, and Plasters**: Practitioners prescribe herbs that need to be applied externally to the skin in any of these types of formulations.

What happens during a treatment?

Herbal practitioners take extensive case histories and perform a physical examination. While patients describe their medical history and current symptoms, practitioners pay particular attention to the state of everyday processes such as appetite, digestion, urination, defecation, and sleep. They then prescribe individualized combinations of herbs, usually taken as tinctures (alcoholic extracts) or teas. Syrups, pills, capsules, ointments, and compresses may also be used. Oral preparations often have an unpleasant taste and odor.

In addition to the herbal prescription, practitioners may work with their clients to improve diet and other lifestyle factors, such as exercise and emotional issues. Follow-up appointments occur after 2 to 4 weeks. Progress is reviewed and changes are made to the choice of drugs, doses, or regimen as necessary.

(Adapted from *ncbi.nlm.nih.gov*, *amcollege.edu*, and *clevelandclinic.org*.)

A2. Words and Expressions

Vocabulary

1. trigram / ˈtraɪɡræm / *n*. 卦;三元
2. antagonistic / ænˌtæɡəˈnɪstɪk / *adj*. 敌对的
3. herbology / hɜːbˈɒlədʒɪ / *n*. 草药学
4. property / ˈprɒpəti / *n*. 属性;特性
5. compendium / kəmˈpendiəm / *n*. (尤指书中某题材事实、图画及照片的)汇编
6. materia medica / məˈtɪərɪə ˈmedɪkə / *n*. 药物学;药物学论著

中草药的历史	**History of the Chinese Herbal Medicine**
八卦图	Bagua / eight trigrams
医学、哲学和占星学思想的基础	the basis of medical, philosophical, and astrological thinking

阴阳	yin and yang
相辅相成而非对立统一	complementary rather than antagonistic
使这两个特性恢复平衡	bring the two qualities back into balance
《神农百草经》	*Divine Husbandman's Classic of Materia Medica*
中医之父	Father of Chinese Medicine
对 365 种草药或药用植物进行分类	classify 365 species of herbs or medicinal plants
草药学的研究基础	the basis of herbology
疗效或毒性	curative or poisonous qualities
《黄帝内经》	*Yellow Emperor's Classic of Internal Medicine*
本草学	herbology
中药学	Chinese materia medica
针灸九针的发明	invention of the nine needles for acupuncture
中华民族的瑰宝	the treasure of the Chinese nation
深厚而博大的知识体系	a deep and immense knowledge system
世界传统医学的重要组成部分	an important part of traditional medicine in the world
《本草纲目》	*Great Compendium of Materia Medica*
最完整和全面的医学书籍之一	one of the most complete and comprehensive medical books
中药材的守护神	patron saint of Chinese herbal medicine
大百科全书式的汇编	encyclopedic compendium
获得全球认可	receive global recognition
被列入联合国教科文组织的《世界记忆名录》	be included in UNESCO's *Memory of the World Register*

Vocabulary

1. microcosm / ˈmaɪkrəʊˌkɒz(ə)m / *n*. 缩影;微观世界
2. meridian / məˈrɪdiən / *n*. 子午线;经线
3. pathology / pəˈθɑːlədʒi / *n*. 病理学;变态
4. pectoral / ˈpekt(ə)rəl / *adj*. 胸部的;胸的
5. metabolism / məˈtæbəˌlɪz(ə)m / *n*. 新陈代谢
6. physiological / ˌfɪziəˈlɒdʒɪk(ə)l / *adj*. 生理学(上)的

中医的基本理论	Basic Concepts of TCM
人类是周围大宇宙的缩影。	Humans are microcosms of the larger surrounding universe.
与大自然相互联系	be interconnected with nature
天人合一	integration of heaven and man
与外部环境相适应	be in tune with the external environment
与自然和谐相处	live in harmony with nature
适应自然规律	adapt to the natural laws
适应变化	adapt to the change
携带能量	carry energy
阴阳平衡	yin-yang balance
阴代表宇宙中黑暗的方面。	Yin represents the aspects of the universe that are dark.
阳代表光明的方面。	Yang embodies the principles of light.
相互依赖	mutually dependent
动态和不断变化	dynamic and constant changing
提供一个病理学的模型	provide a model of pathology
在一个健康的身体中保持平衡	be balanced in a healthy body
五行	wu xing / five phases
木、火、土、金、水	wood, fire, earth, metal, and water
对关系和互动的描述	descriptions of relationships and interactions
表现为两个不同但相关的互动周期	manifest in two distinct but related interaction cycles
相生周期	the creation cycles
木生火。	Wood feeds fire.
火生土。	Fire creates earth.
土生金。	Earth births metal.
金生水。	Metal cradles water.
水生木。	Water feeds wood.
相克周期	the destruction cycles
木克土。	Wood penetrates earth.
土克水。	Earth channels water.
水克火。	Water quenches fire.
火克金。	Fire melts metal.
金克木。	Metal cuts wood.
五行对应着身体中的五个基本系统。	The fire phases equate to five fundamental systems in the body.
木阴为肝;木阳为胆。	Wood yin is the liver; wood yang is gall bladder.

火阴为心;火阳为胃。	Fire yin is the heart; fire yang is the stomach.
金阴为肺,金阳为大肠。	Metal yin is the lung; metal yang is the large intestine.
水阴为肾;水阳为膀胱。	Water yin is the kidney; water yang is the bladder.
气	qi / vital force of life
沿着身体的经络流动	flow along meridians in your body
元气	inborn qi / parental qi
受孕时从父母那里继承的	inherited from parents at conception
宗气	pectoral qi
通过呼吸产生	be produced by breathing
储存在胸部区域	be stored in the chest area
营气	nutritive qi
来自食物	derived from eating food
负责整个身体的营养循环	be responsible for the circulation of nutrition throughout your body
卫气	protective qi
负责保护身体不被疾病侵袭	be responsible for protecting the body from illness
免疫健康	immune health
推神	actuation
保持生命的活力	maintain the vital life energy
温煦	warming
温暖和滋养组织	warm and nourish the tissue
调节体温以实现正常功能	regulate body temperature for normal functions to occur
防御	defending
增强对外部因素的抵抗力	build up resistance against external elements
固摄	containment
中医方法的奥妙	the mystery of TCM methods
医生的直觉和感受	doctors' intuition and sense
医生的悟性	the perception of doctors
可以意会,难于言传	perceivable but inexpressible
类比思维	analogical thinking
心为君子之官。	The heart is a monarch-like organ.
脾为仓廪之官。	The spleen is a granary-like organ.
肝为将军之官。	The liver is a general-like organ.
胆为中正之官。	The gallbladder is a judge-like organ.

Vocabulary

1. immunity / ɪˈmjuːnəti / *n.* 免疫力
2. dysfunction / dɪsˈfʌŋkʃ(ə)n / *n.*(身体)功能障碍
3. primordial / praɪˈmɔːrdiəl / *adj.* 原生的;原始的
4. replenish / rɪˈplenɪʃ / *v.* 补充;重新装满
5. pathogens / ˈpæθədʒənz / *n.* 病原体

中医的益处	**Benefits of TCM**
全面整体的医学健康解决方案	comprehensive holistic medicine solution to wellness
解决健康问题的根本原因	address the underlying root cause of health concern
预防疾病的发生,治未病	prevent illness before its occurrence
防止疾病的出现或发展	keep disorders from appearing or progressing
刺激或调整身体的能量振动	stimulate or adjust the body's energy vibration
更新最佳的健康状况	renew optimal well-being
尽量减少压力和焦虑	minimize stress and anxiety
促进皮肤的年轻化	promote youthful-looking skin
增强健康的气	strengthen the healthy qi
补元气	cultivate the primordial qi
活血化瘀,温通经络	activate blood and warm up the meridians
增强身体对疾病的抵抗力	strengthen the body's resistance to diseases
提高能量和免疫力	boost one's energy and immunity
激活身体的自然自愈能力	activate the natural self-healing ability of the body
重新平衡内在系统	rebalance the inner system
纠正某些器官的功能紊乱	correct dysfunction of certain organs
改善重要器官的健康	improve vital organ health
产生疗效	create a healing effect
减轻症状	alleviate symptoms
增强内在的正气	strengthen the inner upright energy
清肝火	clear liver fire
温补肾脏	warm up the kidney
补气养血	replenish blood and qi
补精益肾	replenish essence and invigorate the kidney
延长寿命	prolong life expectancy

Vocabulary

1. diagnostic / ˌdaɪəɡˈnɒstɪk / *adj*. 诊断的;判断的
2. therapeutic / ˌθerəˈpjuːtɪk / *adj*. 治疗的;医疗的
3. moxibustion / ˌmɒksɪˈbʌstʃən / *n*. 艾灸
4. ceramic / səˈræmɪk / *adj*. 陶器的;制陶的
5. sulphur / ˈsʌlfə(r) / *n*. 硫;硫磺

中医的诊断与治疗	**Diagnosis and Treatment of TCM**
四种诊断方法	four diagnostic methods
望闻问切	inspection, listening and smelling, inquiring and palpation
舌诊	tongue diagnosis
检查舌头的形状、大小和结构	examination of the shape, size, and texture of the tongue
舌苔厚	thick coating
反映是否有湿气	reflect the presence of dampness
脉诊	pulse diagnosis
伸腕	stretch out wrist
放在一个长方形的小米垫子上	lay them on a small oblong rice cushion
用三个手指为病人把脉	use three fingers to take the patient's pulse
针灸	acupuncture
草药疗法	herbal remedy
拔罐	cupping
治疗性按摩	therapeutic massage
艾灸	moxibustion
刮痧	Guasha
食物疗法	food therapy
草药配方	herbal formula
由植物部分制成的有效成分	active ingredients made from plant parts
谨慎使用	use with care and respect
引起意想不到的副作用	trigger unexpected side effect
草药煎剂	herbal decoction
陶瓷容器	ceramic container
化学性质稳定	chemically stable
热量可以均匀地传递。	Heat can be transmitted evenly.

冲洗中草药	rinse the Chinese herbal medicine
流动的水	running water
去除杂质	remove impurity
二氧化硫的残留物	sulphur dioxide residue
滤出煎药	strain the decoction

A3. Speaking Activities

Situational Speech

A program of Traditional Chinese Medicine is designed to provide a deep and thorough understanding of Chinese herbs and formulas, and explain how to apply them to people's physical well-being. You are invited to deliver a **5-minute speech**, introducing TCM and **herbal medicine** to participants. Your speech might cover:

- History of the Chinese Herbal Medicine
- Health benefits of herbal medicine
- Differences between herbal medicine and conventional pharmacotherapy

You may refer to the words and expressions in Part A, but don't confine yourself to them.

Role Play

Anna feels sick recently and she is going to see you, a Traditional Chinese Medicine practitioner. As her doctor, you are supposed to answer her questions. Her questions might include:

- What is Chinese herbalism?
- What should she pay attention to before taking herbal medicine?
- Does herbal medicine have side-effect?
- Others

You may refer to the words and expressions in Part A, but don't confine yourself to them.

Brainstorming

China unveiled a plan to promote the culture of TCM among the public. The plan, jointly issued by five authorities, aims to explain the connotations of TCM culture in modernized, popular, and innovative ways. Among the steps scheduled from 2021 to 2025 are building TCM experience centers, promoting knowledge of health contained in TCM culture, and developing TCM culture products using new technology. **What do you**

think of these steps to promote TCM culture? As a college student, do you have any suggestions for the plan? Please elaborate on your views.

(Adapted from *xinhuanet.com*)

Reading and Sharing

Read the following paragraphs about **Traditional Chinese Medicine in the treatment of COVID-19** and share your views.

Paragraph 1

"TCM is a treasure of China and the whole world as well, and its efficacy has been well proven in the prevention and control of COVID-19," Tang Bei, an international relations researcher at Shanghai International Studies University, said at a seminar on medicine and international relations held in Shanghai on Friday. TCM has been extensively used in COVID-19 prevention and control in China. More than 90 percent of all patients in Hubei province, the hardest hit area by the epidemic in China, received TCM, either independently or in conjunction with modern medicine, and more than 90 percent of them saw their condition improve, according to official data.

(Adapted from *english.scio.gov.cn*)

Paragraph 2

WHO published a report prepared by its Expert Meeting on the evaluation of Traditional Chinese Medicine in the treatment of COVID-19. This report acknowledges the safety and efficacy of the TCM against the coronavirus and encourages the WHO member states to integrate TCM research in their respective planning and implementation of COVID-19 vaccines. It reflects the Chinese potential to develop quick and innovative means to respond to global calamities with its advancement in the field of medicine.

(Adapted from *thediplomaticinsight.com*)

Ideas for Sharing:

- Have you ever had an experience of visiting a TCM practitioner?
- What do you think of the efficacy of TCM in the treatment of diseases?

Interpretation

Interpret the paragraphs below into English with the words and expressions you learned in Part A.

Paragraph 1

有些中药配方已经使用超过2200年，这些成分是被挑选组合而成的，他们通过相互结合的方式发挥着作用。在西医中，药物通常是为特定效果而单独开出的。在经典的中医草药配方中，每种草药都有不同的目的或作用，以帮助身体达到和谐。一种植物要被纳入中国的药房，其每个部分都必须被确定具有明确的治疗目的。中医也以同样的方式看待食物的治疗特性。不同的食物带有不同的能量，可以直接进入特定的器官以帮助它们愈合。

Paragraph 2

中医的一个重要方面是了解人体的“气”(生命力，字面意思是“生命的气息”)，它流经人体无形的经络(通道)。这个能量网络连接着器官、组织、静脉、神经、细胞、原子和意识本身。一般来说，有12条主要经络，每条经络都连接着中医理论中的12个主要器官之一。经络还与各种现象有关，包括昼夜节律、季节和行星运动，以形成额外的隐形网络。

Paragraph 3

在古代，医生用“医者意也”四个字概括了他们是如何广泛运用类比思维的——医学理论的神秘性、治疗方法的灵活性、医生的悟性，都只能以一个“意”字来体现。换言之，中医的魅力就蕴含于“可以意会，难于言传”的韵味当中。近代学者梁启超曾说：“中国任何领域的学问都带有一种‘可以意会不可以言传’的神秘性，而这一神秘性显然是知识扩大的障碍。”而其所举之例，即是中医。的确，较之于任何一种其他古代中国的科技，如天文、数学，中医都更具中国传统文化的特征。

A4. Culture Highlights

Q: *Herbal medicine aims to return the body to a state of natural balance so that it can heal itself. Different herbs act on different systems of the body. Are there any commonly used herbs?*

A: Some herbs that arc commonly used in herbal medicine, and their traditional uses, include:

Echinacea — to stimulate the immune system and aid the body in fighting infection. It was used to treat ailments such as boils, fever and herpes.

Dong quai (dang gui) — used for gynecological complaints such as premenstrual tension, menopause symptoms and period pain. Some studies indicate that dong quai can lower blood pressure.

Garlic — used to reduce the risk of heart disease by lowering levels of blood fats and cholesterol (a type of blood fat). The antibiotic and antiviral properties of garlic mean that it is also used to fight colds, sinusitis and other respiratory infections.

Ginger — many studies have shown ginger to be useful in treating nausea, including motion sickness and morning sickness.

Ginkgo biloba — commonly used to treat poor blood circulation and tinnitus (ringing in the ears).

Ginseng — generally used to treat fatigue, for example during recovery from illness. It is also used to reduce blood pressure and cholesterol levels; however overuse of ginseng has been associated with raised blood pressure.

Hypericum perforatum — commonly known as St John's Wort. Studies have suggested that St John's Wort is just as effective as some pharmaceutical antidepressants in treating mild to moderate depression. It is also used for anxiety and insomnia. However, St John's Wort can interact with a number of prescription medications, including the oral contraceptive pill, and stop them from working properly.

(Adapted from *betterhealth.vic.gov.au*)

Q: *Can herbal medicine interact with other medications?*

A: Herbal medications and supplements may interact in harmful ways with over-the-counter or prescription medicines you are taking.

Taking herbal supplements may increase or decrease the effectiveness of other drugs you are taking or may increase the risk of negative side effects. For example, St John's Wort mostly decreases the effectiveness of other medicines but increases the effects of antidepressants.

If you are considering taking herbal medicines, it is always a good idea to talk to your doctor about possible side effects and interactions with other medications you are taking.

(Adapted from *betterhealth.vic.gov.au*)

Q: *Yin-yang and wuxing have played a significant role in Chinese civilization; as a twentieth-century Chinese scholar puts it, they are "the law of Chinese thinking." What is wuxing? Why is it important in Chinese civilization?*

A: The Chinese term wuxing (wu-hsing, "five processes" or "five phases") refers to a fivefold conceptual scheme that is found throughout traditional Chinese thought. These five phases are wood (mu), fire (huo), earth (tu), metal (jin), and water (shui); they are regarded as dynamic, interdependent modes or aspects of the universe's ongoing existence and development. Although this fivefold scheme resembles ancient Greek discourse about the four elements, these Chinese "phases" are seen as ever-changing material forces, while the Greek elements typically are regarded as unchanging building blocks of matter. Prior to the Han dynasty, wuxing functioned less as a school of thought and more as a way of describing natural processes hidden from ordinary view. During the period of the Han dynasty (202 BCE-220 CE), wuxing thought became a distinct philosophical tradition (jia, "family" or "school"). Since that time, the wuxing system has been applied to the explanation of natural phenomena and extended to the description of aesthetic principles, historical events, political structures, and social norms, among other things. Cosmology, morality, and medicine remain the chief arenas of wuxing thought, but virtually every aspect of Chinese life has been touched by it. As such, wuxing has come to be inseparable from Chinese itself and belongs to no single stream of classical Chinese philosophy.

(Adapted from *iep.utm.edu*)

A5. Extensive Reading

Passage One

Traditional Chinese Medicine Theories

Five concepts or theories are fundamental to an understanding of traditional Chinese medicine. The theories covered here are as follows: Yin and yang, Five Phases, Meridians, Zang / Fu Organs, and External Pathogens.

In Western medicine, specific systems and organs of the body are diagrammed and analyzed in isolation: the circulatory system, the immune system, the liver, etc. In Chinese medicine a basic cosmology or theory of the universe is formed, and mankind is examined and explained as an integral part of this vast system. Yin / yang theory and Five Phase theory are ways of understanding the laws of nature and interrelationships within nature. Meridian and Zang / Fu theories explain human physiology and functionality. Pathogenesis, diagnosis, and treatment theories explain how and why imbalances develop within us and how to go about restoring balance.

Yin and yang. The universe is equally divided between yin and yang. Yin is a philosophical construct representing the aspects of the universe that are dark, receptive, etc. Yang embodies the principles of light, action, etc. Everything that exists in nature can be classified as yin or yang, and is generally a mixed balance of yin and yang. These two "opposites" are mutually dependent, interdependent, and always in a relative balance with each other. The relationship between yin and yang is essentially dynamic, and constantly changing. Yin may change into yang, and vice versa under certain conditions. In traditional Chinese medicine, the theory of yin / yang provides a model of pathology. Yin and yang are balanced in a healthy body. An excess or deficiency of either yin or yang will lead to illness or disease.

Five Phases. This is also called the Five Element theory, because in Western thought the five entities involved (Wood, Fire, Earth, Metal, Water) are considered to be "elements" of nature. However, this label does not convey the idea of action, motion, transformation, and cyclical change that are implied in the Chinese word "xing". As with yin and yang, all things in nature can be classified as one of the Five Phases, or a blending of them: they are the essential constituents of the material universe. Also as with yin and yang, the Five Phases are mutually interdependent, and always in a relative and dynamic balance with each other.

In Traditional Chinese Medicine, the Five Phases are used for explaining the properties of the internal organs (viscera, Zang / Fu) of the human body, including their mutual relations, physiological phenomena, and pathological changes. Five Phase theory is also used as a guide for making diagnosis and treatment.

Meridians. Currently, Western science does not recognize the existence of discrete "energy vessels" in the body that are analogous to blood vessels; but to the Chinese the meridians that carry qi are actual anatomical structures that can be palpated and treated. The function of meridians is to transport qi and Blood, connect the internal organs, and provide pathways between the inside and outside of the body. The meridian system consists of twelve principal meridians which correspond to the five yin and five yang organs, plus the Pericardium (yin) and Triple Burner (yang). So, there is a meridian for the Heart, Lungs, Liver, Spleen, and Kidneys (Zang), and for their paired organs, the Small Intestine, Large Intestine, Gall Bladder, Stomach, and Urinary Bladder (Fu). There are also eight "extraordinary" meridians, a system of tendino-muscular meridians close to the surface of the skin, a system of "divergent" meridians, and "luo" channels that connect paired yin and yang meridians.

Through the meridians, every part of the body is connected to the whole: the internal organs communicate between themselves and have access to the surface of the body; the skin, muscles, and extremities have networks of secondary meridians that circulate energy on the surface and also tap into deeper levels. Each principal meridian is associated with a group of symptoms that appear when the meridian is not functioning properly. For example, cough, dyspnea, asthma, sore throat, and a feeling of fullness in the chest are associated with Lung meridian dysfunction.

Zang / Fu Organs. The internal organs of the body (viscera) are counted as twelve in number, and each is assigned one of the twelve principal meridians. There are six yin and six yang organs, and they are paired into six yin / yang partnerships. Of the twelve viscera, the five Zang, or yin, organs, Heart, Liver, Spleen, Lung, Kidney, are generally considered to be the most significant in terms of pathology, diagnosis, and treatment. In addition to being in a yin / yang relationship with its paired Fu organ, each Zang organ is also assigned to one of the Five Phases. Even though the names of these Zang are the same as the Western names, their functions are markedly different from the Western paradigm, and they can more accurately be considered as "energetic manifestations" rather than as masses of tissue. The functions of the heart are to regulate the circulation of Blood; house the Shen (e.g., regulate mental and emotional activities), and direct speech. The face and the tongue reflect the state of the Heart. The Liver is responsible for storing Blood and causing it to flow smoothly, regulating the smooth flow of emotions, regulating the smooth flow of all Fundamental Substances, controlling the joints and tendons, and regulating digestion. The eyes and the fingernails reflect the state of the Liver. The Spleen transports nutrients for the body, "transforms" food so it will be readily absorbed into cells, assists in making Blood, assists with fluid metabolism, and controls muscles and the four limbs. The Lungs regulate qi in the body (especially Defensive qi), regulate fluid metabolism, regulate and disseminate Air qi in the body, assist the Heart in creating and regulating Blood, and regulate the voice. The skin and body hair reflect the state of the Lungs. The Kidneys store Jing (genetic constitution) and control birth, development, and maturation. They also guide water metabolism and excretion, rule the bones and produce marrow, nourish the brain, and assist the Lungs with the breathing process. The ears, bones (including teeth) and head hair reflect the state of the kidneys.

External Pathogens. The external factors which lead to disease originate in nature. They invade the body via the skin, mouth, and nose. The leading external pathogens include Wind, Cold, Heat, Dampness, and Dryness.

Wind. Wind attacks the yang aspects of the body, namely the upper limbs, torso, head, and the skin. Wind produces a sudden onset of symptoms such as edema and skin irritation with itching. Wind-caused diseases are often accompanied by abnormal movements such as dizziness, tremors, and convulsions.

Cold. Cold damages the yang qi of the body. The nature of yang is to be warm, active, and expansive. When it is damaged by climatic cold, there may be cold, stagnation, and contraction in the body leading to sharp pains, muscular contractions, spasms and limb rigidity. If Spleen yang is damaged, for example, it leads to abdominal coldness and pain.

Heat. Heat is a yang pathogenic factor. Heat causes the depletion of Body Fluids and manifests with such symptoms as dry mouth, scanty urine and constipation. When Heat moves upward, it causes symptoms such as headache, ringing in the ears (tinnitus), and a swollen throat. Heat can damage the Blood and cause it to move "recklessly", leading to nosebleeds, blood in the urine, and excessive menses. Heat can interfere with mental activity and cause anxiety or even coma.

Dampness. Dampness impairs yang qi. If Spleen yang is impaired, it can lead to diarrhea, scanty urine and edema. Dampness-related problems such as edema, gummy eyes, sticky loose stools, and eczema are characterized by heaviness and turbidity. Accumulation of Dampness produces excess phlegm which can lead to many problems — not just profuse sputum production, but also gallstones, strokes, and mental illness in extreme circumstances.

Dryness. Dryness is a yang pathogenic factor. Dryness-related conditions deplete Body Fluids. Dryness especially attacks the Lungs and the Kidneys. Constipation, scanty urine, lusterless hair and dry skin are characteristic symptoms of Body Fluid depletion.

It is the balance and harmony of these various factors that promote health and well-being. If yin and yang are in balance; if the generation and control cycles of the Five Phases are in harmony; if the meridians and Zang / Fu are functioning freely and delivering sufficient qi and Blood to every part of the body, then we are healthy. When these systems become imbalanced through climatic assault, emotional imbalance, improper diet, excessive sexual activity, overwork, etc., our Fundamental Substances are damaged and we fall ill.

(Adapted from *modernherbshop.com*)

Passage Two

Top 10 Traditional Chinese Medicine Herbs List

Chinese herbology, along with treatment techniques like acupuncture, is one of the most important tenets of the ancient wellness practice known as Traditional Chinese Medicine. This holistic tradition, and others from around the world, tap into the power of plants to heal and invigorate the human body.

Here you'll find our most trusted list of 10 all-natural herbs commonly used in Traditional Chinese Medicine to boost overall health and wellness. Each has a unique story and delivers its own remarkable benefits, known for millennia and more recently explored by modern science.

Ren Shen (Red Ginseng Root)

Red Ginseng is a leafy plant, native to Asia, whose root has long been known in Traditional Chinese Medicine as a powerful adaptogen — that's a natural substance that helps the body adapt to stress — with a multitude of health benefits. Research has shown that ginseng can help improve the body's ability to process alcohol. Other interesting studies have demonstrated ginseng's potential as a "beauty food," with a covetable ability to help boost levels of collagen in the skin, reducing the visible effects of aging like wrinkles and discoloration, or dark spots.

Dang Shen (Codonopsis Root)

Codonopsis root, though less well-known in the West than ginseng, is one of the most commonly used herbs in the practice of Traditional Chinese Medicine. It promotes whole-body health by supporting digestion and overall energy levels. It is used to improve vitality and a general feeling of brightness and well-being. One of the many reasons it is so widely used, in addition to the many ailments it treats, is its mildness and gentle effectiveness.

Huang Qi (Astragalus Root)

Astragalus is another Asian root that remains largely unfamiliar to Western consumers, but has been used successfully for thousands of years in herbal treatments developed by Traditional Chinese Medicine. This herb in particular is known as an excellent immune system booster. Chemical compounds found in astragalus, studies have shown, can work to alleviate oxidative stress on the body while decreasing inflammation and regulating the immune response at a cellular level. Astragalus root is thought to work at its highest potential when taken preventatively, and regularly, by those who are in overall good health.

Bai Shao (White Peony Root)

You may already know the peony plant for its colorful petals, especially popular as garden-grown beauties and wedding decor, but the peony's root is where its medicinal properties and health benefits can be found. In Traditional Chinese Medicine, peony root is often used to aid blood circulation, increase energy, and balance mood. In particular, this herb has historically been used to help with anxiety and depression by inhibiting the reuptake of serotonin (one of the nervous system's neurotransmitters, or "happy hormones") in the brain. Improved focus and mental stability are both expected outcomes of a regular regimen of peony root supplementation.

Suan Zao Ren (Jujube Seed)

The jujube fruit, also known as a red date or Chinese date, is a small fruit with a pit at the center. Its seeds have been used medicinally for at least 3,000 years as a remedy for insomnia, and modern studies confirm that this herb works as a natural sedative, helping you to feel like resting when your mind, body, or both can't seem to slow down on their own. This fruit, modern science now understands, is rich in compounds called saponins, which have a soothing effect on the nervous system, which regulates the body's ability to relax (and ultimately drift into slumber).

Wu Wei Zi (Schisandra Berry)

Also known as the "five-flavor fruit" because its berries are said to contain an entire spectrum of salty, sweet, sour, spicy, and bitter tastes, this Asian plant is widely respected in Traditional Chinese Medicine. Schisandra is part of a family of herbs called adaptogens, which help the body to adapt to stressors and ultimately weather life's physical and emotional challenges. It's been used for millennia to fight the symptoms of stress and fatigue, and newer research suggests that schisandra berry may improve endurance in particular by preventing a buildup of acid in the lungs. With the power to ease breathing in this way, schisandra berry may help you exercise longer and even feel physically calmer in the face of anxiety or panic.

Jin Yin Hua (Honeysuckle Flower)

Honeysuckle is a beautifully vibrant flowering plant, growing widely across East Asia. It also has a delightfully warm, sweet scent that's sometimes used in relaxing aromatherapy treatments (or even pleasantly scented cleaning products). But in Traditional Chinese Medicine, its most coveted characteristic is its ability to support the immune system with anti-inflammatory, antibacterial and antiviral effects. It's understood to help the body fight off certain ailments, like fevers, sore throats, and even skin rashes.

Bai Zhu (Atractylodes Root)

The root of the atractylodes plant, which is part of the sunflower family that grows abundantly in the southeastern part of China, has a long history as one of the most important herbs in Traditional Chinese Medicine. With many medical uses, it's especially well known for its ability to support metabolism and improve the function of the digestive tract. Atractylodes root is an invigorating herb that supports overall mood and well-being by targeting the flow of qi, TCM's concept of essential energy.

Bai Zhi (Fragrant Angelica Root)

This herb is one with quite a range of powers, and as such, has long been used in Chinese herbal medicine — as well as traditional European, particularly Russian, medicine — to tackle multiple symptoms at the same time. To many TCM practitioners, fragrant angelica root's core use is working to open up the nasal passages. This in turn helps alleviate the discomfort of congestion, cold symptoms, and headaches. In addition, many patients find that fragrant angelica root reduces related tension in the head, neck, and shoulders, along with all over body aches. Interestingly, fragrant angelica root is known to have a synergistic effect with another traditional Chinese herb called corydalis.

He Huan Pi (Mimosa Tree Bark)

With a nickname like "happy bark," it shouldn't come as a surprise that this particular Chinese herb works wonders for mood. The mimosa tree, also called the Chinese silk tree or pink silk tree for its delicate, wispy flower petals. For thousands of years, holistic practitioners have known that mimosa tree bark helps with feelings of overwhelm and restlessness. We now know that the herb does this by regulating the body's hypothalamic-pituitary-adrenal axis, which is the nervous system's central hub of stress response. Mimosa tree bark is thought to help the nervous system balance the way it taps into both sympathetic and parasympathetic functions, which control active, danger-response reactions and restful, return-to-calm processes, respectively.

"Although there are several studies that prove the safety and effectiveness of Chinese herbal medicine," notes certified and licensed Chinese herbalist Galina Roofener, LAc. "But just because it's natural does not mean it's problem-free. Treat Chinese herbs like a prescription — first get an evaluation from a qualified practitioner before taking anything." She discusses what you should know before taking Chinese herbs.

(Adapted from *wthn.com*)

A6. Assignment

Poster Design

Form **groups of 3 or 4 and design an English poster for Traditional Chinese Medicine (TCM)**. You need to cover:

- The history of TCM
- The diagnostic principles of TCM
- The benefits of TCM

Part B Acupuncture

B1. Introduction

Acupuncture

Contrary to popular Western belief, acupuncture is not just a system for inserting very fine needles into specific body locations to alleviate pain. Acupuncture is a complete medical protocol focused on correcting imbalances of energy in the body. From its inception in China more than 2,500 years ago, acupuncture has been used traditionally to prevent, diagnose, and treat disease, as well as to improve general health.

The traditional explanation for acupuncture's effectiveness is that it modifies the flow of energy (known as qi or chi) throughout the body, but there is no scientific consensus that this is actually its mechanism of action. Research published in the May 30, 2010 online edition of Nature Neuroscience demonstrated that the effects of acupuncture needling include influencing the activity of adenosine, an amino acid which becomes active in the skin after an injury to ease pain. This may explain in part why pain relief is often experienced as one of the benefits of acupuncture. In fact, much research in the West has focused on this pain-relieving effect, rather than acupuncture's traditional role of balancing energy to address a wide range of disorders, and the more subtle mechanisms that may be responsible for its overall benefits to health.

Acupuncture was popularized in the United States during the early 70s after President Nixon opened relations with China. At the time, a *New York Times* reporter, James Reston, had an appendectomy in a Chinese hospital using acupuncture as a means to decrease his post-surgical pain.

What is acupuncture used for?

Because the goal of acupuncture is to promote and restore the balance of energy, which flows throughout the body, the benefits of acupuncture can extend to a wide variety of conditions, from emotional disorders (anxiety, depression) to digestive complaints (nausea, vomiting, irritable bowel syndrome). It can be beneficial for pain syndromes due to an injury or associated with chronic degenerative diseases such as rheumatoid arthritis. It can also be helpful in treating neurological problems like migraines or Parkinson's disease, or as a rehabilitation strategy for individuals who suffered a stroke. Respiratory conditions, including sinusitis and asthma have been relieved with acupuncture, as have many gynecologic disorders and infertility. Acupuncture has also proved beneficial for reducing fatigue and addictions, and for promoting overall well-being.

Studies in the U.S. indicate that acupuncture can help relieve chronic low back pain, dental pain, migraine headaches, fibromyalgia, and symptoms of osteoarthritis. It has been shown to assist in the treatment of emotional pain syndromes such as post-traumatic stress disorder, as well as controlling chemotherapy-induced nausea and vomiting. It has also demonstrated clinical success in achieving pregnancy when used in conjunction with in-vitro fertilization.

What to expect on a visit to a practitioner of acupuncture?

Typically, the first acupuncture visit involves a comprehensive health history assessment. Questions that are included may seem strange, but in Traditional Chinese Medicine (TCM) — which encompasses acupuncture, herbal medicine, massage and other modalities — energy flow and whole-body interaction are the keys to diagnosing all physical diseases. For example, the practitioner may ask to examine your tongue, feel your pulse to help determine energy flow, or ask many questions related to bowel habits and diet, even if these seem to have nothing to do with the primary complaint.

After the initial acupuncture consultation and assessment, the needles are placed in very specific locations. Upon insertion, one may feel a momentary sharp or stinging sensation; however, many report they don't even feel the majority of the insertions. It is common to experience a deep ache for a short time at some of the points. The acupuncture needles may then be gently manipulated and some practitioners may use heat or even electricity with the needles.

The depth to which the acupuncture needles are inserted varies according to the treatment and the practitioner; however, needles should never be positioned deep enough to puncture organs (other than the skin). The needles are usually left in place for 5 to 20 minutes, usually no longer than 60 minutes, and then removed. Following an acupuncture treatment, practitioners will usually reassess the client and often give suggestions for home care. It is also typical to suggest supplemental Chinese herbs to enhance the achievement of energetic balance. Acute symptoms may require only two to four treatments; whereas for chronic cases, it is common to have as many as 12 or more treatments, usually over a course of 8 to 10 weeks. Regular monthly visits may be suggested as preventive measures to decrease stress, improve energy or boost immunity.

(Adapted from *drweil.com*)

B2. Words and Expressions

Vocabulary

1. induce / ɪnˈduːs / *v*. 导致;引起
2. collagen / ˈkɒlədʒ(ə)n / *n*. 胶原蛋白
3. neurological / ˌnjʊərəˈlɒdʒɪk(ə)l / *adj*. 神经系统的;神经(病)学的
4. asthma / ˈæsmə / *n*. [病]气喘
5. chemotherapy / ˌkiːməʊˈθerəpi / *n*. 化疗
6. sympathetic / sɪmpəˈθetɪk / *n*. 交感神经系
7. bowel / ˈbaʊəl / *n*. 肠

针灸的作用	**Functions of Acupuncture**
触发身体的自然愈合反应	trigger the body's natural healing response
促进和恢复能量的平衡	promote and restore the balance of energy
改善身体的血液流动	improve blood flow in the body
刺激中枢神经系统	stimulate the central nervous system
减少手术后的疼痛	decrease post-surgical pain
改变整个身体的能量流动	modify the flow of energy throughout the body
平衡能量以解决广泛的疾病	balance energy to address a wide range of disorders
促进胶原蛋白的产生	induce collagen production
减少面部细纹和皱纹的出现	reduce the appearance of fine lines and wrinkles on the face
没有科学共识	no scientific consensus
作用机制	the mechanism of action
影响腺苷的活性	influence the activity of adenosine
减轻疼痛	alleviate pain
缓解疼痛的作用	pain-relieving effect
治疗神经系统问题	treat neurological problem
管理慢性疼痛	manage chronic pain
治疗过敏性哮喘	tame allergic asthma
控制化疗引起的恶心和呕吐	control chemotherapy-induced nausea and vomiting
改善睡眠质量	improve sleep quality
缓解交感神经系统紧张	calm the sympathetic nervous system
副作用的风险小	carry little risk of side effect

情绪紊乱	emotional disorder
消化系统问题	digestive complaints
肠易激综合征	irritable bowel syndrome
创伤后应激障碍	post-traumatic stress disorder

Vocabulary

1. penetrate / ˈpenətreɪt / *v*. 渗透；进入
2. acupoint / ˈækjʊˌpɔɪnt / *n*. 穴位
3. acute / əˈkjuːt / *adj*. 十分严重的；(疾病)急性的
4. chronic / ˈkrɒnɪk / *adj*. 长期的；慢性的

针灸的使用	**The Usage of Acupuncture**
全面的健康史评估	a comprehensive health history assessment
诊断所有身体疾病	diagnose all physical diseases
确定能量流	determine energy flow
与肠道习惯和饮食有关的问题	questions related to bowel habits and diet
初步的针灸咨询和评估	initial acupuncture consultation and assessment
插入细针	insert thin needle
用细的金属针头刺入皮肤	penetrate the skin with thin, metallic needles
穴位	acupoint
通过轻柔和特殊的运动进行激活	activate through gentle movement
体验深层疼痛	experience a deep ache
用热甚至用电进行针刺	use heat or even electricity with the needles
定位到足够深的位置	be positioned deep enough
留在原位 5 至 20 分钟	be left in place for 5 to 20 minutes
拔针	remove the needle
重新评估患者的情况	reassess the patient
建议补充中草药	suggest supplemental Chinese herbs
加强能量平衡	enhance the achievement of energetic balance
急性症状	acute symptom
慢性症状	chronic symptom
每月定期访问	regular monthly visit
预防措施	preventive measure
减少压力	decrease stress
提高能量	improve energy

Vocabulary

1. anatomy / əˈnætəmi / *n*. 解剖;解剖学
2. physiology / ˌfɪziˈɑlədʒi / *n*. 生理学;生理机能
3. permeate / ˈpɜː(r)mieɪt / *n*. 渗透;弥漫
4. intricate / ˈɪntrɪkət / *adj*. 错综复杂的

经络	**Meridian**
经络通道	meridians channels
解剖学和生理学	anatomy and physiology of the physical body
能量通过经络的流动。	Energy flows through the meridians.
中医的整体能量分布系统	overall energy distribution system of Traditional Chinese Medicine
渗透到整个身体	permeate the whole body
携带、保持或运输身体周围的气、血和体液	carry, hold or transport qi, blood, and body fluids around the body
循环系统	circulatory system
全身基本物质的分布	distribution of the basic substances throughout the body
识别这些通道	identify these pathways
能量分布网络	energetic distribution network
以相应的对数存在	exist in corresponding pairs
每条经络都有许多针灸点。	Each meridians has many acupuncture points along its path.
如何以及在何处获取身体的气能	how and where to access the qi energy of the body
12 条主要经络	12 main meridians
隐形的通道	invisible channels
肺经	lung meridian
大肠经	large intestine meridian
脾经	spleen meridian
胃经	stomach meridian
心经	heart meridian
小肠经	small intestine meridian
肾经	kidney meridian
膀胱经	bladder meridian
心包经	pericardium meridian

三焦经	san jiao meridian
肝经	liver meridian
胆经	gall bladder meridian
与器官相对应	corresponds to the organs
阴阳配对	yin yang pair
每个阴性器官都与相应的阳性器官成对。	Each yin organ is paired with its corresponding yang organ.
气在胸部区域沿手三阴经流向手部。	Qi flows in the chest area along the three arm yin channels to the hand.
与成对的手三阳经相连	connect with the three paired arm yang channels
向上流动到头部	flow upward to the head
与其对应的足三阳经相连	connect with their three corresponding leg yang channels
沿着身体向下流动到脚	flow down the body to the feet
它们与相应的足三阴相连接	connect with their corresponding leg yin channels
再向上流到胸部,完成气的循环	flow up again to the chest to complete the cycle of qi
气和血的储存库	reservoirs of qi and blood
循环身体周围的精气或精华	circulate jing or essence around the body
与肾脏有密切联系	have a strong connection with the kidneys
在身体的主干上循环防御性的卫气	circulate the defensive wei qi over the trunk of the body
精确的,但错综复杂的相互连接的能量线的网络	delicate, yet intricate web of interconnecting energy lines

B3. Speaking Activities

Situational Speech

Lectures of Traditional Chinese Medicine will be held at your university next month. You are invited to deliver a **5-minute speech**, introducing **acupuncture** briefly to international students. Your speech might cover:

- A brief history of acupuncture
- Health benefits of acupuncture
- The contribution of acupuncture to Traditional Chinese Medicine

You may refer to the words and expressions in Part B, but don't confine yourself to them.

Role Play

Acupuncture is used mainly to relieve discomfort associated with a variety of diseases and conditions. Your foreign friend John has neck pain and he is planning to undergo the acupuncture therapy. As his doctor, you are supposed to answer his questions. His questions might include:

- Does acupuncture hurt?
- What health problems can acupuncture address?
- How does it work?
- Others.

Brainstorming

Acupuncture is a technique in which practitioners stimulate specific points on the body —most often by inserting thin needles through the skin. Some people are not willing to try acupuncture because they hold that as with any treatments, acupuncture may cause side effects. The World Health Organization maintains an extensive list of diseases and conditions (mostly pain related) possibly treatable by acupuncture. Many doctors now do not discourage their patients from receiving acupuncture when conventional medicine fails them or when convention treatment entails too many adverse side effects. **What do you think of the side effects of acupuncture**? **How to make the best use of acupuncture**? Please elaborate on your views.

(Adapted from *livescience.com*)

Reading and Sharing

Read the following paragraphs about **globalization of acupuncture** and share your views.

Paragraph 1

Acupuncture and Massage College (AMC) was established in 1983 as the first acupuncture school in Florida. Today, it is considered one of the leading colleges of Oriental Medicine in the nation and is known for its distinguished professors of Traditional Chinese Medicine, Asian Bodywork Therapy specialization, and its holistic approach to teaching integrative medicine.

(Adapted from *amcollege.edu*)

Paragraph 2

Bastyr University's comprehensive approach of acupuncture medicine prepares students to work in collaboration with practitioners of conventional Western medicine. With courses taught by some of the premier Chinese medicine educators, the acupuncture and east Asian medicine programs at Bastyr are strongly inspired by the contemporary model of health care education and practice in China, which combines traditional Chinese medicine with modern Western medicine. As a student, you will be trained in co-management of patients with Western medicine providers. You will build the skills and confidence to practice and to inform both patients and other providers on the practice of traditional Chinese medicine.

(Adapted from *bastyr.edu*)

Ideas for Sharing:

- What can you learn from the above paragraphs?
- Why is acupuncture becoming popular in the West?
- What qualities are you looking for when choosing an acupuncturist?

Interpretation

Interpret the paragraphs below into English with the words and expressions you learned in Part B.

Paragraph 1

针灸是中医的重要治疗方法，它的神奇疗效已为世人所知。如肩背痛这类疾病，西医很难处理，但中医通过针灸疗法，疏通脉络，可以有效地缓解疼痛，甚至治愈此类疾病。由于针灸治病不用开刀吃药，只是在病人身体的一定部位用细针刺入，简便易行，而且可以减少病人的痛苦，所以受到人们的欢迎。在针灸疗法中，有一个重要术语叫穴位，针灸就是根据病情对不同的穴位进针。

Paragraph 2

中医在长期的经验积累中，发现了大量的连通身体的穴位，并通过对穴位的针灸来治疗疾病。比如一个人身体虚弱，记忆力减退，中医认为可能是肾脏出了问题。肾脏是人体内部主管生长发育的脏器，一个人肾功能正常，就会精力充足，头发乌亮，思维活跃。如果肾脏出了问题，身体就会向相反方面发展。中医的针灸疗法，不是对肾脏进行直接治疗，而是对足底的一个穴位进行针灸，以求缓解或治愈该病。

Paragraph 3

中医认为，人体的生命能量（气）是通过经脉和络脉（经络）循环的，经络有很多分支，与身体器官和功能相连。中医主要关注人体的功能，如消化、呼吸、体温维持、衰老等，而不太注重人体的解剖结构。健康被看作不同功能实体与外界之间和谐的相互作用，而疾病被解释为相互作用中的不和谐。中医诊断的目的是，通过把脉，检查舌、皮肤和眼睛，以及观察一个人的饮食和睡眠习惯等，来追踪症状内在的不和谐。

B4. Culture Highlights

Q: *Is acupuncture safe?*

A: When performed by a suitably trained practitioner, acupuncture is generally considered to be safe for most people, but any procedure that involves puncturing the skin with needles or manipulating the human body carries some risks.

Potential side effects of acupuncture can include:

- bleeding or bruising at puncture sites
- infection at puncture sites
- contact dermatitis
- nerve damage
- transmission of blood-borne diseases, such as hepatitis C and HIV/AIDS
- puncture of organs

Acupuncturists should use sterile, disposable needles to prevent the transmission of blood-borne diseases and reduce the likelihood of infection at the puncture site.

(Adapted from *healthdirect.gov.au*)

Q: *What happens during an acupuncture treatment?*

A: A typical acupuncture session begins with a discussion of your problem and a physical examination.

The acupuncturist may then stimulate certain points on the body, either by inserting fine metal needles or using a laser.

The needles used in acupuncture are typically much finer than the needles used to take blood, and the process is usually painless. Once the needles are inserted, they will be left in place while you lie still, and hopefully relaxed. As many as 20 needles may be used in one session.

The needles may be turned or wobbled as part of the treatment. The needles will be removed at the end of the session.

(Adapted from *healthdirect.gov.au*)

Q: *What is the difference between acupuncture and dry needling?*

A: The difference between dry needling and acupuncture goes further than that they both use needles. Dry needle treatment, also known as myofascial point dry needling, is a remarkable and completely natural treatment for chronic and acute pain. Often used as part of a larger treatment plan, it is widely misunderstood by many patients who have questions about dry needling who liken the procedure to acupuncture. The differences between dry needling and acupuncture actually outweigh the similarities by far.

Both dry needling and acupuncture involve the insertion of thin needles into certain parts of the body, but the similarities stop there. The difference is that during an acupuncture session, needles are inserted into points along meridian lines. These lines represent the body's organs, and they are based on ancient Chinese medicine. Acupuncture is based on the idea of balance and restoring proper flow of energy throughout the body.

During acupuncture, the needles are usually left in place for 15 to 30 minutes. It is most often used to treat internal ailments, including digestive problems, insomnia, stress and chronic pain.

Dry needle treatment is a relatively new treatment based on modern Western medicine. This treatment was developed in the 1980s, and during treatment, needles are inserted into trigger points, or tender bands of muscle located within larger muscles. When needles are inserted into trigger points, they elicit a response that releases the trigger point and restores normal function.

Another difference between dry needling and acupuncture is that dry needling is used to treat cases of chronic and acute pain without the use of medication, surgical procedures, etc.

(Adapted from *denverphysicalmedicine.com*)

B5. Extensive Reading

Passage One

Acupuncture Meridians

So, what is a meridian anyway? This is one of the first questions students of Traditional Chinese Medicine want to understand. Simply put, a meridian is an "energy highway" in the human body. Qi energy flows through this meridian or energy highway, accessing all parts of the body. Meridians can be mapped throughout the body; they flow within the body and not on the surface. Meridians exist in corresponding pairs and each meridian has many acupuncture points along its path.

The term "meridian" describes the overall energy distribution system of Traditional Chinese Medicine and helps us to understand how basic substances of the body (qi, blood and body fluids) permeate the whole body. The individual meridians themselves are often described as "channels" or even "vessels" which reflect the notion of carrying, holding, or transporting qi, blood and body fluids around the body.

It is tempting to think of the meridians of the human body the same way as we think of the circulatory system, as the meridians are responsible for the distribution of the basic substances throughout the body just like the circulatory system, but here is where the similarities end. Conventional anatomy and physiology would not be able to identify these pathways in a physical sense in the way that blood vessels can be identified.

It is more useful to consider the meridian system as an energetic distribution network that in itself tends towards energetic manifestation. Meridians can be best understood as a process rather than a structure.

Practitioners of Traditional Chinese Medicine must be as knowledgeable about these meridian channels as the Western Doctor is about the anatomy and physiology of the physical body. Without this thorough understanding, successful acupuncture treatments would be difficult. A practitioner of Traditional Chinese Medicine must know how and where to access the qi energy of the body to facilitate the healing process.

There are twelve main meridians, or invisible channels, throughout the body with qi or energy flows. Each limb is traversed by six channels, three yin channels on the inside, and three yang channels on the outside. Each of the twelve regular channels corresponds to the five yin organs, the six yang organs as well as the pericardium and san jiao. These are organs that have no anatomical counterpart in Western medicine but also relate to processes in the body. It is also important to remember that organs should not be thought of as being identical to the physical, anatomical organs of the body.

Each meridian is a yin yang pair, meaning each yin organ is paired with its corresponding yang organ: the yin lung organ, for example, corresponds with the yang large intestine. Qi flows in a precise manner through the twelve regular meridians or channels. First, qi flows from the chest area along the three arm yin channels (lung, pericardium, and heart) to the hands. There they connect with the three paired arm yang channels (large intestine, san jiao, and small intestine) and flow upward to the head. In the head they connect with their three corresponding leg yang channels (stomach, gall bladder, and bladder) and flow down the body to the feet. In the feet they connect with their corresponding leg yin channels (spleen, liver, and kidney) and flow up again to the chest to complete the cycle of qi. For example:

- Arm Tai Yin channel corresponds to the lung
- Leg Tai Yin channel corresponds to the spleen
- Arm Shao Yin channel corresponds to the heart
- Leg Shao Yin corresponds to the kidney
- Arm Jue Yin corresponds to the pericardium
- Leg Jue Yin corresponds to the liver
- Arm Yang Ming corresponds to the large intestine

- Leg Yang Ming corresponds to the stomach
- Arm Tai Yang corresponds to the small intestine
- Leg Tai Yang corresponds to the bladder
- Arm Shao Yang corresponds to the san jiao
- Leg Shao Yang Channel corresponds to the gall bladder

The arm and leg channels of the same name are considered to "communicate" with each other in Traditional Chinese medicine. Thus, problems in a given channel or organ can be treated by using various points on the communication "partner". As an example: a problem with the lungs can be treated by using points on the spleen channel as they are both Tai yin channels.

In addition to the twelve regular meridians there are "Extraordinary Meridians" that are not directly linked to the major organ system but have various specific functions:

- They act as reservoirs of qi and blood for the twelve regular channels, filling and emptying as required.
- They circulate jing or "essence" around the body because they have a strong connection with the kidneys.
- They help circulate the defensive wei qi over the trunk of the body and, as such, play an important role in maintaining of good health.
- They provide further connections between the twelve regular channels.

The meridian system of the human body is a delicate, yet intricate web of interconnecting energy lines. If a person masters an understanding of this meridian system they will know the secrets of the flow of qi energy in the body.

(Adapted from *kootenarycolumbiacollege.com*)

Passage Two

Definition of Qi in Traditional Chinese Medicine

In English, qi (also known as chi) is usually translated as "vital life force", but qi goes beyond that simple translation. According to Classical Chinese Philosophy, qi is the force that makes up and binds together all things in the universe. It is paradoxically, both everything and nothing.

Unless you're enrolled at an acupuncture school, this concept may seem strange and inapplicable to medicine and healing. As such, in this article, we will explore the concept and definition of qi, as it relates to Traditional Chinese Medicine (TCM).

Understanding what qi is in TCM

In Traditional Chinese Medicine, the concept of qi or chi has two main branches. There is the physical or nourishing portion of qi that makes up the air, water, and food that we take in. The other branch of chi is more insubstantial. It is the vital fluids and the energy itself that flow through our bodies.

The first, as stated above, could be thought of as those things we take in and make a part of us while the second is what has already become part of us and is then released to continue the cycle of life. It is the imbalances and interruptions of this flowing force that are responsible for most human ailments whether physical, mental, or emotional.

In this article, we will explore the concept of qi in the human body and how it relates to Oriental Medicine.

Maintaining balance of qi

As with yin-yang, qi needs to balance in order to maintain good health. If there is an imbalance of qi, illness can arise, with varying symptoms according to the type of qi and whether there is a deficiency or excess of qi. Curing the imbalance of qi is usually the main work of the different healing modalities in Traditional Chinese Medicine, such as acupuncture and tui na.

Qi Deficiency: In Chinese medicine, a qi deficiency can take many forms. It could be a lack of sleep, food shelter, clean water, fresh air or other physical things the body needs to function properly. It can also be a lack of sufficient mental stimulation, social interaction, and love.

Excess Qi: Excess qi can be as detrimental as a qi deficiency if not worse. It can arise as a result of environmental toxins, like polluted air or water. It can also arise from excessive physical activity, overeating, stress, or strong negative emotions.

To avoid disharmony, it is important to maintain a proper balance of all the different forms of qi that make up life. There are four types of qi within the human body.

- Parental Qi: Our parental or yuan qi is the qi that is inherited from our parents at conception. After conception occurs, parental qi is stored in the kidneys.

- Pectoral Qi: Pectoral or zong qi is qi that is produced by breathing. It is stored in the chest area.

- Nutritional Qi: Nutritional or ying qi is derived from eating foods and is responsible for the circulation of nutrition throughout the body.

- Defensive Qi: Defensive or wei qi is responsible for protecting the body from illnesses.

It is the yang of nutritional qi, meaning that it is also derived from eating foods, but serves a different purpose. Each of the vital substances has Five Cardinal Functions: actuation, warming, defense, containment, and transformation. The five cardinal functions of qi are:

- Actuation: Qi is responsible for maintaining the vital life energy that is necessary for the body to grow and develop properly. This includes all the body's functions, such as the Zang / Fu organs, meridians, and Xue (Blood). If there is a qi deficiency, then the functional entities and vital substances will be negatively impacted, which can cause illness.

- Warming: Qi helps produce heat and regulates body temperature for normal functions to occur. A deficiency in qi can result in a lowered body temperature, cold limbs, and a disposition to hot drinks, as means to combat this.

- Defending: Qi defends the body against external elements, such as pathogens and environmental factors that can cause illness.

- Containment: Qi is responsible for ensuring that the body's organs and fluids kept in their proper places. In the case of Xue, qi is responsible for regulating blood flow within the vessels and ensuring that they don't leak out. Qi also regulates Jinye (body fluids-sweat, saliva, etc.) and makes sure that only the proper amount is allowed to leave the body. Qi deficiency can result in symptoms related to body fluids and organ problems.

- Transformation: Qi is also responsible for transforming nutrition and air into different subsets of qi, such as blood.

(Adapted from *amcollege.edu*)

B6. Assignment

Poster Design

Form **groups of 3 or 4 and design an English poster to introduce acupuncture.** Your poster might include:

- How does acupuncture work?
- What happens during an acupuncture treatment?
- What happens to your body after acupuncture?

References

Ananya Mandal. (2019). Acupuncture History. *News Medical Life Sciences*. Retrieved from https://www.news-medical.net/health/Acupuncture-History.aspx on May 20th, 2022.

Cathy Wong. (2022). The Benefits and Side Effects of Acupuncture. *verywellhealth.com*. Retrieved from https://www.verywellhealth.com/acupuncture-health-uses-88407 on May 14th, 2022.

China Daily. (2020). TCM Offers a Healthy Path for Belt and Road Countries. *China Daily*. Retrieved from http://english.scio.gov.cn/beltandroad/2020-10/27/content_76847422.htm on April 15th, 2022.

Chinese Dietary Therapy. (2022). Chinese Dietary Therapy Concepts and Principles. *Modern Herb Shop*. Retrieved from https://www.modernherbshop.com/Chinese_Dietary_Therapy_Concepts_and_Principles_s/533.htm on May 6th, 2022.

Editors of AMC. (2022). About Acupuncture and Massage College in Miami, FL. *Acupuncture and Message College*. Retrieved from https://www.amcollege.edu/ on May 14th, 2022.

Editors of AMC. (2017). What Is Qi? Definition of Qi in Traditional Chinese Medicine. *Acupuncture and Message College*. Retrieved from https://www.amcollege.edu/blog/qi-in-traditional-chinese-medicine on May 25th, 2022.

Editors of Bastyr University. (2022). Acupuncture and East Asian Medicine Programs. *Bastyr University*. Retrieved from https://bastyr.edu/academics/acupuncture-east-asian-medicine on May 15th, 2022.

Editors of Better Health Channel. (2021). Herbal Medicine. *Better Health*. Retrieved from https://www.betterhealth.vic.gov.au/health/conditionsandtreatments/herbal-medicine on April 30th, 2022.

Editors of Encyclopedia Britannica. (2022). Traditional Chinese Medicine. *Britannica*. Retrieved from https://www.britannica.com/science/traditional-Chinese-medicine on April 4th, 2022.

Editors of Healthdirect. (2021). Acupuncture. *healthdirect*. Retrieved from https://www.healthdirect.gov.au/acupuncture on May 18th, 2022.

Editors of TCM Wiki. (2012). China Promotes Traditional Chinese Medicine Culture. *TCM Wiki*. Retrieved from https://tcmwiki.com/wiki/the-five-elements on May 8th, 2022.

Program Manager. (2018). Acupuncture Meridians — The Central Meridian System in Chinese Medicine. *Kootenay Columbia College of Integrative Health Sciences*. Retrieved from https://kootenaycolumbiacollege.com/the-chinese-medicine-meridian-system/ on May 8th, 2022.

Wang Zhiru, Lu Xiaoli. (2017). *Introducing Chinese Culture in English*. Beijing: Foreign Language Teaching and Research Press. pp. 238-253.

Andrew Weil. (2022). Acupuncture. *drweil.com*. Retrieved from https://www.drweil.com/health-wellness/balanced-living/wellness-therapies/acupuncture/ on May 7th, 2022.

What You Should Know about Chinese Herbs. (2022). *Clevelendclinic.org*. Retrieved from https://health.clevelandclinic.org/what-you-should-know-about-chinese-herbs/ on June 1st, 2022.

Wu H. (2022). An Introduction to Traditional Chinese Medicine Herbs. *Acupuncture Message College*. Retrieved from https://www.amcollege.edu/blog/introduction-traditional-chinese-medicine-herbs on June 6th, 2022.

Wthn Team. (2022). Traditional Chinese Medicine Herbs List to Improve Overall Health. *Wthn.com*. Retrieved from https://wthn.com/blogs/wthnside-out/traditional-chinese-medicine-herbs-list on October, 1st, 2022.

Xinhua. (2021). China Promotes Traditional Chinese Medicine Culture. *English.gov.cn*. Retrieved from http://english.www.gov.cn/statecouncil/ministries/202107/07/content_WS60e5aa05c6d0df57f98dc8d2.html on April 24th, 2022.

Yang Zhi, Gan Shengnan. (2013). *TCM Listening and Speaking*. Shanghai: World Publishing Shanghai Corporation Limited. pp. 36-41.

Ronnie Littlejohn. (2021). Wuxing (Wu-hsing). *Internet Encyclopedia of Philosophy*. Retrieved from https://iep.utm.edu/wuxing/ on May 4th, 2022.

Sissi Wachtel-Galor, Iris F. F. Benzie. (2011). Herbal Medicine: A Growing Field with a Long Tradition. *National Library of Medicine*. Retrieved from https://www.ncbi.nlm.nih.gov/pmc/articles/PMC3486438/ on May 5th, 2022.

TDI. (2022). TCM: Revolutionary Approach towards COVID-19. *The Diplomatic Insight*. Retrieved from https://thediplomaticinsight.com/tcm-revolutionary-approach-towards-covid-19/on April 23rd, 2022.

Elizabeth Peterson. (2017). What Is Acupuncture? *Livescience.com*. Retrieved from https://www.livescience.com/29494-acupuncture.html on April 23rd, 2022.

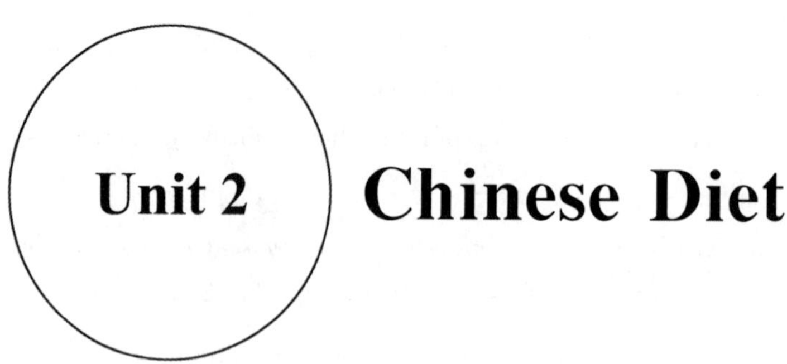

Unit 2 Chinese Diet

Part A Chinese Cuisine

A1. Introduction

Eight Chinese Cuisines

How many Chinese cuisines are there? The most influential and typically known by the public are the "8 Chinese Cuisines". Actually, Chinese cuisine has more than 8 genres. China is large and the climate, ingredients, history and dining customs vary from place to place, leading to the differences in cooking methods and dish flavors and forming the different cuisines.

As early as in the Shang dynasty (17th century BCE-1046 BCE) and Zhou dynasty (1046 BCE-256 BCE), China's dietary culture had taken shape. In the Tang dynasty (618-907) and Song dynasty (960-1279), the northern and southern food already had their own characteristics: generally sweet in south and salty in north. By the early Qing dynasty (1644-1911), four most influential cuisines prevailed. What are the four main styles of Chinese cuisine at that time? They are cuisines of Shandong, Sichuan, Guangdong, and Jiangsu respectively. By the end of the Qing dynasty, the four new cuisines — Zhejiang cuisine, Fujian cuisine, Hunan cuisine, and Anhui cuisine appeared, together with former four cuisines, they were listed as "8 Chinese Cuisines".

Today, the hot and spicy Sichuan and Hunan cuisines are the most popular in China. The Cantonese cuisine with light taste and delicate cooking methods is not only sought after in China, but also popular around the world.

Sichuan Cuisine / Szechuan Cuisine / Chuan Cuisine

Chinese:川菜

Popular in China's Sichuan Province, Chongqing

Features: hot and spicy, mouth-numbing; using a lot of pepper, chili, garlic, and Pixian bean chili paste

Originated in Southwest China, Sichuan cuisine is the most popular cuisine in China. Sichuan dishes are famous with its spicy, pungent and hot flavor, and red color. Sichuan chefs prefer seasonings like various pepper and chili, garlic and broad bean paste which is the soul of Sichuan dishes. Hot Pot is the most popular Sichuan dish in China and is the first choice when dining together with friends.

Cantonese Cuisine / Guangdong Cuisine / Yue Cuisine

Chinese:粤菜

Popular in China's Guangdong Province, Hong Kong, and Macao

Features: mild, fresh, and natural taste; wide use of materials and rich cooking methods

Cantonese cuisine is popular around the world and is the representative Chinese cuisine. The cooking methods of Cantonese dishes are always complex, flexible, exquisite, and creative. Most Cantonese dishes taste mild and fresh, preserving the natural taste of food materials. The food materials are extremely rich which include poultries, birds, seafood, land animals and various vegetables and fruits.

3 Major Styles in Cantonese Cuisine: Guangzhou Cuisine, Teochew Cuisine (Chaoshan Cuisine), and Hakka Cuisine (Dongjiang Cuisine).

Hunan Cuisine / Xiang Cuisine

Chinese:湘菜

Popular in China's Hunan Province

Features: spicy, hot, and salty; preference for chili & fermented soya beans; dark dish color

Originated in Eastern Zhou dynasty (770 BCE-56 BCE), Hunan cuisine, also called Xiang cuisine, is another cuisine popular throughout China with the spicy taste. Hunan dishes are even hotter and spicier than Sichuan cuisine since they have even more dried or fresh chili in dishes. Hunan people also invent sour and spicy taste and numb and spicy taste, and they like pickled and preserved vegetables and meats very much.

Shandong Cuisine / Lu Cuisine

Chinese:鲁菜

Popular in China's Shandong Province and Southern Liaoning Province

Features: umami, salty, sweet and sour flavors; using much soup, scallion, ginger and garlic; good at cooking seafood

Originated in the Spring and Autumn Period (770 BCE-476 BCE), Lu cuisine is the only self-originated cuisine among 8 Chinese cuisines which has the longest history of 2, 500 years, hence seen as the No. 1 of 8 great cuisines of China. Shandong dishes pay much attention to the quality and natural taste of food. Soup and scallion are key seasonings and seafood plays a crucial role in Shandong cuisine. Most Shandong dishes taste fresh, umami and moderately salty.

Jiangsu Cuisine / Su Cuisine

Chinese:江苏菜，苏菜

Popular in China's Jiangsu Province

Features: umami, mild, slightly sweet, and natural; exquisite cuttings and precise control of heat; delicate dish appearance

Jiangsu cuisine, the representative food in the south of China, is famous for its delicate appearance and lightly sweet, umami, natural and mild taste. Jiangsu dishes preserve much original flavor of food materials. The main food materials are mainly freshwater fishes and seafood. The cutting is extremely exquisite and changeful and the control of heat is precise. The dishes are always served delicately.

4 Major Styles in Jiangsu Cuisine: Nanjing Style, Huaiyang Cuisine, Suxi Style, Xuhai Style

Zhejiang Cuisine / Zhe Cuisine

Chinese:浙菜

Popular in China's Zhejiang Province

Features: light and fresh, crisp and tender; good control of fire heat; yellow wine as special seasoning

Popular in Zhejiang, Zhejiang cuisine is often lightly seasoned with appealing appearance. Zhejiang cuisine chefs prefer fresh food materials like seafood, freshwater fishes, and vegetables in season and they are extremely strict in the selection of raw materials. In addition, Zhejiang cuisine is well-known for its varied cooking methods and frying is the most frequently used.

Fujian Cuisine / Min Cuisine

Chinese:闽菜

Popular in China's Fujian Province

Features: light, fresh, sweet, and sour; special condiment red vinasse; woodland delicacies and seafood widely used for ingredients

Originated in Fuzhou, Fujian cuisine dishes are light, fresh, mellow, and non-greasy in general. The food materials used are pretty rich, containing both materials in land and seas. The common seasonings include red vinasse, sugar, and vinegar. Like Jiangsu cuisine, Fujian cuisine attaches great importance to cutting techniques as well.

Anhui Cuisine / Hui Cuisine

Chinese:徽菜

Popular in China's Anhui Province

Features: salty and fresh, light, preserving the original flavor of ingredients; preference for hams; light cooking methods including braising, stewing and steaming

Popular in Anhui Province, Hui dishes taste salty, fresh, and light and have the unique flavor of ingredients. Hui cuisine attaches importance to dietetic invigoration with natural ingredients. It is noteworthy that Anhui cuisine dishes have the effect of nourishing body for multiple ingredients with varied nutrition are matched scientifically.

(Adapted from *travelchinaguide.com*)

A2. Words and Expressions

Vocabulary

1. pockmarked / ˈpɒkmɑːkt / *adj*. 有麻子的,有痘痕的
2. bean curd / ˈbiːnˌkɜːd / *n*. 豆腐(同 tofu)
3. aromatic / ˌerəˈmætɪk / *adj*. 有香味的,有香气的,芳香的
4. diced / daɪst / *adj*. 切粒的
5. tingly / ˈtɪŋgəli / *adj*. 刺痛的
6. culinary / ˈkʌlɪnəri / *adj*. 烹饪的;厨房的

川菜	**Sichuan Cuisine**
麻婆豆腐	"Pockmarked Granny" Bean Curd (Mapo Tofu)
麻辣	spicy-hot
软嫩	tender and soft
酥香	aromatic and flaky
宫保鸡丁	Spicy Diced Chicken (Kung Pao Chicken)
受西方人欢迎	popular among Westerners
四川火锅	Sichuan Hot Pot
味蕾	taste bud
回味,余韵	aftertaste
辣椒和花椒	chilies and Sichuan pepper
唇齿发麻	lip tingling sensation
多种味道	diversity of flavor
甜、酸、辣、麻	sweet, sour, spicy, and tingly-numbing
必备调味品	must-have seasonings
混合的烹饪风格	a mix of culinary styles

Vocabulary

1. crispy / ˈkrɪspi / *adj*. 酥脆的
2. exquisite / ɪkˈskwɪzɪt / *adj*. 精美的;精致的;卓越的
3. syrup / ˈsɪrəp / *n*. 浓糖水,糖浆
4. umami / uːˈmaːmi / *adj*. 鲜味的
5. scallion / ˈskæliən / *adj*. 葱(同 spring onion)

鲁菜	**Shandong Cuisine**
擅长烹煮海鲜	good at cooking seafood
咸、脆	salty and crispy
各种醋	kinds of vinegar
酱油	soy sauce
高温油炸	fry in high heat
锁住味道	lock the flavors
保持形状、颜色和味道	preserve the cut, color, and taste
精湛的刀工	exquisite cutting skills
首屈一指	second to none
爆(一种烹饪方式)	extreme heat stir frying
扒(一种烹饪方式)	fried dough coating method
拔丝	crisp frying with syrup

糖醋鲤鱼	Sweet and Sour Carp
外皮酸甜酥脆	sweet, sour, and crispy outside
寓意吉祥	an auspicious sign
葱烧海参	Braised Sea Cucumber with Scallion
减轻海参的腥味	release the fishy smell of the sea cucumbers
增添独特风味	add a special flavor
蒸酿豆腐	Steamed Stuffed Tofu
颜色雪白	snow white in color
柔滑、鲜嫩	smooth, umami, and tender
油焖大虾	Braised Prawns in Oil
馒头	steamed bun

Vocabulary

1. stir-fry / ˈstɜːfraɪ / *v.* 煸炒,翻炒
2. grill / ɡrɪl / *v.*(在火焰或烧热的煤上)烧烤
3. seasoning / ˈsiːzənɪŋ / *n.* 调味品,作料
4. crunchy / ˈkrʌntʃi / *n.*(食物)脆生生的,松脆的,鲜脆的
5. dim sum / ˌdɪmˈsʌm / *n.*(港式)点心

粤菜	**Cantonese Cuisine**
追求菜肴的原味和鲜味	pursue the original flavor and umami taste of dishes
原料广泛	have the widest range of ingredients
清、淡、脆、鲜	clear, light, crisp, and fresh
蒸、炒	steaming and stir-frying
注重菜肴的艺术呈现	pay much attention to the artistic presentation of dishes
叉烧	Char Siu (Barbecued Pork)
放在炉子上烤	grilled on the stove
叉烧包	Char Siu Bao (Barbecued Pork Buns)
白斩鸡	White Cut Chicken
简单烹饪,不加调味	simple cooking without seasoning
肉质细嫩,口味清淡	smooth meat and mild flavor
煲仔饭	Claypot Rice
金黄酥脆的锅底	the crunchy golden base
烟熏味和香气	smoky flavor and aroma
广东烤鹅	Cantonese Roasted Goose
粤式点心	Cantonese dim sum

Vocabulary

1. greasy / ˈgriːsi / *adj*. 沾满油脂的;含脂肪的;油腻的
2. pickled / ˈpɪkəld / *adj*.(用醋)腌的,腌制的
3. ferment / fəˈment / *v*. (使)发酵
4. fragrant / ˈfreɪgrənt / *n*. 芳香的,芬芳的
5. stinky / ˈstɪŋki / *adj*. 产生臭味的
6. braise / breɪz / *v*. (用文火)炖,焖

湘菜	**Hunan Cuisine**
气候潮湿	humid climate
纯粹的辣	pure spicy
热身并祛湿	warm up and expel dampness
辣、酸、干、腻	spicy, sour, dry, and greasy
煎、炖、烤、蒸	frying, stewing, roasting, and steaming
泡菜	pickled vegetables
红辣椒	chili peppers
辣椒粉	chili powder
豆豉	fermented black soybeans
开胃	stimulate appetite
消除天然原料的难闻气味	dispel the unpleasant smell of the natural ingredients
带来一种特殊的芳香酸味	bring a special fragrant sour taste
熏肉	smoked meat
长沙臭豆腐	Changsha Stinky Tofu
剁椒鱼头	Steamed Fish Head with Diced Pepper
毛氏红烧肉	Mao's Braised Pork
半肥半瘦	half fat and half lean

Vocabulary

1. simmer / ˈsɪmər / *v*. 炖,煨
2. marinate / ˈmærɪneɪt / *v*. 在肉(或鱼)上浇些腌泡汁
3. stew / stjuː / *v*.(通常由肉或鱼加蔬菜制成的)炖菜,煨菜
4. nutritive / ˈnjuːtrətɪv / *adj*. 营养丰富的,营养价值高的

苏菜	Jiangsu Cuisine
独特的天然风味	distinct natural flavors
精细的烹饪方法	elaborate and precise cooking methods
美丽精致的外观	beautiful and delicate appearance
如同艺术品般精致地奉上	be served delicately like artworks
保持食材的原始风味	preserve the original flavor of food materials
煨、烩、炖	simmering, braising, and stewing
注重对火候的把握和刀工	focus on the controlling of fire heat and the art of cutting
南京盐水鸭	Nanjing Salted Duck
用炒盐腌制	be marinated with fried salt
红烧狮子头	Braised Meat Balls in Brown Sauce
由巨大的肉团子做成,有如“雄狮之头”	be made of giant balls of meat, like the head of a lion
叫花鸡	Beggar's Chicken
据说由乞丐所发明,以此命名	be invented by and named after beggars
用荷叶和泥包裹	be wrapped with lotus leaves and mud
霸王别姬	Stewed Tortoise and Chicken
主要食材为甲鱼和鸡	the main ingredient is soft-shelled turtle and chicken
纪念项羽和虞姬	in memory of Xiang Yu and Yu Ji
具有很高的营养价值	have high nutritive value

Vocabulary

1. sauté / ˈsəʊteɪ / *v.* 煎,煸,炒
2. brine / braɪn / *n.*(尤指用于腌制食物的)盐水
3. condiment / ˈkɒndɪmənt / *n.* 调味品
4. shoot / ʃuːt / *n.* 芽;苗;新枝
5. dainty / ˈdeɪnti / *v.* 小巧玲珑的,娇小的,小巧精美的
6. refined / rɪˈfaɪnd / *adj.* 精炼的;精制的;提纯的

浙菜	Zhejiang Cuisine
精致和优雅	dainty and refined
鱼米之乡	land of milk and honey
各种海鲜	a wide variety of seafood
艺术精致性	the artistic refinement
清淡、新鲜	light and fresh

保持原料的原汁原味	maintain the original taste of raw materials
讲究时间和火候	particular about time and fire
甜点	sweet desserts
宁波年糕	sweet Ningbo rice cake
煎、焖、炖	sautéing, braising, and stewing
浸在盐水中	soak in brine
宁波咸膏蟹	Ningbo salty crab
东坡肉	Dongpo Pork (Stir-Fried Pork)
绍兴黄酒	Shaoxing yellow wine
增进滋味	promote the flavor
浙菜特有的调味品	unique condiment of Zhejiang food
油焖春笋	Braised Bamboo Shoot
春笋	spring bamboo shoots
西湖醋鱼	West Lake Fish in Vinegar Gravy
龙井虾仁	Fried Shrimps with Longjing Tea
用西湖龙井茶叶炒虾仁	stir-fry shrimps with West Lake Longjing tea leaves

Vocabulary

1. vinegar / ˈvɪnɪgər / *n.* 醋
2. impart / ɪmˈpaːt / *v.* 赋予,给予
3. glutinous / ˈgluːtɪnəs / *adj.* 黏的
4. yeast / jiːst / *n.* 酵母;酵母菌
5. vinasse / vɪˈnæs / *n.* 酒糟;酿酒蒸馏后之残渣
6. chop / tʃɒp / *n.* 带骨的肉块;排骨

闽菜	**Fujian Cuisine**
清淡、酸甜	light, sweet, and sour
虾酱	shrimp sauce
白醋	white vinegar
红米酒	red rice-wine
糯米经红曲发酵制成	be made from glutinous rice fermented with red yeast
红糟	Red Vinasse
用红糟腌渍	pickle with red vinasse
红酒糟腌鱼	Steamed Fish in Red Vinasse
使闽菜具有独特的风味	impart a unique flavor to Fujian Cuisine

使菜肴有酒香和漂亮的红色	give the dishes a wine aroma and beautiful red color
佛跳墙	Buddha Jumps over the Wall
用夸张的名字突出其美味程度	with exaggerated names to highlight its delicacy
由 10 种以上的食材文火煨制而成	simmer over 10 ingredients
醉排骨	Drunken Chops
香味浓郁,令人陶醉	the fragrance is strong and intoxicating
鸡焖蛤	Braised Sea Clam with Chicken Soup
蚵仔煎(闽南语,普通话译作“海蛎煎”)	Oyster Omelet

Vocabulary

1. partridge / ˈpaːtrɪdʒ / *n*. 山鹑,鹧鸪
2. yam / jæm / *n*. 薯蓣,山药;(北美)番薯,山芋
3. intoxicating / ɪnˈtɒksɪkeɪtɪŋ / *adj*. 醉人的,令人陶醉的
4. omelette / ˈɒmlət / *n*. 煎鸡蛋,煎蛋饼,摊鸡蛋

徽菜	**Anhui Cuisine**
细心调节火候,使所有食材充分均匀煮熟	adjust heat carefully to fully cook all the ingredients evenly
重视天然食材的营养滋补	attach importance to dietetic invigoration with natural ingredients
炖、焖、蒸	stew, braise, and steam
油腻色深	greasy and deep color
火候掌握是关键。	Fire control is the key.
偏爱火腿	preference for hams
火腿炖甲鱼	Stewed Soft-Shelled Turtle with Ham
臭鳜鱼	Stinky Mandarin Fish
闻着臭	smell stinky
虎皮毛豆腐	Fried Hairy Tofu
表面长有白毛的发酵豆腐	the fermented tofu with white hair on the surface
清蒸石鸡	Steamed Partridge
营养丰富	rich in nutrition
汤汁清香,肉质鲜嫩	aromatic light soup and fresh tender meat
黄山炖鸽	Huangshan Stewed Pigeon
爽口山药	Refreshing Chinese Yams

A3. Speaking Activities

Situational Speech

Your school is organizing a Chinese Cuisine Culture experiencing activity, and you are invited to deliver a **5-minute speech** on the **"eight great" regional cuisines.** Your speech may cover:

- The features of the eight regional cuisines;
- The signature dish of each cuisine;
- The factors associated with the development of the dish.

You may refer to the words and expressions in Part A, but please don't confine yourself to them.

Role Play

Chinese food has historically been divided into "eight great" regional cuisines, a term used to designate the country's most important culinary traditions. But these categories don't even come close to capturing Chinese regional cuisines, and some popular cuisines are not included, like Dongbei Cuisine. Imagine that you invite your bestie to your home town, and you are introducing local food to him or her.

Interview

There are many factors we must consider when choosing a dining place, like online reviews, quality of food, the proximity of the restaurant, waiting time, hygiene, service quality, prior experience, menu (price + offering). **What do you value most among the above-mentioned factors when choosing a restaurant? Put five factors you care most in order and give the reasons.** Interview your groupmates, and select one group member to summarize your findings.

You may refer to the words and expressions in Part A, but please don't confine yourself to them.

Read and Retell

Study the text below and try to retell the main information in your own words. You will be given 5 minutes to prepare, and may add more details as necessary.

Chinese food culture can be loosely defined into two camps: North and South. Within the two camps, the Eastern and Western regions of each have their own distinctions. Broadly speaking, the climate in north of the Yangtze River is colder and the south warmer, resulting in different choices of staple food (wheat in the North and rice in the

South), ingredient options (the South has more seafood and river fishes, while the North has more red meat), and palates (Northern food is stronger and heavier, many Southern foods are subtler and more complex, and Southwestern food is spicier partially due to the humidity).

For example, known for a variety of dim sum, char siu, wonton noodles, and seafood, Cantonese food is one of the longest-standing Chinese cuisines in the South. Guangdong, where Cantonese food comes from, is a rich and coastal province with plenty of seafood and local produce. Compared to heavier Northern food, Cantonese cooking has a mantra to retain the freshness and original flavor of ingredients.

Another example is that dumplings are the most important festive dish to many Northerners — they appear in so many traditional Northern holiday celebrations that it became a running joke in Chinese food debates. Unlike the steamed dumplings served in Guangdong and Shanghai, Northern dumplings are boiled instead. Classic dumpling stuffings include pork, lamb, Chinese cabbage, leek, and combinations among them.

(Adapted from *opentable.com*)

Interpretation

Interpret the paragraphs below into English with the words and expressions you learned in Part A.

Paragraph 1

春卷可能是外国中餐馆最受欢迎的开胃菜之一。它是一种中国民间庆祝节日时吃的传统食品,流行于中国各地,在江南等地尤盛。表面上看,春卷有金黄色的、酥脆的外壳,其实它脆而不硬、油而不腻。春卷馅料丰富,有豆沙馅的,也有蔬菜馅的,我最爱吃的是豆芽和卷心菜馅的春卷。在中国南方一些地区,过春节不吃饺子,吃春卷和芝麻汤圆。在东南沿海一带,清明时节人们也吃春卷,而且常常用于招待客人。

Paragraph 2

虽然川菜以大量使用辣椒和令人唇齿发麻的四川花椒而闻名,但其精髓在于将多种口味巧妙融合。川菜厨师擅长将辣、麻、甜、酸、咸以及稀奇古怪的调味料结合在一起,烹饪出各种不可思议的美味。四川人常说:“一菜一格,百菜百味。”有些川菜特别辣,比如又麻又辣的四川花椒和干辣椒。有的菜则是微辣的,比如泡椒鱼香口味的菜,而糖醋口味的菜就一点儿都不辣。

Paragraph 3

饺子、麻辣烫、宫保鸡丁……除了顶流吉祥物冰墩墩,北京冬奥会上让运动员和工作人员流连忘返的,还有中国美食!北京冬奥会期间,运动员们在媒体采访中分享了冬奥村的美食,让数道中国美食走红。有些人甚至被拍到在比赛现场“品尝”美食。中国的元宵也是一道广受国内外欢迎的美食,其外形圆圆的,外皮由糯米制成,内馅或甜或咸。人们都说汤圆有两个象征之意,一为农历的第一个月圆,二为家庭团聚圆满。

A4. Culture Highlights

Q: *What is seasonal eating?*

A: Seasonal eating means eating fruits and vegetables that are grown in your area in a particular time period. Fruits and vegetables that are produced locally can be tastier, fresher, and loaded with essential nutrients, and not like the out-of-season produce that is harvested early. So, if you ever feel like buying your favorite non-seasonal fruits, then try and go for the seasonal local production, which will surely be tastier, healthier, and fresher. Seasonal eating most is not just for privileged people or developed countries. It is an important part for millions of people around the world who count on growing their own crops to feed themselves and their families. Even many experts also suggest you to consume seasonal foods.

(Adapted from *www.onlymyhealth.com*)

Q: *Chinatowns are almost everywhere! For a nation that topped the population chart for years, it has made its presence felt in almost every aspect. What is the charm of Chinatown? And what is its significance for locals and immigrants?*

A: They're a whole different world in the different cultures blending in and yet standing out. In most cities where their shades are all subtle and gray, Chinatowns add some colors to them. The neon signs, Chinese language boards, Chinese supermarkets and restaurants, and so much more now make them inseparable attributes of Chinatown. Chinatowns have a legacy. Some of them have generations staying in them. It all started in the trading years. All the main trading centers started getting Chinese population. Due to frequent trading and easy migrating policies, Chinese men set themselves in different places for better opportunities. The main purpose behind the settlements of Chinatowns was to provide a transitional place into a new culture. Initially, the capability of the Chinese to engage in business and entrepreneurship such as wholesale and retail in their new host country boost not only the growth of their migration but also local economy. Now, the immigrants are no more limited to only Chinese. In fact, Chinese are observed to be dropping in numbers overall. Chinatowns now usually observe Vietnamese, Indians and South Asians.

(Adapted from *www.veenaworld.com*, *gradesfixer.com*)

Q: *What are Chinese Manhan Quanxi ? What is its origin and significance ?*

A: Manhan Quanxi, literally Manchu Han Imperial Feast, was one of the grandest meals ever documented in Chinese cuisine. It consisted of at least 108 unique dishes from the Manchu and Han Chinese culture during the Qing dynasty (1644-1911), and it is only reserved and intended for the emperors. The meal was held for three whole days, across six banquets. The culinary skills consisted of cooking methods from all over ancient China.

Its name shows the feast originated from the combination of the traditional catering cultures of the Han nationality and the Manchu nationality. Meanwhile, it fully affects the harmonious coexistence of these two nationalities. Manchu Han Imperial Feast was ever popular throughout China and many other foreign countries, such as Japan, South Korea, and Singapore.

Today, Manchu-Han Imperial Feast is but a faint reflection of the extreme extravagance of the first Manchu-Han Imperial Feast. Many of the exotic dishes on the original menu can no longer be made because they used animals that are now considered endangered species.

(Adapted from *infogalactic.com*, *en.g-photography.net*, *kenmorepines.com*)

Q: *What is the making process of a century egg and what does it look like ?*

A: A century egg, also known as a hundred-year egg, is a Chinese delicacy. If you're used to the sight of clear, transparent egg whites and golden yolks, the look and aroma of a newly-cracked century egg may come as a shock.

A century egg is made by preserving an egg, usually, from a duck, such that the shell becomes speckled, the white becomes a dark brown gelatinous material, and the yolk becomes deep green and creamy. The surface of the egg white may be covered with beautiful crystalline frost or pine-tree patterns. The white supposedly doesn't have much flavor, but the yolk smells strongly of ammonia and sulfur and is said to have a complex earthy flavor. The most common type of century eggs is made from duck eggs. However, other types, such as chicken eggs, goose eggs, and quail eggs can be preserved the same way.

There's an old rumor that century eggs are soaked in horse urine, which is thankfully not true. There isn't any solid evidence that horse urine is involved in the curing, especially considering the fact that urine is slightly acidic, not basic. So, don't let that deter you from being adventurous and trying this food.

(Adapted from *www.thoughtco.com*, *redhousespice.com*)

A5. Extensive Reading

Passage One

What is Chinese Hot Pot? — The Perfect Guide

Chinese cuisine is full of variety. From stir-fries to soups and steamed dishes to deep-fry, there seems to be a dish for everyone. One of the most popular meals is Chinese hot pot.

What is Chinese hot pot?

Chinese hot pot is a style of eating where a pot of simmering broth sits in the middle of the table with raw ingredients placing all around it. People add and cook whatever they want from these ingredients in the broth. It's sometimes referred to as "Chinese fondue".

Although it's generally favored in winter since it's very warming, Chinese hot pot is still enjoyed in the summertime. It also has a long history in Chinese culture, going all the way back to the Zhou dynasty (1046 BCE-256 BCE). Emperors and empresses even held hot pot banquets to welcome winter.

Chinese hot pot meals are extremely popular because they enhance friendship and unite family, colleagues, and friends. The meal itself is inherently social because several people sit around a pot, talking and eating. The warm atmosphere also creates a cozy, comfortable, and relaxed environment. The unique way of eating has also spurred the popularity of hot pot, especially in North America.

Many hot pot restaurants have opened up in Toronto including, Macao Doulao, Chongqing Liuyishou Hot Pot and Xiaobiandan. Some of these restaurants have added a new flare to eating hot pot. Unique ingredients, new broth flavors, and even individualized hot pots are all part of the mix now.

Components

Chinese hot pot can include a variety of ingredients and broths. It varies from restaurant to restaurant and region to region.

Hot pot varieties are usually differentiated by the type of broth used. The most popular type of hot pot is Sichuan hot pot. It is most famous for the numbing and spicy flavor of the broth.

Popular ingredients include lamb, beef, shrimp, fish, fish balls, shellfish, tofu, Chinese cabbage, bok choy and mushrooms. This is only a small preview of the different ingredients you can add to the hot pot.

To add to all the variety, there are dipping sauces for the cooked food. You can combine whatever you'd like to create your perfect sauce. Some people enjoy the typical sesame paste sauce with their food, while others enjoy a spicier and salty one made with soysauce. Some people add in a raw egg!

Hot Pot Etiquette

Hot pot sounds easy enough. Just put the ingredients in and let them cook, right? There's a special way to eat Chinese hot pot to make sure it's as enjoyable as possible.

Something to keep in mind before digging in is to cook your ingredients gradually and pace it with the group's eating speed. The food is best enjoyed hot and as soon as you scoop it out of the broth. It's also no fun waiting for it to cook during the middle of the meal.

Speaking of cooking the food, remember to cook the food that takes the longest first. This includes hearty vegetables and some of the meat. Try not to throw everything in at once, or the pot will overflow, and it will take longer to cook everything. A good rule of thumb is to make sure the soup is boiling again before adding more.

Since you are cooking raw meat and seafood, it's important to use designated chopsticks or scoopers. This also helps with keeping things sanitary since you are sharing a pot with others.

Hot pot is a naturally social meal, so there are some unspoken rules too. Sharing is the most important one. Dole out meatballs to your friends, don't double-dip and don't hog all the sauce to yourself!

Now you're all ready to enjoy a great meal with some friends and family!

(Adapted from *www.dumplingconnection.com*)

Passage Two

Introducing Dim Sum, the Traditional Chinese Brunch

Rhonda Parkinson

Originally a custom in Cantonese cuisine, dim sum is inextricably linked to the Chinese tradition of yum cha or drinking tea. Teahouses sprung up to accommodate weary travelers journeying along the famous Silk Road. Rural farmers, exhausted after long hours working in the fields, would also head to the local teahouse for an afternoon of tea and relaxing conversation.

Still, it took several centuries for the culinary art of dim sum to develop. At one time, it was considered inappropriate to combine tea with food: a famous third-century Imperial physician claimed this would lead to excessive weight gain. As tea's ability to aid in digestion and cleanse the palate became known, tea house proprietors began adding a variety of snacks, and the tradition of dim sum was born.

Dim sum and Chinese brunch

In the west, dim sum came about as a natural result of 19th-century Chinese immigrants — most of whom were from the Canton region — settling on the East and West coasts. Some gourmands believe that dim sum inspired the whole idea of "brunch", the combination of breakfast and lunch into one large midmorning meal. It is true that the word brunch only came into existence in the late 1800s.

Dim sum food

Many of the dishes that compose a dim sum-inspired lunch are either steamed or deep-fried. Among the former, you'll find everything from steamed pork spareribs, char siu bao (steamed buns with roast pork), and har gaw (shrimp dumplings). Deep-fried treats include mini spring rolls and wu gok, a type of taro turnover.

Finally, there's dessert. Egg custard tarts are a must; you may also have a choice between almond or mango pudding.

All of these delicious foods are washed down with copious amounts of green tea.

Ordering dim sum dishes

If you enjoy browsing through a menu, a restaurant that serves dim sum in the traditional style is not for you. Instead of ordering from a menu, you choose from an assortment of dishes that servers push around on carts.

While it may not be evident in the hustle and bustle of the carts rolling by, there is a certain order to how dim sum is served. Lighter, steamed dishes come first, followed by items such as chicken's feet, then deep-fried dishes, and finally dessert.

Starting with lighter fare not only leaves room for the heavier delicacies but also makes a lot of sense. If you were to begin dim sum with heavier deep-fried food, it would be a little like serving rice for dinner as the first course.

Today, most restaurants have dispensed with the cart system. Instead, when you are first seated, the waitress will hand you a menu, and you use a pencil to mark off which items you want and the number of orders. The food is still served at the table in steamer baskets to keep it warm.

Restaurants that continue to use the traditional cart system — including a major restaurant chain in Hong Kong — have made this type of service a selling point.

Dim sum as a group activity

If you're looking to have a romantic lunch, a dim sum restaurant probably isn't the best choice. First off, the atmosphere is hardly conducive to romance, what with the clattering of trays, people calling out their orders, and large groups of people talking at each table.

Besides, the best way to enjoy dim sum is with a group; otherwise, you'll fill up on a few items and miss the opportunity to sample everything. On the other hand, you can always take home the leftovers.

For the novice, the noisy atmosphere in a dim sum restaurant can take a bit of getting used to. It's a great way to sample a variety of intriguing tastes and flavors. Somehow, the typical Sunday brunch can't match the culinary appeal of Chinese dim sum.

(Adapted from *www.thespruceeats.com*)

A6. Assignment

Poster Design

Imagine that you are going to start a Chinese restaurant in Chinatown, New York. Please **design an English menu** for your restaurant. The major parts might include:

- Specialties
- Set meals
- Drinks and wine
- Prices and discounts

Part B Dining & Drinking Etiquette

B1. Introduction

Chinese Table Manners

As is well-known, China is a country with a time-honored civilization and a land of ceremony and decorum. According to the traditional Chinese etiquette, there are strict rules about people's daily life, like the way of walking, standing, and the polite behaviors when meeting up with people, as well as the table manners. Chinese table manners are part of Chinese catering culture, and include a series of rules, such as the chopstick etiquette, how to order dishes, seating arrangements, and so forth.

Seating arrangements

Generally speaking, the best seat is that on the left, east and facing the gate, and will be arranged for the main guest, the elder or boss. Those next to the best are also good ones. The worst is where waiters serve the dishes. If attending a banquet, the most important table serving for the main guests will be in the front and in the middle of the restaurant hall. It is better to be seated after the elders are seated.

How to order dishes in China

Ordering dishes is the most significant part of Chinese table manners. If time permits, the menu will be circulated among the people in attendance. If you are the host, you should make the final decision after asking for the others' opinions. If you are one of the guests, you may order an inexpensive and commonly-favorite dish. Chinese table manners advocate that we must consider the others' dietary restrictions. For example, the monks are vegetarians who don't eat any kinds of meat.

When in China, you are encouraged to respect and follow the local dining etiquette. Therefore, make sure you also try the local specialties and have an interesting food tour. The most popular dishes at a Chinese banquet are fried spring rolls, dumplings, large meatballs, and spicy diced chicken with peanuts. If you are traveling around, don't miss the Pita Bread Soaked in Lamb Soup in Xi'an, hot pot in Chengdu or Chongqing, instant-boiled mutton in Beijing, beer fish in Yangshuo, etc.

Eating etiquette in China

In ancient China, each person had his / her own table, with his / her own food. This is somewhat like Western table manners. But the individual dining habit has been changed since the Yuan dynasty (1271-1368). However, the essence of Chinese dining etiquette is still kept today.

Chinese are particular about food, as well as what they look like when eating food. After being seated, the waiter will give you a towel to wipe the hands. When there are dishes about lobster, chicken or fruit, a bowl of water may be served with some rose petals or lemon slices, which is not drinks but to wash your hands. At a standard Chinese banquet, the cold dish will be served first, then the soup, the hot dish, the main dish, and dim sum and fruits at last. Here are some important tips for the table manners in China.

- Be graceful and polite when taking food with chopsticks.
- Don't make much noise when eating or drinking soup.
- Don't talk with food in the mouth.
- Don't point someone with chopsticks or play with chopsticks.

- Pick the teeth with a toothpick.
- Don't insert chopsticks in the bowl with rice, as it indicates worshipping ancestors.

Drinking etiquette in China

As far back as the West Zhou dynasty (1046 BCE-771 BCE), China has established a complete drinking etiquette, which advocates people to drink wine at the right time, be moderate in drinking, and comply with the etiquette. It is common to propose a toast at a banquet in China. How to propose a toast is important for learning Chinese table manners.

- There must be something for which you'd like to propose a toast.
- To propose a toast, it is polite for you to stand up, and hold the glass with your two hands.
- If you want to offer a toast to the people in attendance one by one, make sure you know the order, according to age and status.

Tea etiquette in China

In China, tea is always served when guests come to visit. As an important medium of etiquette, tea plays a significant role in Chinese interpersonal relationships. Knowing the tea etiquette, being polite and showing respect when drinking tea can not only reflect your good self-cultivation, but also bring you the pleasantness and peacefulness from tea. There are four tips for your attention when drinking tea.

- Do not drink up the tea at once.
- Do not spit the tea out of your mouth.
- Do not smoke.
- Do not be absent-minded.

Leave the dinner

Don't forget the etiquette when leaving the dinner. Show your appreciation to the host and invite the host for a dinner. If you have to leave halfway, you should explain the situation and analogize to the host.

(Adapted from *topchinatravel.com*, *teavivre.com*)

B2. Words and Expressions

Vocabulary

1. solo / ˈsəʊləʊ / *adj*. & *adv*. 独自的(地),单独的(地)
2. centric / ˈsentrɪk / *adj*. 中心的;重要的
3. glee / gliː / *n*. 快乐,兴奋,高兴

餐食	**Meals**
一日三餐	eating three meals a day
一人食	meal for one
独自用餐	dine solo
套餐	set meals
家庭餐	family centric meals
吃团圆饭	have a family reunion dinner
吃大锅饭	eat from the big pot
满月酒	one-month-old celebration
生日宴	birthday dinner
升学宴	graduation dinner
婚宴	wedding feast
庆功宴	glee feast

Vocabulary

1. catering / ˈkeɪtəɪŋ / *n*. (会议或社交活动的)饮食服务,酒席承办
2. courtesy / ˈkɜːtəsi / *n*. 谦恭有礼的举止,礼貌;礼节;客气话
3. livelihood / ˈlaɪvlɪhʊd / *n*. 生活来源;饭碗,生计
4. congratulatory / kənˌgrætʃəˈleɪtəri / *adj*. 祝贺的,恭喜的

就餐礼仪	**Dining Etiquette**
饮食文化	catering culture
民以食为天。	Food is the people's livelihood.
请客吃饭	treat people to dinner
贺礼	congratulatory gift

厚礼	generous gift
回礼	a return present
迎客	welcome guest
就餐指引	dining guidance
主陪	main host
副陪	assistant host
主宾	main guest
副宾	second guest
餐桌礼仪	table manners
入乡随俗	a guest should suit the convenience of the host
社会公德	common courtesy
八仙桌	old-fashioned square table for eight people
圆形餐桌	round / circular dining table
圆转盘(便于取食)	lazy Susan / rotating tray
座次安排	seating arrangement
上座	the seat of honor
点菜	order dishes
上菜	serve the dishes
细嚼慢咽	take one's time in eating

Vocabulary

1. communal / ˈkɒmjənəl / *adj*. 公共的;共有的;集体的;公用的
2. spit / spɪt / *v*. 唾,吐(尤指唾液)
3. utensil / juːˈtensɪl / *n*. (尤指厨房或家用的)器具,用具
4. disinfection / ˌdɪsɪnˈfekʃən / *n*. 杀菌,除菌,消毒

餐饮习惯	**Dining Habits**
做客	be a guest of
打包带走	take away / pack up
堂食	dine / eat in
点外卖	order take-out
分餐制	individual serving
集体用餐	communal meal
一客一用一消毒	disinfection after each serving
公筷	serving chopsticks

公勺	serving spoon
私人用具	personal utensils
光盘行动	"Clear your plate" campaign
打包剩菜	pack up leftovers
使用二维码扫码点餐、结账	use QR codes for placing orders and paying bills
把骨头吐在旁边的盘子里	spit out the bones on the side plate
用公筷为长辈夹菜	pick up food for elders with serving chopsticks

Vocabulary

1. stab / stæb / *v*. (用刀等锐器)戳,捅,刺
2. tap / tæp / *v*. (常指连续)轻拍,轻叩,轻敲
3. lick / lɪk / *v*. 舔,舐
4. smack / smæk / *v*. (尤指作为惩戒孩子的方式)掌掴,打;撞
5. slurp / slɜːp / *v*. 咕嘟咕嘟地喝,出声地喝

饮食禁忌	**Dining Taboos**
忌口	dietary restrictions
不要用筷子戳食物。	Don't stab food with personal chopsticks.
不要把筷子插在碗里。	Don't insert chopsticks in the bowl with rice.
不要用筷子敲碗。	Don't tap on your bowl with your chopsticks.
不要舔黏在筷子上的食物。	Don't lick the food attaching on the chopsticks.
不要把筷子竖插在碗里。	Don't stick your chopsticks vertically into your food.
不要用筷子指着他人。	Don't use chopsticks to point at other people.
不要吃掉在桌子上的食物。	Don't eat the food which is dropped on the table.
不要(吃东西时)咂嘴。	Don't smack one's lips.
喝汤不要咕噜咕噜响。	Don't slurp one's soup.

Vocabulary

1. spirits / ˈspɪrɪts / *n*. 烈酒
2. medicinal / məˈdɪsɪnəl / *adj*. 药用的,用于治疗的
3. ceramic / səˈræmɪk / *n*. 陶瓷制品;陶瓷器 *adj*. 陶瓷的

酒与酒器	Alcoholic Drinks and Drinking Utensils
中国白酒	Chinese spirits / Baijiu
黄酒	yellow rice wine
啤酒	beer
果酒	fruit wine
药酒	medicinal liquor
配制酒	compound wine
海波杯	highball / Hi-ball
品脱杯	pint
司令杯	sling
高脚杯	goblet
马提尼杯	martini
水晶杯	crystal cup
陶瓷杯	ceramic cup
酒杯	wine glass
酒壶	wine pot
高脚杯	goblet

Vocabulary

1. wager / ˈweɪdʒə / *n*. 赌注；赌博
2. clink / klɪŋk / *v*. 发出叮当声 *n*. 叮当声
3. forfeit / ˈfɔːrfɪt / *v*. 丧失，被没收 *n*. 罚金，没收物
4. bosom / ˈbʊzəm / *adj*. 知心的，亲密的

饮酒礼仪	Drinking Etiquette
酒令	drinkers' wager game
猜拳	finger-guessing game
斟酒	pour wine
斟酒八分满	fill a wine glass to 80 percent full
斟满酒	refill glasses to the brim
祝酒词	words for the toast
敬酒	make / offer / propose a toast
回敬某人	toast somebody in return
互敬	toast each other
碰杯	clink glasses

干杯	bottoms up
一饮而尽	drink it all in one gulp / drink up
酒量	alcohol tolerance / capacity for liquor
酒量好	have a high tolerance for alcohol
酒量差	have a low tolerance for alcohol
适度饮酒	be moderate in drinking
酒逢知己千杯少。	A thousand cups of wine are not too much when bosom friends meet.
举杯时酒杯要低于长者	raise one's glass lower than those of the respected elder
干杯以示尊重	empty cup as a sign of respect
用右手表示敬意	use the right hand as a sign of respect
左手放在杯子的下面	the left hand be placed underneath the cup
在主人敬酒之前喝酒是不礼貌的	impolite to drink before the host makes a toast

Vocabulary

1. underage / ˌʌndəˈeɪdʒ / *adj*. 未满法定年龄的;未成年的
2. concentration / ˌkɑːnsənˈtreɪʃən / *n*. 浓度
3. antibiotics / ˌæntɪbaɪˈɒtɪk / *n*. 抗生素

饮酒禁忌	**Drinking Taboos**
未成年人饮酒	underage drinking
最低法定饮酒年龄	minimum legal drinking age (MLDA)
酗酒	hit the bottle
烂醉	get / be wasted
宿醉	have a hangover
大醉	be hammered / blasted
酒驾	drunk driving
醉驾	drunken driving
血液酒精浓度	blood alcohol concentration
空腹饮酒	drink on an empty stomach
饮酒后吃抗生素	take antibiotics after drinking

Vocabulary

1. scented / ˈsentɪd / *adj*. 有香味的;有气味的;洒了香水的
2. fermented / fəˈment / *adj*. 酿造;已发酵的
3. sample / ˈsæmpəl / *v*. 尝;品尝;尝试;体验
4. saucer / ˈsɑːsə / *n*. 茶碟,茶托,碟状物

茶和茶具	Tea and Tea Set
绿茶	green tea
白茶	white tea
黄茶	yellow tea
乌龙茶	oolong tea
红茶	black tea
黑茶	dark green tea
花茶	scented tea
非发酵茶	non-fermented tea
半发酵茶	semi-fermented tea
发酵茶	fermented tea
养生茶	healthy tea
茶具	tea set
茶壶	teapot / tea kettle
盖碗	covered tea bowl
闻香杯	tea aroma smelling cup
品茗杯	sample tea cup
杯托	cup saucer

Vocabulary

1. rinse / rɪns / *v*.(用清水)冲洗,洗涮
2. brew / bruː / *v*. 沏(茶);煮(咖啡);酿制(啤酒)
3. refreshments / rɪˈfreʃmənt / *n*. 茶点;点心和饮料
4. aroma / əˈrəʊmə / *n*. 芳香;香味

饮茶礼仪	**Drinking Tea Etiquette**
选茶	tea selection
布置茶席	arrange tea table
洁具	rinse tea sets
温壶	warm teapot
取茶	put tea leaves into teapot
洗茶	wash the tea leaves
泡茶	brew tea
斟茶	pour tea soup into tea cups
敬茶	serve / offer tea
品茶	savor tea
提供茶点	provide refreshments
茶馆	tea house
递茶礼	serving tea etiquette
叩指礼	finger kowtow / finger tapping
及时换茶叶	renew tea leaves in time
斟茶七分满	fill a tea cup to 70 percent full
及时续茶	refill the tea in time
小口喝茶	take a small sip of tea soup
忌一口闷	do not drink up the tea at once
第一冲茶	the first steeping of tea
修养	self-cultivation
抱拳	hold fists
合掌	put palms together
鞠躬	make a bow
闻香	smell the tea's aroma

B3. Speaking Activities

Role Play

You invite your friend Amy, an American girl, to your family reunion party. Please introduce the dining etiquettes, the dos and don'ts of dining in your hometown to her.

You may refer to the words and expressions in Part B, but don't confine yourself to them.

Brainstorming

China has a rich and complex history with alcohol, with long-established traditions and etiquette when it comes to alcohol consumption. One of the drinking etiquettes in China is that a guest's glass will probably never be empty. It's a custom for the host or friends to automatically refill each other's glasses to the brim whenever it's empty or a toast has been made, even when it is not requested. The overarching Chinese value of "saving face" applies in its drinking culture. **How to turn down drinks without causing loss of face**? Please brainstorm with your teammates and share your ideas.

(Adapted from *daxueconsulting.com*)

You may refer to the words and expressions in Part B, but don't confine yourself to them.

Discussion

A report by the China Academy Science found that in 2015 residents in big cities, including Beijing and Shanghai, wasted 17 to 18 million tons of food, or enough to feed 30 to 50 million people. President Xi Jinping said the amount of food wasted nationally was shocking and distressing, declaring in a speech that: "Waste is shameful and thriftiness is honorable". Under the campaign "Operation empty plate", local authorities quickly embarked on programs to reduce waste and encourage food outlets to limit orders to one less dish than the number of diners in a group. The popular phenomenon of mukbang videos — performative eating videos which originated in Korea and often feature excessive binge eating — were also banned. Apart from these measures Chinese government are taking, discuss with your partners and come up with **ways to reduce food waste.**

(Adapted from *theguardian.com*)

You may refer to the words and expressions in Part B, but don't confine yourself to them.

Debate

In China, dishes are usually served on separate plates either at restaurants or at homes. No matter whether it is a quick meal or an elaborate banquet, people will sit around a table and clip food from the center with their own chopsticks. However, such an act probably increases the risk of spreading diseases. But some people may find it emotionally difficult to reject the food from tablemates, regarding it as a "betrayal" of tradition, even viewing it as a behavior of destroying Chinese food culture.

(Adapted from *china.org*)

Topic for Debate:

Individual portions should replace communal plates for dining in China.

Read and Retell

Study the text below and try to retell the main information in your own words. You will be given 5 minutes to prepare, and may add more details as necessary.

Tips of Effective Tea Drinking

Drinking tea offers numerous benefits. It refreshes the mind, clears heat within the human body and helps people lose weight. As you add a cup of tea to your daily routine, please check the following tips which help you reap the maximum health benefits.

- Drink it hot. Tea oxidizes quickly after brewing, and its nutrients diminish overtime. It is suggested that you drink it hot to get the best out of tea.
- Do not drink too much strong tea. It is likely to upset your stomach and cause insomnia if you make the tea too strong. No more than 12-15 grams of tea leaves is suitable for daily consumption.
- The best time to drink is in between meals. Do not drink tea soon after or before meals. Otherwise, it may suppress appetite when your stomach is empty, or cause indigestion when your stomach is full.
- Do not drink with medication. Tea contains large amount of tannin, which will react with certain elements in the medicine, thus reduce medical effects. You can drink tea a couple of hours after you take medicine.
- Green tea is the best option for office workers. Green tea contains catechins that help prevent computer radiation and supplement moisture content of the human body.

(Adapted from *chinahighlights.com*)

Interpretation

Interpret the paragraphs below into English with the words and expressions you learned in Part B.

Paragraph 1

俗话说得好,民以食为天。在中国,一日三餐不仅是为了填饱肚子,还是人与人沟通的桥梁。因此,遵守良好的餐桌礼仪往往会给别人留下良好的印象。首先是长幼有序,无论是坐在八仙桌还是圆桌,都需在长者落座之后再就座,并等长辈先动筷。其次,吃东西不能咂嘴,喝汤不能咕噜作响,要细嚼慢咽。最后,社会新风尚促成了新的餐桌礼仪,如分餐制、使用公筷公勺等,这均有助于减少疾病的传播;光盘行动、饭后打包等行为也大大减少了粮食浪费。

Paragraph 2

中国是酒的故乡，酒也融入了中国人生活的方方面面。在六大酒类之中，中国人尤其钟情白酒，而西方人则更喜爱葡萄酒。酒桌上，敬酒似乎是一个无法避免的环节。寒暄之后，主人往往先向客人敬酒以表尊敬，而客人也会礼貌地回敬以示感谢。需要注意的是，敬酒不能只说"我敬你"，还需要根据实际场景说出相应的敬酒词。有时，大家还会玩起酒令游戏来活跃气氛，输的人则要喝罚酒。另外，就算酒量再好，饮酒后也绝对不能开车！

Paragraph 3

茶在中国已有三千多年的历史，备受中国人喜爱。中国乃礼仪之邦，以茶待客是最常见的待客之道，这不仅是对客人的尊重，也体现了自身的修养。泡茶的茶具可繁可简，一个盖碗也能泡出好茶。茶叶主要分为六类，有绿茶、白茶、黄茶、乌龙茶、红茶、黑茶，从左到右发酵程度依次升高。因此，泡茶前需根据个人喜好进行选茶，选茶之后便是洗茶、斟茶、敬茶。当主人向客人敬茶时，客人作叩指礼表示谢意。

B4. Culture Highlights

Q: *Unlike most foreigners who like drinking cold water, most Chinese people like drinking hot water. Why?*

A: The Chinese custom of drinking hot water goes beyond simple preference. According to traditional Chinese medicine, every human body is made up of yin elements and yang elements. A person remains healthy when the yin and yang are balanced. However, if the yang gets too strong, the body's internal temperature rises, and that person becomes susceptible to any number of illnesses.

To treat these illnesses, the person must get rid of the extra yang, or the excess heat. The best way to do so is by consuming food and drinks in the yin category. Hot water, for example, is a yin beverage. It is believed to actually lower the body's internal temperature, restoring the balance and the person's health.

Chinese have been drinking hot water since at least the 4th century BCE. At that time, hot beverages were seen to expel humidity from the body, while cold beverages could, naturally, cool the body down. But not everyone had access to the luxury of fuel for a stove. Thus, hot water was reserved for those who needed it the most, namely pregnant women, the elderly, and the sick. And so, gradually, there grew to be a connection between health and hot water.

It wasn't until 1862, however, that this connection was cemented as the golden rule of traditional medicine. That year, a cholera epidemic broke out in Shanghai, killing up to 3,000 people a day, many of whom were refugees from the ongoing Taiping Rebellion. From Shanghai, the disease spread northward, reaching the capital of Beijing.

The south, on the other hand, remained untouched by the disease. It was well known at the time that southerners drank more hot water than northerners. And while hindsight has made it clear that the real cause of cholera's northward travel was mail boats, the myth that hot water had spared the south spread as fast as the disease itself.

By the time of 1949, drinking hot water had already become a widespread preference among people of every geographic position and party affiliation. In 1952, the nationwide Patriotic Health Campaign was launched, with posters hung in schools declaring that "Children should cultivate the habit of drinking boiled water three times a day!"

(Adapted from *theculturetrip.com*)

Q: *Since chopsticks play an irreplaceable role in many Asian countries, what are the characteristics of chopsticks used in different countries? Moreover, in China, what do chopsticks symbolize or represent in gift-giving?*

A:

- **Different Styles of Chopsticks**

In China: Chinese chopsticks are round or square in cross-section with tapered eating ends. They are much longer than other styles. Most Chinese chopsticks are about 25-30 centimeters long. In Chinese restaurants, melamine, steel, or plastic chopsticks are often provided, because they are inexpensive and durable. Bamboo and wood chopsticks are commonly seen in individual households or with takeaways. There has been a drive to reduce one-use chopsticks in China.

In Japan: Japanese chopsticks are shorter and sharper than Chinese ones. It is common for women to use shorter chopsticks. There are also small-sized chopsticks designed for children. Many Japanese chopsticks have round grooves at the eating end, which keeps the food from slipping.

In Korea: Different from other Asian countries, metal chopsticks are much more popular than other materials in Korea. Most of them are made of stainless steel. Wealthy families use silver or bronze chopsticks. To get around metal's slippery nature, most Korean chopsticks have a flat side for better grip.

In Vietnam: Vietnamese chopsticks are much longer than other styles in Asian countries. They are often thicker and bigger than other ones. The ends for eating are smaller. Most Vietnamese chopsticks are made of bamboo or wood, with bamboo being most popular in villages of Vietnam.

In Thailand: Compared with other Asian countries, knives, forks, and spoons are much more popular than chopsticks in Thailand, as Western cuisines are more popular there. Since Chinese immigrants introduced the use of chopsticks, many Thai restaurants today offer chopsticks for Asian cuisines.

- **Chopsticks as a Gift: Meanings**

For new couples: Sending chopsticks to a new couple (as a wedding present) means they are a perfect match for marriage (as two chopsticks are perfectly match for one another) and it expresses hopes they will soon give birth to a son (the Chinese for chopsticks is kuaizi, which sounds like kuai zi meaning "quickly a son").
For friends: Giving chopsticks to a teacher speaks of honesty and integrity, as well as great rewards.
For elders: Chopsticks mean eternal happiness and longevity when given to seniors.
(Adapted from *chinahighlights.com*)

Q: *Why do people say cheers and clink glasses when drinking with others?*
A: This ritual that has transcended time has its origins in the following:

- **To chase away evil spirits and demons**

This stems from the medieval times when glasses were banged on the table or clinked, followed by loud cheering to ward off any bad spirits in the room.

- **A form of poison control**

When glasses that are filled to the brim are clinked, a bit of alcohol from each glass would spill into the other glasses, proving that none was poisoned. This mixing of drinks would prevent anyone from attempting to tamper with the drink.

- **To elevate the senses**

Aside from sound, all the other senses are involved when drinking. You can taste it, touch it, smell it, and of course see it. So, the clinking of glasses was a way to involve hearing into the drinking experience.

- **A glass is lifted to the heavens**

This upward action of raising our glasses is as if an offering is made to the gods and a declaration of health for the living.

Q: *List 10 other creative ways to say cheers.*

A:

Bottoms up!	Good Health!
Down the hatch!	Skol!
Salud!	Mate!
Good luck!	Prosit!
Here's to you (us)!	Chin-chin!

(Adapted from *araioflight.com*)

B5. Extensive Reading

Passage One

Major Differences between Chinese and Western Drinking Culture

Speaking of drinking, compared to the freestyle drinking in the west, Chinese drinking culture is controlled and ritualized. For the following discussion, let's focus on these aspects.

Emphasis

Chinese people mainly emphasize on the people who drink tighter with them, while western people put a heavier emphasis on the beverage itself. In Chinese drinking culture, the taste of the liquor or wine isn't so important as the people involved. When it comes to some social events, Chinese care more about whom they drink with, no matter for business meetings, family gatherings or celebrations. This phenomenon also indicates the collectivistic culture in China.

For western people, the taste of the actual drink means a lot to them, as they concern more about individual's feeling. Moreover, for some westerners, wine-tasting is enjoyable, which plays an important role in their life.

Choices

Compared to China, there are more options in western countries, and each country has its own drinking traditions. In general, you can choose from beer, white/red wine, champagne, rum, cider, brandy, whisky, vodka, cocktails, and plenty more drinks. Chinese brands are not so popular in the west.

In China, beer and Chinese White Liquor (known as Baijiu) are enjoyed by the majorities. Nowadays, some foreign drinks are increasing in popularity among lots of young adults, but it's a far cry from local alcohol in China. There are many kinds of famous brands of Chinese beers and liquors, yellow wine and fruit wine are also popular in China.

Famous Chinese beers like Snow Beer and Tsingtao Beer are very famous in China, and for Chinese Liquor brands, there is a full array of liquors available, such as Maotai, Wu Liang Ye, Luzhou Laojiao, Jian Nan Chun, Xifengjiu, Fenjiu, Gujing Gongjiu, Dongjiu, Yanghe Daqu, Langjiu, etc.

Additionally, each area of China may have some other local brands. In some districts, locals make wine at home, generally are yellow wine, made from rice or sticky rice, and fruit wine, mainly made from grapes, waxberries, oranges and litchis.

Tasting some local wine is highly recommended during your trip in China, especially when you're traveling in Tibet, for you can try the highland barley wine in no other place but on the plateau. You'd better not miss this amazing experience.

Etiquette

In Chinese culture, people show great respect to elders and authorities, and it may also be applied to the Chinese drinking culture, just hold the glass lower than them when clinking glasses. What's more, you'd better finish your glass.

Chinese people will say "Ganbei" for the toast, it's similar to "cheers" in English, but the actual meaning is to dry your glass, or bottom up. Thus, it's more polite to finish your drink when someone proposes a toast, rather than just take a sip, this is the best way to show your respect.

The drinking rules for each social activity may vary from each other, the key is to follow what others do and show your respect all the time. Don't worry too much about it, Chinese people are kind to foreign friends, they won't force you to drink if you're not willing to.

Wine games

There are more wine games in China than in western countries. As Chinese people prefer communal eating, wine games are really popular in any social activities that involves alcohol, as wine games may easily liven up the atmosphere. When you enter a bar or a KTV in China, you may find there are dice and cards on the table, moreover, finger-guessing game is one of the most popular drinking games among most Chinese people.

In some ethnic villages, there are some special toasting songs, tourists should have a drink before entering the village. Also, they will sing during the meal and have some interesting games. It will be an amazing experience to visit ethnic villages. Additionally, wine they serve is generally home-made, so don't hesitate to have a try.

Survival tips

How to survive from Chinese drinking frenzy? If you're going to a Chinese meal, you can hardly get rid of drinking. By knowing some tips, you may enjoy the meal better.

Never be late. You will be "punished" for more glasses of wine if you're the last one for the party.

Be aware that you may need a couple of hours until the end. Make sure you eat some food, and remember to take less Baijiu. If you really have to drink, you can choose beer instead.

Once you're in, you're in. If you don't refuse at the beginning of the dinner, maybe you will be encouraged to drink more till the end. You can wisely pretend that you can't drink and politely request a pot of tea, so that you could participate in the toasts and cheers.

Take it easy. Your Chinese friends won't blame on you if you're unable to drink, but you'd better let them know the fact at the very beginning. They care more about whether you enjoy the time with them.

(Adapted from *topchinatravel.com*)

Passage Two

Chinese Tea Culture: History and Etiquette

The history of Chinese tea is a long and gradual story of refinement. Generations of growers and producers have perfected the Chinese way of manufacturing tea, and its many unique regional variations. And along the refinement of tea, tea etiquette developed. Now let's look into the history and etiquette of tea culture.

History of Chinese tea

The history of Chinese tea is a long and gradual story of refinement. Generations of growers and producers have perfected the Chinese way of manufacturing tea, and its many unique regional variations.

The original idea is credited to the legendary emperor Shennong, who is said to have lived 5,000 years ago. His far-sighted edicts required, among other things, that all drinking water be boiled as a hygienic precaution. A story goes that, one summer day, while visiting a distant part of his realm, he and the court stopped to rest. In accordance with his ruling, the servants began to boil water for the court to drink. Dried leaves from a nearby bush fell into the boiling water, and a brown substance was infused into the water. As a scientist, the emperor was interested in the new liquid, drank some, and found it very refreshing. And so, according to this legend, tea was created in 2737 BCE.

Traditional Chinese tea etiquette

- **Seating etiquette**

Conventionally, the host's left-hand side should be the first guest of honor. The importance of the seats is in descending order from the host's left hand to the right. It is the iron law to follow regardless of the table shapes. Besides, the old and teachers are most revered to take the first ranked seat, among them ladies have the priority when age differences are small. In addition, it would be inappropriate to sit opposite to the host. If it is inevitable, children should be allowed to take this seat.

- **Gratitude for the first steep**

It is the first time that the guests express appreciation to the host when they're invited to taste the first steep, it is one of the most important etiquette in traditional tea ceremony. The formal and standard gesture is to stand up, men hold fists (left over right), women put palms together, make a bow, sit down, and take over the tea cups, smell the tea's aroma first, then take a sip and savor the tea.

- **Finger kowtow**

Finger kowtow, otherwise known as finger tapping, is a ritual performed as a silent gratitude to the person serving the tea. According to legend, emperor Qianlong of Qing dynasty (1644-1911) used to travel incognito to the south and once he went into a teahouse with his companions. The tea house owner used a long pot and poured the water three ups and downs with rhythm to make a cup of tea without even spilling a drop. Emperor Qianlong was impressed yet didn't understand, "What was that movement?" he asked. The owner smiled and said: "This is the tradition of our tea house called 'Three Nods of the Phoenix'". Heard that, emperor Qianlong took over the long pot and tried to do the same, but that cup was his servant's, normally the servant would get down on knees and kowtow to the emperor for this great honor. However, to do so would reveal the identity of the emperor, so the quick-thinking servant bent his two fingers and tapped on the table as if he was kneeing and kowtowing to the emperor. From then on, finger kowtow has been the practice. Nowadays, instead of the implication of kowtow, people just tap their two fingers on the table to pay silent thanks to the tea server.

(Adapted from *chinahighlights.com*, *teavivre.com*)

B6. Assignment

Poster design

Work in a team to compare the differences in food serving order between China and a western country you are interested in. You are supposed to design a poster to present the differences you have found.

References

Eight Chinese Cuisines. *Travelchinaguide*. Retrieved from https://www.travelchinaguide.com/intro/cuisine_drink/cuisine/eight_cuisines.htm on September 17th, 2022.

Tony Lin. (2020). Chinese Food 101: Learn the Varied, Delicious Regional Cuisines of China. *Opentable*. Retrieved from https://blog.opentable.com/chinese-food-cuisines-explainer-restaurants// on September 17th, 2022.

Navya Kharbanda. (2021). What Is Seasonal Eating?: Here Are The Reasons Why You Should Practice It. *Onlymyhealth*. Retrieved from https://www.onlymyhealth.com/what-is-seasonal-eating-here-are-the-reasons-why-you-should-practice-it-1617103295 on September 17th, 2022.

Priyanka Tawde. (2019). Why Are Chinatowns Everywhere? *Veenaworld*. Retrieved from https://www.veenaworld.com/blog/why-are-chinatowns-everywhere on September 17th, 2022.

Chinatown: Understanding Its Impact and Origin. *Gradesfixer*. Retrieved from https://gradesfixer.com/free-essay-examples/chinatown-understanding-its-impact-and-origin/ on September 17th, 2022.

Manchu Han Imperial Feast. *Infogalactic*. Retrieved from https://infogalactic.com/info/Manchu_Han_Imperial_Feast on September 17th, 2022.

Jane. (2016). The Manchu Han Imperial Feast. *en.g-photography*. Retrieved from http://en.g-photography.net/china/related/ethnicarts_man_10514.html#:~:text=Manchu%20Han%20Imperial%20Feast%20%28a%20full%20formal%20banquet%29, of%20the%20Han%20Nationality%20and%20the%20Manchu%20Nationality. on September 17th, 2022.

Natalie Claire. (2021). The History of the Manchu-Han Imperial Feast: A Chinese Thanksgiving. *Kenmorepines*. Retrieved from https://kenmorepines.com/the-history-of-the-manchu-han-imperial-feast-a-chinese-thanksgiving/ on September 17th, 2022.

Anne Marie Helmenstine. (2019). What Are Century Eggs? Are the Eggs Soaked in Horse Urine? *Thoughtco*. Retrieved from https://www.thoughtco.com/century-eggs-chinese-delicacy-3976058 on September 17th, 2022.

Wei Guo. (2021). Century Eggs, The Myths and Recipe (Pi Dan, 皮蛋). *Redhousespice*. Retrieved from https://redhousespice.com/century-eggs/ on September 17th, 2022.

What Is Chinese Hot Pot? — The Perfect Guide. *Dumplingconnection*. Retrieved from https://www. dumplingconnection. com/articles/what-is-chinese-hot-pot-the-perfect-guide/ on September 17th, 2022.

Rhonda Parkinson. (2020). Introducing Dim Sum, the Traditional Chinese Brunch. *Thespruceeats*. Retrieved from https://www. thespruceeats. com/delicious-dim-sum-chinese-brunch-694544 on September 17th, 2022.

Chinese Table Manners. *TCT*. Retrieved from https://www.topchinatravel.com/china-guide/chinese-table-manner.htm. on September 17th, 2022.

Armstrong. (2019). The Twelve Stages of the Human Life Cycle. *American Institute for Learning and Human Development*. Retrieved from https://www.institute4learning. com/resources/articles/the-12-stages-of-life/ on September 17th, 2022.

Traditional Chinese Tea Etiquette. *teavivre*. Retrieved from https://www. teavivre. com/info/traditional-chinese-tea-etiquette.html on September 17th, 2022.

Individual Meals and Serving Chopsticks: Changing Dining Table Habits. *china*. Retrieved from http://www.china.org.cn/video/2020-03/26/content_75862841.htm on September 17th, 2022.

Fercility Jiang. (2021). Chinese Tea, Discover Chinese Tea Culture and History. *chinahighlights*. Retrieved from https://www. chinahighlights. com/travelguide/chinese--tea/ on September 17th, 2022.

Rachel Deason. (2018). Why Do Chinese People Drink Hot Water? *theculturetrip*. Retrieved from https://theculturetrip. com/asia/china/articles/why-do-chinese-people-drink-hot-water/ on September 17th, 2022.

Mike Ho. (2021). Chinese Chopsticks — Legends, How to Use Them, and Taboos. *chinahighlights*. Retrieved from https://www. chinahighlights. com/travelguide/chinese-food/chopsticks.htm#style on September 17th, 2022.

100+Ways to Say Cheers in Different Languages Around the World. *araioflight*. Retrieved from https://www. araioflight. com/cheers-in-different-languages-world/#:~:text=10%20Other%20Creative%20Ways%20to%20Say%20Cheers%201,7%20Skol%208%20Mate%209%20Prosit%2010%20Chin-chin on September 17th, 2022.

Major Differences between Chinese and Western Drinking Culture. *topchinatravel*. Retrieved from https://www. topchinatravel. com/china-guide/major-differences-between-chinese-and-western-drinking-culture. htm#:~:text=Chinese%20people%20mainly%20emphasis%20on%20the%20people%20who, wine%20isn%E2%80%99t%20so%20important%20as%20the%20people%20involved on September 17th, 2022.

Ganbei! An Indepth Guide to Chinese Drinking Culture. *Daxue Consulting*. Retrieved from https://daxueconsulting. com/understand-drinking-culture-china/ on November 10th, 2022.

China to Bring in Law Against Food Waste with Fines for Promoting Overeating. *The Guardian*. Retrieved from https://www. theguardian. com/world/2020/dec/23/china-to-bring-in-law-against-food-waste-with-fines-for-promoting-overeating on November 10th, 2022.

Unit 3 Historic Sites in China

Part A Ancient Palaces

A1. Introduction

The Forbidden City

The Forbidden City is an imperial palace complex at the heart of Beijing, China. Commissioned in 1406 by the Yongle emperor of the Ming dynasty, it was first officially occupied by the court in 1420. It was so named because access to the area was barred to most of the subjects of the realm. Government functionaries and even the imperial family were permitted only limited access; the emperor alone could enter any section at will. The 178-acre compound was designated a UNESCO World Heritage site in 1987 in recognition of its importance as the center of Chinese power for five centuries, as well as for its unparalleled architecture and its current role as the Palace Museum of dynastic art and history.

The architecture of the walled complex adheres rigidly to the traditional Chinese geomantic practice of fengshui. The orientation of the Forbidden City, and for that matter all of Beijing, follows a north-south line. Within the compound, all the most important buildings, especially those along the main axis, face south to honor the sun. The buildings and the ceremonial spaces between them are arranged to convey an impression of great imperial power while reinforcing the insignificance of the individual. This architectural conceit is borne out to the smallest of details — the relative importance of a building can be judged not only from its height or width but also by the style of its roof and the number of figurines perched on the roof's ridges.

Among the more notable landmarks are the Wu Gate, the Hall of Supreme Harmony, and the Imperial Garden. The Wu Gate is the imposing formal southern entrance to the

Forbidden City. Its auxiliary wings, which flank the entryway, are outstretched like the forepaws of a guardian lion or sphinx. The gate is also one of the tallest buildings of the complex, standing 125 feet high at its roof ridge. One of its primary functions was to serve as a backdrop for imperial appearances and proclamations. Beyond the Wu Gate lies a large courtyard, 460 feet deep and 690 feet wide, through which the Golden Water River runs in a bow-shaped arc. The river is crossed by five parallel white marble bridges, which lead to the Gate of Supreme Harmony.

North of the Gate of Supreme Harmony lies the Outer Court, heart of the Forbidden City, where the three main administration halls stand atop a three-tiered marble terrace overlooking an immense plaza. The area encompasses some seven acres — enough space to admit tens of thousands of subjects to pay homage to the emperor. Towering above the space stands the Hall of Supreme Harmony, in which the throne of the emperor stands. This hall, measuring 210 by 122 feet, is the largest single building in the compound, as well as one of the tallest (being approximately the same height as the Wu Gate). It was the center of the imperial court. To the north, on the same triple terrace, stand the Hall of Central Harmony and the Hall of Preserving Harmony, also loci of government functions.

Farther north lies the Inner Court, which contains the three halls that composed the imperial living quarters. Adjacent to these palaces, at the northernmost limit of the Forbidden City, is the 3-acre Imperial Garden, the organic design of which seems to depart from the rigid symmetry of the rest of the compound. The garden was designed as a place of relaxation for the emperor, with a fanciful arrangement of trees, fish ponds, flower beds, and sculpture. In its center stands the Hall of Imperial Peace, a Daoist temple where the emperor would retreat for contemplation.

After being the home of 24 emperors, 14 of the Ming dynasty and 10 of the Qing dynasty, the inauguration of the new Republic of China under Sun Yat-sen in 1912 meant that the Forbidden City was no longer the palace of the emperor. Puyi, the last Qing emperor, was permitted to live there after his abdication, but he left the palace in 1924.

The Chinese now call the Forbidden City *gugong*, which means "Former Palace". It is now also known as the "Former Palace Museum". The Palace Museum is the the world's most visited museum with approximately 16.7 million visitors in 2017. This is about twice as many visitors as the next most visited museum, the Louvre in France.

At the end of 2016, the Palace Museum announced that 55132 previously unlisted items were discovered in an inventory check. It's estimated that the number of items in the Palace Museum collection now totals 1862690, which makes it the best place to see

China's imperial treasures, artifacts and other cultural relics, including paintings, calligraphy, jade, embroidery, lacquer wares, pottery, etc.

(Adapted from *britannica.com*)

A2. Words and Expressions

Vocabulary

1. epitome / ɪˈpɪtəmi / *n*. 典型,典范;缩影
2. commission / kəˈmɪʃən / *v*.(正式地)安排……做,委托……做;委任
3. culmination / ˌkʌlməˈneɪʃən / *n*. 顶点;关键点;高潮
4. hereditary / həˈredəteri / *adj*. (特点或疾病)遗传的;(称号或爵位)世袭的
5. consolidate / kənˈsaːlədeɪt / *v*. 巩固,加强;联合,合并
6. symmetry / ˈsɪmətri / *n*. 对称(性);匀称
7. statuette / ˌstætʃuˈet / *n*. 小雕像,小塑像
8. tranquility / træŋˈkwɪləti / *n*. 平静,宁静

紫禁城	**The Forbidden City**
皇宫	imperial palace
故宫博物院	the Palace Museum
旅游胜地	tourist attraction
中国历史文化的缩影	an epitome of Chinese history and culture
被指定为世界遗产	be designated a World Heritage site
受到良好保护的历史文化遗产	well protected historical and cultural heritage
具有不可替代的文化意义	be of irreplaceable cultural significance
世界已存的最大的古代木质结构建筑群	the largest collection of preserved ancient wooden structures in the world
世界最大的古代宫殿建筑	the world's largest ancient palatial structure
中国五千年历史和文明的有形证据	tangible evidence of five-thousand years' history and civilization of China
由明朝永乐皇帝委托(建造)	be commissioned by the Yongle emperor of the Ming dynasty
为许多艺术作品提供灵感	provide inspiration for many artistic works
作为许多电影的场景	serve as the scene to many films
无与伦比的建筑	unparalleled architecture

严格遵守中国传统的风水习俗	adhere rigidly to the traditional Chinese geomantic practice of fengshui
体现中国传统建筑的精髓和最高水准	display the essence and culmination of traditional Chinese architecture
展示最高的建筑技术和工艺	show the supreme techniques and craftsmanship on construction
举办隆重仪式和政治事件	hold grand ceremonies and political events
占地178英亩的建筑群	the 178-acre compound
遵循一条南北主线	follow a north-south line
沿着主轴线	along the main axis
面朝南向太阳致敬	face south to honor the sun
有围墙的建筑	walled complex
中国的权力中心	the center of Chinese power
世袭制度	hereditary system
政府官员	government functionaries
皇室家族	royal families
皇家宅邸	royal residence
夺取王位	seize the throne
加强帝国力量	consolidate the imperial power
特定条件下允许进入	be permitted only limited access
保持洁净和华丽	retain the cleanliness and magnificence
背离刻板的对称	depart from the rigid symmetry
后花园	side garden
欧洲和阿拉伯风格的建筑	European and Arabic style buildings
促进中外文化交流	promote Sino-foreign cultural communication
奇特的布局	a fanciful arrangement
雕刻着祥云和飞龙的大理石块	a huge block of marble carved with cloud and dragon designs
五座平行的大理石桥	five parallel white marble bridges
石狮和铜狮	stone lions and bronze lions
象征性的守护者	symbolic guardians
屋顶上的神秘动物雕像	mystical animal statuettes on the roofs
屋脊上(陶瓷)小雕像的数量	the number of figurines perched on the roof's ridges
外朝	the Outer Court
内廷	the Inner Court
冷宫	the Cold Palace
午门	the Wu (Meridian) Gate
太和殿	the Hall of Supreme Harmony

中和殿	the Hall of Central Harmony
保和殿	the Hall of Preserving Harmony
乾清宫	the Hall of Heavenly Purity
坤宁宫	the Hall of Earthly Tranquility
养心殿	the Hall of Mental Cultivation
军机处	the Office of Privy Council
御花园	the Imperial Garden
钟楼和鼓楼	bell tower and drum tower
金水河	the Golden Water River
以弓形弧线运行	run in a bow-shaped arc
在第二次鸦片战争期间	during the Second Opium War
被英法联军占领	be occupied by Anglo-French allied forces
有这样一个传说……	Legend has it that...
它的收藏是首屈一指的。	Its collections are second to none.

Vocabulary

1. blend / blend / *v*. 混合,交融
2. Mecca / ˈmekə / *n*. 麦加(伊斯兰教圣城);令人向往的地方
3. ingenious / ɪnˈdʒiːnɪəs / *adj*. 制作精巧的,巧妙的
4. expel / ɪkˈspel / *v*. 驱逐;开除;排出
5. scripture / ˈskrɪptʃə / *n*. 宗教经文
6. stupa / ˈstuːpə / *n*. 佛塔,浮屠(用于珍藏佛的舍利或供奉佛像、佛经)
7. incarnation / ˌɪnkaːrˈneɪʃən / *n*. (宗教观念中人的)化身;道成肉身(神以人的形式出现);特殊体现
8. panorama / ˌpænəˈræmə / *n*. 全景,全貌;概述,概论

布达拉宫	**The Potala Palace**
俯瞰拉萨市	overlook the Lhasa city
与景观融为一体	blend in with the landscape
感到与自然融为一体	feel immersed by and at one with nature
在山坡上形成平台	terrace up hillsides
看一眼它的壮丽与庄严	catch a glimpse of its magnificence and stateliness
最初作为松赞干布的宫殿而建造	be first built as the palace of Songtsan Gambo

世界各地佛教徒的麦加	a Mecca for Buddhists around the world
宗教圣地和陵墓	a religious sanctuary and a mausoleum
防御性的堡垒	a defensive fortress
每个历史爱好者的梦想	a fantasy for every history buff
西藏起源的遗产	legacies of Tibet's origins
精神家园	the spiritual home
点燃一盏祈祷灯	light a lamp for prayer
将名字添加到祈祷墙上	add one's name to the Prayer Wall
寻求祝福、真理和启迪	seek blessings, truth, and enlightenment
政府议会厅	governmental assembly halls
佛堂	Buddhist chambers
礼拜堂,朝拜堂	house of prayer / house of worship
晨祷和晚祷	morning prayer and evening prayer
巧妙的西藏建筑	ingenious Tibetan architecture
对称的建筑布局	asymmetrical architectural layout
象征天地合一	symbolize the union of the earth and the sky
白宫和红宫	the White Palace and the Red Palace
冬季住所	winter residence
金色屋顶	golden roofs
红墙和白墙	crimson and white walls
由镀金的青铜制成	be made of gilded bronze
花朵和钟形的尖顶	flower-and-bell-shaped spires
冬季吸收热量	absorb heat in the winter
夏季驱散热量	expel heat in the summer
巨大的文物宝库	a huge treasure house of cultural relics
具有很高的文化艺术价值	be of great cultural and artistic value
大量的壁画收藏	a large collection of murals
佛经	Buddhist scriptures
宗教神话	religious myths
佛祖的化身	Buddha incarnations
民俗	folk customs
雕塑珍品	sculpture treasures
石雕、木雕和黏土雕刻	stone carvings, wood carvings, and clay carvings
铸铁佛像	cast-iron Buddha statues
古董和文物	antiques and artifacts
远眺宫殿	see the palace from afar
欣赏这座壮观建筑的全景	appreciate the panorama of this spectacular building
在高海拔爬台阶	climb steps at high altitudes

避免高山症和其他不适	avoid altitude sickness or other discomforts
把包放在入口处	deposit your bag at the entrance
禁止拍摄。	Photography is not allowed.
提倡朴素穿着。	Modest clothing is encouraged.
历史名胜点缀着拉萨。	Lhasa is dotted with historic attractions.

Vocabulary

1. ensemble / ˌɑːnˈsɑːmbəl / *n*. 整体，全体；剧团，乐团
2. sacrifice / ˈsækrəfaɪs / *n*. 献祭，祭品；牺牲，献出
3. bumper / ˈbʌmpə / *adj*. 丰盛的；(数量)异常大的
4. concubine / ˈkɑːnkjəbaɪn / *n*. 妃子；妾
5. requisition / ˌrekwəˈzɪʃən / *v*. 征用

其他古代建筑	**Other Ancient Architecture**
沈阳故宫	Shenyang Imperial Palace
保存最完好的皇宫式建筑之一	one of the best-preserved imperial palace-like constructions
仿造紫禁城	resemble the Forbidden City
体现满洲和藏族元素	exhibit Manchurian and Tibetan elements
颐和园	the Summer Palace
中国园林设计的杰作	a masterpiece of Chinese landscape garden design
形成具有卓越审美价值的和谐体	form a harmonious ensemble of outstanding aesthetic value
承德皇家避暑山庄	Imperial Mountain Resort of Chengde
著名的皇家避暑胜地	a famous summer resort of emperors
享受极美的自然环境	enjoy a breathtaking natural environment
装饰精美的建筑	be built with exquisite decoration
占地面积是……	cover an area of...
必须参观的景点	a must-visit attraction
天坛	Temple of Heaven
祭祀天神	offer sacrifice to heaven
皇家祭坛	an imperial sacrificial altar
祭祀仪式	sacrificial rites and ceremonies
在冬至进行一年一度的朝圣	undertake an annual pilgrimage during the winter solstice

向天祈求来年大丰收	pray to heaven for bumper harvests for the following year
象征天地之间的关系	symbolize the relationship between earth and heaven
华清宫	the Huaqing Palace
皇陵建筑	imperial mausoleum architecture
秦始皇陵	the mausoleum of emperor Qinshihuang
(秦始皇)兵马俑	the Terracotta Army
候选为"世界第八大奇迹"	be candidate for "the Eighth Wonder of the World"
真人大小的兵马俑	life-size terracotta soldiers and horses
出土青铜武器	unearth bronze weapons
从中国各地征用劳工	requisition laborers from all over China
清东陵	the Eastern Qing Tombs
建成底部宽大的土质金字塔	be built into an earth pyramid with a wide base
显示皇室的威严气势	reveal the imposing majestic manner of royalty
见证中国历史的兴衰	witness the rise and decline of Chinese history

A3. Speaking Activities

Situational Speech

As a tour guide, you are leading a group of foreign tourists on a visit to the Forbidden City in Beijing. Prepare a **5-minute opening speech**, briefly introducing the **scenic spot.** Your speech might cover:

- Why is it called the Forbidden City?
- Its historical background.
- Its layout and architecture.
- The tour time and best spots to take pictures.

You may refer to the words and expressions in Part A, but don't confine yourself to them.

Role Play

You are video-chatting with your friend Zhuoma, a Tibetan girl who is living in Lhasa. You are asking her for travelling advice as you are planning to visit the Potala Palace in Lhasa. Your questions might include:

- Its location and height;
- Its layout and structure;
- Its history and collections;
- Its religious significance;

- Important travelling tips.

Prepare possible answers to the questions above and role play the conversation with your partner.

Debate

Read the following paragraphs about the preservation of historic buildings and conduct a team debate: **Should historic buildings be preserved or demolished**?

Paragraph 1

The reason for preserving historic buildings, aside from their architectural value, is that they embody our values, our cultural identity and historic continuity. Protecting our patrimony helps remind people of their historic roots and identity and can serve to bind the nation together. More often than not, famous historic buildings represent influential and important people who have lived in this world. They thereby promote respect for our past and the extraordinary individuals who have lived in different times and societies.

(Adapted from *timesmojo.com*)

Paragraph 2

Having survived hundreds of years, historic buildings usually provide us with valuable lessons about construction methods and technologies. Restoring or retrofitting older buildings is much more economical than constructing a completely new structure. The carbon footprint of restored structures is much lesser than newly erected buildings due to minimum requirement of transportation of materials and tools. Additionally, some historic buildings can also be converted to museums, galleries, restaurants, or hotels, attracting tourists and generating business.

(Adapted from *wallthought.com*)

Paragraph 3

When it comes to tearing an old historic building down, several benefits can be attributed or tied to such action. Sometimes, it doesn't matter whether an old building has historical value or not. Having it pulled down tends to be more advantageous when there's a more beneficial use for such land to the community. Here, a new house, local park, or community garden may occupy or replace the old structure. Apart from that, certain historic buildings increasingly become unstable and may crumble. A proactive step like demolition prevents or forestalls any danger that may be posed by the presence of the structure. Also, renovation or maintenance of a historic building may become counterproductive when it becomes too frequent. Rather than channeling more resources and time than necessary into maintenance, it's best to have the building demolished.

(Adapted from *safeandsanitaryhomes.org*)

Interpretation

Interpret the paragraphs below into English with the words and expressions you learned in Part A.

Paragraph 1

紫禁城是位于中国北京市中心的皇宫建筑群。1406 年由明朝永乐皇帝命令建造,1420 年被朝廷正式启用。之所以这样命名,是因为皇宫禁止普通人进入。政府工作人员甚至皇室成员,只有经过许可才能进入指定区域;皇帝则可随意出入任何区域。紫禁城的主色调是黄色和红色,象征着皇权的至高无上。宫殿内的墙壁、柱子和门窗也大多涂成红色,这在中国文化中被认为是好运和幸福的象征。

Paragraph 2

这个占地 178 英亩的建筑群在 1987 年被列为世界遗产,以彰显它在五个世纪里作为中国权力中心的重要性,以及它无与伦比的建筑风格和艺术价值。目前,它作为故宫博物院对公众开放,前来访问的游客络绎不绝。故宫博物院藏有一百多万件珍贵的艺术品,占中国文物总数的六分之一。收藏品包括陶瓷、绘画、书法、青铜器、钟表、玉器、古籍和历史文献。

Paragraph 3

布达拉宫位于拉萨河谷的红山上,它是拉萨的标志性建筑,也是西藏的象征。它曾经是整个西藏的宗教、政治和文化中心。布达拉宫宏伟的建筑、悠久的历史和伟大的宗教影响力使其享誉世界。布达拉宫是一个高 130 多米的巨大建筑群,其中主体建筑高达 117 米,共 13 层,宫殿主要由石头和木头建造而成。

Paragraph 4

布达拉宫一直是藏传佛教最神圣的地标之一,每年都吸引许多来自世界各地的游客和虔诚的朝圣者来此观光和朝拜。人们必须通过安检才可进入宫殿,禁止携带打火机和任何液体,包括瓶装水。布达拉宫是宗教场所,因此宫殿内禁止拍照,游客也不宜穿着奇装异服。这座古老的建筑内部比较寒冷,所以即使在阳光明媚的夏日,带上一件外套也不失为一个好主意。

A4. Culture Highlights

Q: *There are several fun facts about the Forbidden City. To begin with, it is divided into the Outer Court and Inner Court. What are the differences between the two?*

A: The Outer Court and Inner Court are architecturally and functionally different. Emperors had absolute godly power and held solemn public ceremonies in the Outer Court. The buildings here look solemn and grand. In contrast with the Outer Court, the Inner Court was where emperors enjoyed domestic bliss and did mundane tasks. The architectural styles are less formal with gardens and courtyards. Apart from the halls and palaces along the central axis, there are buildings on the two sides to accommodate lesser nobles.

Q: *There are no trees in the Outer Court, why?*

A: The Hall of Supreme Harmony, the Hall of Central Harmony, and the Hall of Preserved Harmony in the Outer Court are the prime structures for holding important rites and events. To show the imperial dignity and supreme authority, and for safety reasons as well, it was forbidden to plant trees around these halls. In fact, it was not permitted to plant trees along the imperial pavement from the Tiananmen Gate to the Wu Gate either. All the trees you see today are from a more recent era. None has passed down from the times of monarchy.

Q: *Why are many gates decorated with 9 rows of doornails?*

A: Many gates inside the imperial city, especially the huge red gates of the major structures, are decorated with gilded doornails. If you study them carefully, you will find that most of the gates have nine rows of doornails and each row consists of nine. That's because the number nine implied supremacy in monarchist China and was reserved for the emperor's use.

Q: *What are the ranks that the Forbidden City has gained?*

A: It was declared a World Cultural Heritage Site in 1987. It's among the top 5 palaces in the world: The others are the Versailles Palace in France, the Buckingham Palace in Britain, the White House in America, and the Kremlin Palace in Russia. It's one of the most visited museums in the world: About 15 million visitors every year. It's among the museums with the greatest variety of exhibitions in the world. It's also the largest and best-preserved palace complex in the world: It covers an area of 72 hectares and the living quarters inside are well preserved.

(Adapted from *travelchinaguide.com*)

Q: *Culture plays a significant role when it comes to associating symbolic or hidden meanings with different colors. China is a country rich with heritage, and uses colors symbolically within every ceremony, festival, and ritual. In imperial times, builders and architects relied on certain colors like red, yellow, and blue to add life to their creations. Were these colors just aesthetic choices?*

A: These colors were not just aesthetic choices; each was associated with a complex schematic that involved everything from astrology and metaphysics to food and medicine. This concept sought to explain all phenomenon as an interaction between five different elements: metal, wood, water, fire, and earth. Later each element became associated with different colors, which then became the dominant palette in Chinese architecture, especially imperial constructions.

Q: *Why was red a prominent color in traditional Chinese architecture?*

A: Red has long been important in Chinese symbolism. It is a popular color in Chinese culture, symbolizing luck, joy, and happiness. It also represents vitality and fertility. Traditionally, red represented warmth and the highest amount of yang — as in yin-yang — energy. The association of red with positive mojo and good fortune is why the color red is prominent in weddings, New Years, and other important celebrations. Think of "red envelopes" given out each year to children at the Lunar New Year. Red is believed to ward off evil too.

Q: *Yellow was another prominent color, right?*

A: Yes, yellow was an imperial color in traditional Chinese color symbolism, representing power, royalty and prosperity. Yellow figures prominently in the Forbidden City and other examples of imperial architecture. The rooftops of most imperial palaces are made of glazed yellow tiles. Yellow was also the color of the imperial robes, and the interior walls of many palace rooms were washed with yellow clay from Hebei province. Yellow was so associated with the emperor, that by court decree the color could only be used for imperial palaces, temples, and tombs.

Q: *What about the color blue?*

A: Blue symbolized heaven and heavenly blessings with the best example being the deep cobalt tiles adorning the rooftops of structures at the Temple of Heaven. This wasn't always the case. When the Temple of Heaven was first laid out in the Ming era, most of the temple structures had green rooftops. This was changed during renovations ordered by the Qianlong emperor in the 18th century. In fact, the famous triple-tiered Hall of Prayer for Good Harvests was once a tri-color mash-up of symbolic colors. The first tier was green, symbolizing the earth, the second tier yellow for the emperor, and only the upper level, representing heaven, had the now characteristic blue tiles. When the structure was remodeled by the Qianlong emperor (and then again when it was rebuilt following an 1889 fire) all the tiers were tiled a uniform blue.

(Adapted from *thebeijinger.com*)

A5. Extensive Reading

Passage One

The Forbidden City

Dr. Ying Chenpeng

The Forbidden City is a large precinct of red walls and yellow glazed roof tiles located in the heart of China's capital, Beijing. As its name suggests, the precinct is a micro-city in its own right. Measuring 961 meters in length and 753 meters in width, the Forbidden City is composed of more than 90 palace compounds including 98 buildings and surrounded by a moat as wide as 52 meters.

The Forbidden City was the political and ritual center of China for over 500 years. After its completion in 1420, the Forbidden City was home to 24 emperors, their families and servants during the Ming (1368-1644) and the Qing (1644-1911) dynasties. The last occupant (who was also the last emperor of imperial China), Puyi (1906-1967), was expelled in 1925 when the precinct was transformed into the Palace Museum. Although it is no longer an imperial precinct, it remains one of the most important cultural heritage sites and the most visited museum in the People's Republic of China, with an average of eighty thousand visitors every day.

Construction and layout

The construction of the Forbidden City was the result of a scandalous coup d'état plotted by Zhu Di, the fourth son of the Ming dynasty's founder Zhu Yuanzhang, that made him the Chengzu emperor (his official title) in 1402. In order to solidify his power, the Chengzu emperor moved the capital, as well as his own army, from Nanjing in southeastern China to Beijing and began building a new heart of the empire, the Forbidden City.

The establishment of the Qing dynasty in 1644 did not lessen the Forbidden City's pivotal status, as the Manchu imperial family continued to live and rule there. While no major change has been made since its completion, the precinct has undergone various renovations and minor constructions well into the twenty-first century. Since the Forbidden City is a ceremonial, ritual, and living space, the architects who designed its layout followed the ideal cosmic order in Confucian ideology that had held Chinese social structure together for centuries. This layout ensured that all activities within this micro-city were conducted in the manner appropriate to the participants' social and familial roles. All activities, such as imperial court ceremonies or life-cycle rituals, would take place in sophisticated palaces depending on the events' characteristics. Similarly, the court determined the occupants of the Forbidden City strictly according to their positions in the imperial family.

The architectural style also reflects a sense of hierarchy. Each structure was designed in accordance with the Treatise on Architectural Methods or State Building Standards (Yingzao Fashi), an eleventh-century manual that specified particular designs for buildings of different ranks in Chinese social structure.

The Forbidden City architecture

The Forbidden City is outstanding not only because of its magnitude, but also for its unique architectural design. Here are five key features.

- Axial symmetry and south-north orientation: To represent the supreme power of the emperor, given from Heaven, and the place where he lived being the center of the world, all the important gates and halls of the Forbidden City were arranged symmetrically on the north-south central axis of old Beijing. Heaven was thought to be Polaris (the North Star), the only seemingly stationary star in the northern sky, and the Forbidden City's layout points its visitors straight at "Heaven".
- Wooden structures without nails: The Forbidden City is the largest and most complete complex of ancient wooden structures in the world. The main frames of all buildings were built with high-quality wooden beams and columns, including whole trunks of precious Phoebe zhennan wood from the jungles of southwest China. The carpenters used interlocking mortise and tenon joints to build its great palace buildings "harmoniously", without nails. Nails were considered violent and inharmonious.
- The yellow and red color scheme: The main colors of the Forbidden City are yellow and red. The walls, pillars, doors, and windows were mostly painted in red, which is regarded as a symbol of good fortune, and happiness in Chinese culture. During the Ming and Qing dynasties, yellow was a symbol of supreme power and only used by the imperial family. If you climb up to the top of "Scenery Hill" in Jingshan Park and overlook the Forbidden City, you will see an expanse of yellow glazed tile roofs.
- Mystical animal statuettes on the roofs: There is a row of mystical animal statuettes placed along the ridge line of halls that were only for official use. The animals, like dragons, phoenixes, and lions, have powerful meanings in Chinese culture. The number of animals is different based on the importance of the buildings. You can see 10 animals on the Hall of Supreme Harmony, the most important structure in the Forbidden City, and seven on the Palace of Earthly

Tranquility, the residence of the Empress.

- Stone / bronze lions: In Chinese culture, the lion is the king of the animals, and is regarded as a symbol of power and strength. Stone and bronze lions are popular as symbolic guardians, and can be seen beside the gates of many Forbidden City palace compounds. The lions are always in pairs, with the female lion on the left and the male on the right.

Public and private life

Public and domestic spheres are clearly divided in the Forbidden City. The southern half, or the outer court, contains spectacular palace compounds of supra-human scale. This outer court belonged to the realm of state affairs, and only men had access to its spaces. It included the emperor's formal reception halls, places for religious rituals and state ceremonies, and also the Wu Gate (Wumen) located at the south end of the central axis that served as the main entrance.

Upon passing the Meridian Gate, one immediately enters an immense courtyard paved with white marble stones in front of the Hall of Supreme Harmony (Taihedian). Since the Ming dynasty, officials gathered in front of the Meridian Gate before 3 a.m., waiting for the emperor's reception to start at 5 a.m.

While the outer court is reserved for men, the inner court is the domestic space, dedicated to the imperial family. The inner court includes the palaces in the northern part of the Forbidden City. Here, three of the most important palaces align with the city's central axis: the emperor's residence known as the Palace of Heavenly Purity (Qianqinggong) is located to the south while the empress's residence, the Palace of Earthly Tranquility (Kunninggong), is to the north. The Hall of Celestial and Terrestrial Union (Jiaotaidian), a smaller square building for imperial weddings and familial ceremonies, is sandwiched in between.

Although the Palace of Heavenly Purity was a grand palace building symbolizing the emperor's supreme status, it was too large for conducting private activities comfortably. Therefore, after the early 18th century Qing emperor, Yongzheng, moved his residence to the smaller Hall of Mental Cultivation (Yangxindian) to the west of the main axis, the Palace of Heavenly Purity became a space for ceremonial use and all subsequent emperors resided in the Hall of Mental Cultivation.

The residences of the emperor's consorts flank the three major palaces in the inner court. Each side contains six identical, walled palace compounds. It is the symbol of mother and earth, and thus is a metaphor for the proper feminine roles the occupants of these palaces should play. Such architectural and philosophical symmetry, however, fundamentally changed when the empress dowager Cixi (1835-1908) renovated the

Palace of Eternal Spring (Changchungong) and the Palace of Gathered Elegance (Chuxiugong) in the west part of the inner court for her fortieth and fiftieth birthday in 1874 and 1884, respectively. The renovation transformed the original layout of six palace compounds into four, thereby breaking the shape of the symbolic trigram and implying the loosened control of Chinese patriarchal authority at the time.

The eastern and western sides of the inner court were reserved for the retired emperor and empress dowager. The emperor Qianlong built his post-retirement palace, the Hall of Pleasant Longevity (Leshoutang), in the northeast corner of the Forbidden City. It was the last major construction in the imperial precinct. In addition to these palace compounds for the older generation, there are also structures for the imperial family's religious activities in the east and west sides of the inner court, such as Buddhist and Daoist temples built during the Ming dynasty. The Manchus preserved most of these structures but also added spaces for their own shamanic beliefs.

The Forbidden City now

Today, the Forbidden City is still changing. As a modern museum and an historical site, the museum strikes a balance by maintaining the structures and restoring the interiors of the palace compounds, and in certain instances transforming minor palace buildings and hallways into exhibition galleries for the exquisite artwork of the imperial collections. For many, the Forbidden City is a time capsule for China's past and an educational institute for the public to learn and appreciate the history and beauty of this ancient culture.

(Adapted from *smarthistory*, *chinahighights.com*)

Passage Two

The Potala Palace

Ivana

The Potala Palace, which is now on the list of Chinese national key protected cultural relics, is the most valuable depot in Tibet. It is a huge treasure house of ancient materials and articles of Tibetan history, religion, culture, and arts. The palace is widely known for its countless precious sculptures, murals, scriptures, Buddha figures, murals, antiques, and religious jewelry housed in its many rooms, all of great cultural and artistic value. In 1994, the Potala Palace has declared a UNESCO World Cultural Heritage Site.

External appearance and structure

The Potala Palace is 3,756.5 meters above sea level, covering an area of over 360,000 square meters, measuring 360 meters from east to west, and stretching 270 meters from south to north. It has a total of 13 stories and is 117 meters high. The walls of the palace are over 1 meter in thickness, with the thickest sections being 5 meters wide. Moreover, the walls are covered with huge, colorful, carefully painted murals, allowing history to seep back into the building beautifully and gracefully.

The magnificent palace is made of sturdy wood and stone; all the walls are of granite, and all the roofs and windows are of wood. The overhanging eaves and upturned roof corners, not to mention the gilded brass tiles and gilded pillars inscribed with Buddhist scriptures, bottles, Makara fish designs, and gold-winged birds decorating the roof ridges all contribute much to the beauty of the hip-and-gable roofs.

This grand structure consists of over 1,000 rooms including seminaries, chanting halls, temples, chambers for worshipping Buddha, and chambers covered with gold leaf and studded with jewels housing the stupas of several Dalai Lamas. Throughout the rooms, there can be found tens of thousands of Buddha figures. Walking in, it is difficult not to be struck by the figures' vibrancy, given off by their different sizes and complex designs.

History

The Potala Palace was built in the 7th century with a long history of over 1,300 years. In 641, Songtsan Gambo, ruler of the Tubo Kingdom, had the Potala Palace built for Princess Wencheng of the Tang dynasty, whom he was soon to marry. It was later rebuilt in the 17th century by the fifth Dalai Lama. From then, repeated repairs and expansions until 1645 finally brought the palace to its present scale. Over the past 3 centuries, the palace gradually became a place where the Dalai Lamas lived and worked, as well as a space for keeping the remains of successive Dalai Lama.

The Potala Palace has also always been the political center of Tibet since the fifth Dalai Lama. In 1645, the fifth Dalai Lama, feeling too confined at Drepung Monastery just outside Lhasa, ordered the construction of a new structure that would accommodate his new role as both a religious and political leader. This was what led the Potala Palace to be built, as the imposing and self-confident expression of the new theocracy. With the ascension of the seventh Dalai Lama, the Summer Palace was established at Norbulingka (a stunning garden just outside of Lhasa). The Potala Palace then transitioned to be used predominantly during winter, earning its other name, "Winter Palace."

White Palace and Red Palace

The White Palace, comprising halls, temples, and courtyards, serves as the living quarters of the Dalai Lama and the political headquarter of the Potala Palace. There are

3 ladder stairs reaching inside of it; the central one was reserved for only Dalai Lamas and central government magistrates dispatched to Tibet. In the first hallway, there are huge murals describing the construction of the Potala Palace and Jokhang Temple, and the procession of Princess Wencheng reaching Tibet.

The Red Palace, with 7 golden roofs on its flat top, is renowned for its religious status, gorgeous stupas, and precious cultural relics. The dominant buildings of the Red Palace are the stupa-tombs halls of Dalai Lamas and all kinds of halls for worshiping Buddha. The center of the elaborate Red Palace is the Great West Hall, which records the great fifth Dalai Lama's life in its fine murals. There is a gallery that houses a collection of 698 murals, portraying Buddhas, bodhisattvas, Dalai Lamas, and great adepts narrating jataka stories and significant Tibetan historic events.

Stupa tombs

Among the 7 stupa-tombs in the Potala Palace, that of the fifth Dalai Lama, built in 1691, is known as the oldest and largest. Records say that it is made of sandalwood, wrapped in gold foil, and decorated with thousands of diamonds, pearls, agates, and others gems. The stupa, with a height of 14.86 meters, consists of more than 3,700 kilograms of gold. Delicately designed, the intricate patterns on the stupa-tombs are truly amazing and striking. Mainly decorated with amber, pearl, coral, agate, diamond, and other precious stones, these designs add even more value to the whole stupa-tombs.

Apart from the patterns, precious items housed in the stupas also make them priceless. There is a large number of cultural relics; for example, the stupa of Sakyamuni includes a thumb from his figure, a piece of a posthumous decree by King Songtsan Gambo, a portrait embroidered by Princess Wencheng, things left by previous high-ranking monks, and so on. According to Tibetan custom, the mummified and perfumed bodies of Dalai Lamas and Panchen Lamas are well kept in stupas, which is known as Stupa Funerals.

Around the stupa-tomb chapel of the fifth Dalai Lama, there are also some chapels in which thousands of precious books and numerous scriptures written in Chinese, Manchu, and Mongolian are carefully kept. In addition, there are many handwritten copies and printed books about history, medicine, culture, Buddhism, and more. It is recorded that the total number of those books is over 200,000.

Legend

The Potala Palace is said to have been built in the 7th century for Princess Wencheng, a very famous princess in China's history. It was King Songtsan Gambo who had the palace built. It was said that he was a wise, handsome, and brave man, with a strong body, charming figure, and heavy features.

It was in 629, the 3rd year of emperor Li Shimin's reign, that a coup d'etat took place in Tubo. The kingdom was seized with a movement of separatism championed by the aristocrats bent on returning to the old system. Songtsan Gambo became the 32nd tsampo. Though he was only 13 years old at the time, he had already been a resourceful statesman. Calmly exploiting his diplomatic and military clout, he crushed the separatist movement, and in 3 years Tubo became an integrated kingdom again. Then Songtsan Gambo crossed the Yalutsangbo River and established the capital at Lhasa. Ever since King Songtsan Gambo has been a national hero of the Tibetans and worshiped like the revered Lamas.

Visiting tips

There is no heat inside this ancient building. So be aware that it can be very cold inside the Potala Palace. It would not be a bad idea to take a coat with you even on the sunny Lhasa summer days.

As this is a religious site, it is hard to find an adequate bathroom during your tour. So make sure you try to take care of business before you leave your hotel in Lhasa. If you do end up finding one of the few bathrooms along the tour, it is said the bathroom at the right side of the White Palace Square is the most beautiful one on earth with an excellent view out onto Lhasa. Lucky you if you make it here!

The tour time in the Potala Palace is normally limited to 1 hour. So don't dilly dally and make sure you stay close to your guide. It might be easy to get lost amidst the many steps and the labyrinth of rooms and holy sites if you were separated from your tour guide.

Entering the palace is like entering airport security. You will have to check your bags through an X-ray machine, and lighters and any kind of liquid are forbidden. (You can buy bottles of water inside the palace for about twice as much as they are sold for in Lhasa).

The best spot to take pictures of the Potala Palace is Chakpori Hill, across the square from the palace. I highly recommend visiting this place at night because seeing the palace all lit up in the dark is pure magic!

(Adapted from *chinatravel.com*, *elevatedtrips.com*)

A6. Assignment

Travel Plan

Form **groups of 3 or 4 and plan a 6-Day Beijing tour with your friends.** You need to make a detailed plan which may cover:

- Must-see attractions in Beijing;
- Brief introductions of scenic spots;
- Package tour or free walker;
- Accommodation and transportation;
- Reservation and budget;
- Time allocation.

Part B Buddhist Caves

B1. Introduction

China's Buddhist Caves: The Enduring Art of the Silk Road

Tess Humphrys

The Silk Road is well-known as being one of the world's earliest trade routes, allowing the exchange of goods between China and Europe, via Central Asia. And it was along the Silk Road that Buddhism began spreading into China from India as early as the first century. With it came the idea of constructing temples and holy sites by hollowing out rock faces: Buddhist caves and mural art spread across China in this way.

Hundreds of these magnificent cave art sites, or grottoes, still dot mountainsides and rock faces across China, housing impressive sculptures and vivid murals that are thousands of years old. Not only are these sites evidence of their creators' dedication to their faith, they also offer a fascinating glimpse into the multicultural society that thrived for a thousand years along the once mighty Silk Road trade route that connected east and west.

Stories of the Silk Road

China's Buddhist caves were often chosen for their scenic beauty, sometimes by travelling monks who had had visions at a particular spot or who were attracted by its spiritual aura. Within the excavated caves, which would take years to hollow out, monks and other followers would carve thousands of Buddhas, bodhisattvas (spiritual beings on the path to becoming Buddhas), apsaras (heavenly nymphs) and celestial musicians. These would be painted and highlighted in explosions of color made from precious materials like lapis lazuli, indigo and real gold traded along the Silk Road. Alongside these heavenly beings, however, more down to earth details were also depicted — Central Asian merchants, Indian monks in white robes and Chinese peasants working in the fields. These portraits of average travelers from bygone times have sat quietly in grottoes throughout western China, preserved for generations to come.

Many Buddhist caves in China became the focus of worship and meditation not only for the communities of monks who would reside there, but also for visiting pilgrims and traders. Indeed, many of the temples and holy sites on the Silk Road were used by merchants as banks or warehouses. They would be centers of religious practice and cultural exchange, as well as valued stop-off points on the long, dangerous routes through central China. Over the years, more and more cave sites, stretching further away from the Silk Road and deeper into China, would be excavated and decorated, matching closely the spread and acceptance of Buddhism across the country and showing an incredible development and change in artistic style as they moved.

As the millennia passed, however, and trade along the Silk Road lessened (thanks to increased sea transportation), many of the caves were abandoned or fell into disrepair. Others were destroyed as cultural shifts in China meant that different religions and new ways of worship came to dominate certain parts of the country. Many Silk Road caves were looted for their treasures or cast from the cultural consciousness, becoming buried by the desert sands from which they were carved. It wasn't until the 19th century that the caves began to be opened up again, as explorers and archaeologists from China and around the world started to rediscover their hidden treasures.

Most well-preserved Buddhist Caves in China today

The enduring Buddhist caves in China are mainly scattered throughout the far west, mainly in Xinjiang, Gansu and the Yellow and Yangtze River regions. Many are listed as UNESCO World Heritage Sites, housing unique sculptures and murals in varying states of preservation. What connects them all is their important place in the story of Buddhism and multiculturalism in China. They are among the world's greatest monuments to faith and the way in which humans always have, and continue to, share and transmit new ideas. There are many grottoes and cave art sites across the country that are open to the public. Here are our choices of some of the most interesting Buddhist caves in China.

Mogao Grottoes

Hewn into eastern slope of the vocatively named Rattling Sand Mountain near Dunhuang in Gansu province, the Mogao Grottoes are one of the most important collections of Buddhist art in the world. Situated at a strategic point along the Silk Road, at a crossroads of trade as well as religious, cultural and intellectual influences, the grottoes first began being carved in 366 by a monk named Yue Seng. The artwork here reached its creative peak during the Tang dynasty (618-907), when the area housed 18 monasteries, more than 1400 monks and nuns, and countless artists, translators and calligraphers.

Nowadays, around 500 cave cells and sanctuaries survive and are prized for the statues and wall paintings, spanning 1,000 years of Buddhist art, preserved within. Protected under UNESCO World Heritage status, the caves at Mogao show the evolution of religious art along this part of the Silk Road, and provide a literal vivid picture of medieval politics, economics, culture, arts, religion, ethnic relations and daily dress in western China.

Bingling Si

Accessible mainly by boat, and hidden in an arid gorge formed by the Yellow River, Bingling Si in Gansu province certainly wins the prize for most spectacular location. The site's desert isolation not only provides an adventurous journey to reach it, but it also means it is one of the few Buddhist cave sites to have survived the ravages of time and human interference relatively intact.

Over a period of 1600 years, starting from around 420, daring sculptors dangled from ropes to carve almost 200 niches and 700 sculptures into the steep canyon walls. Their sculptures show differing cultural and physical features, with the earliest carved with clear Indian influence. The most spectacular sculpture here is the 27 m-high seated statue of Maitreya, the future Buddha, but some of the smaller bodhisattvas and guardians are equally impressive in their tiny detailing. It's a challenge to find the smallest one, which measures just 25 centimeters in height!

Kizil Thousand Buddha Caves

The Kizil Thousand Buddha Caves in the far western Xinjiang Uyghur Autonomous Region are believed to be the earliest Buddhist cave complex in China. They were started in the 3rd century BCE and reached their height between the 5th and 13th centuries, when Buddhism was the dominant faith in the area.

While not many of the caves are open to the public, those that are contain colorful murals depicting a variety of religious themes, ranging from the life of the Buddha to stories about the nature of karma. Many of these are painted in the shocking blue tinge of lapis lazuli, a semi-precious rock prized for its intense color — one of the most precious commodities traded on the Silk Road at that time. What's particularly interesting about the murals here is that most lack any clear Chinese influence in their style. The presence of Afghan, Persian and Indian elements in the murals indicate that they were produced at an early date by western travelers passing just passing through.

Yungang Caves

The 51,000 statues and carvings in the 5th-century Yungang Caves, in Shanxi province, are simply magnificent. They were predominately carved during the Northern Wei dynasty (386-534), when nearby Datong was the capital of the Turkic-speaking Tuoba clan that ruled China. The dynasty was one of the earliest in Chinese history to adopt Buddhism as their state religion and many of the caves at Yungang were constructed under the supervision and support of the imperial court.

The sculptors here drew inspiration from Indian, Persian and even Greek influences to create their masterpieces. Despite the centuries that have passed since their creation, many of the statues and frescoes at Yungang still retain their gloriously vivid colors. Beautifully painted images of animals, birds and angels fill the walls, while almost every cave contains depictions of tiny Buddhas seated in niches, also known as the "1000-Buddha motif".

Longmen Grottoes

The grottoes at Longmen, located a few kilometers south of Luoyang in Henan province, were started in around 494, after the capital was moved from Datong. As well as being some of the most beautiful representations of ancient Chinese stone art, the statues and inscriptions within the caves provide a window into the political, cultural and artistic environments of that early time. Many of the statues in the oldest grottoes were commissioned by the royal court as a way to honor their ancestors.

The grottoes were maintained and developed over a period of around 200 years, reaching their zenith in 675 with the completion of the extraordinary Fengxiansi Cave. It's an awe-inspiring experience to gaze up at the cave's colossal statue of Vairocana Buddha, flanked on one side by disciples and bodhisattvas, and by heavenly kings and guardians on the other. The face of the Buddha is said to have been modelled on Tang empress and Buddhist patron Wu Zetian, the first empress regnant in China, who funded its carving.

Maijishan Grottoes

Another series of grottoes set into a cliff face so steep you genuinely wonder how they were carved in the first place, Maijishan has over 221 caves and niches that hold around 7800 sculptures. A series of vertiginous scaffolding walkways and stairwells connects visitors up and around the site, to peer into tiny caves for glimpses at Buddhas and bodhisattvas, some dating all the way back to the 4th century. The site was continually added to as trade through the region brought visitors — he towering 15.7m Buddha flanked by two bodhisattvas carved into the cliffside was added a little "later" during the Sui dynasty (581-618). During the 1980s, restoration works on the site revealed a treasure folded away within the Buddha's fan: a handwritten copy of the Sutra of Golden Light.

(Adapted from *lonelyplanet.com*)

B2. Words and Expressions

Vocabulary

1. grotto / ˈgrɑːtəʊ / *n*. 小洞穴;(尤指用于美化的)人工洞穴
2. pre-eminent / ˌpriːˈemənənt / *adj*. 杰出的,卓越的,出类拔萃的
3. antiquity / ænˈtɪkwəti / *n*. 古代;古物,古董
4. oasis / əʊˈeɪsɪs / *n*. (沙漠中的)绿洲;宁静宜人之地
5. medieval / ˌmediˈiːvəl / *adj*. 中世纪的,中古时代的

地理位置和历史意义	**Geographic Position and Historical Significance**
莫高窟	the Mogao Grottoes / Caves; the Thousand-Buddha Caves
著名的佛教石窟遗址	a pre-eminent Buddhist grotto site
被列入世界遗产名录	be inscribed on the World Heritage List
丝绸之路上的中途停留地	a stopover on the Silk Road
沿着古代最伟大的贸易路线之一	along one of the great trade routes of antiquity
从中国一直延伸到地中海	stretch from China to the Mediterranean Sea
河西走廊以西	west of Hexi Zoulang
在戈壁沙漠边缘	on the edge of the Gobi desert
敦煌绿洲东南部约25公里处	some twenty-five kilometers southeast of the Dunhuang oasis
在中国最西北的地方	in the far northwest of China
见证十六个朝代的兴衰	see the rise and fall of sixteen dynasties
见证中国古代文明	bear exceptional witness to the civilizations of ancient China
跨越一千多年	span over one thousand years
追溯到很久以前	extend far back into history
作为连接南亚和东亚的佛教中心而蓬勃发展	thrive as a Buddhist center connecting South and East Asia
与洲际关系史有关	be linked to the history of transcontinental relations
被一个道士发现	be discovered by a Taoist abbot
被誉为世界上最伟大的古代东方文化大发现	be acclaimed as the world's greatest discovery of ancient Oriental culture
在中国、中亚、印度的艺术交流中发挥举足轻重的作用	play a decisive role in artistic exchanges between China, Central Asia, and India

更广泛地了解中世纪早期的中国	comprehend more broadly the early medieval China
具有无与伦比的历史价值	be of unmatched historical value

Vocabulary

1. trove / trəʊv / *n*. 宝库；宝藏
2. repository / rɪˈpɑːzɪtɔːri / *n*. 仓库，储藏室；智囊，知识宝典；知识渊博的人
3. Bodhisattva / ˌbəʊdɪˈsɑːtvə / *n*. 菩萨；开悟的人（在佛教中指运用自己的智慧帮助他人获得觉悟和解脱者）
4. mural / ˈmjʊrəl / *n*. 壁画
5. sutra / ˈsuːtrə / *n*. （佛教中的）经；箴言
6. embroider / ɪmˈbrɔɪdə / *v*. 刺绣；（对故事等）润饰，渲染
7. meditate / ˈmedəteɪt / *v*. 冥想，默念；沉思

艺术、宗教和文化价值	**Artistic, Religious, and Cultural Value**
佛教艺术宝藏	a treasure trove of Buddhist art
宗教文化财富	religious-cultural riches
宗教的见证	a testimony to religion
佛教、道教和儒教	Buddhism, Taoism, and Confucianism
了解佛教传播的巨大文化影响	understand the considerable cultural impact of the transmission of Buddhism
让人们深入了解佛教在亚洲的传播	offer an insight into the spread of Buddhism throughout Asia
让人们一窥古代佛教徒所践行的信仰和传统	offer a glimpse into the beliefs and traditions practiced by ancient Buddhists
沿着丝绸之路向西行进	travel westward along the Silk Road
包含一个佛教经文宝库	comprise a repository of Buddhist scriptures
用砂岩峭壁雕刻而成	be carved out of the sandstone cliffs
凿开石窟	chisel out the grottoes
佛教主题和图像	Buddhist themes and iconography
佛经	Buddhist texts
佛祖和菩萨的雕像	statues of Buddha and Bodhisattva
佛祖的弟子和僧侣	students of Buddha, monks
神圣的勇士	divine warriors

精美的雕塑和手稿	exquisite statues and manuscripts
珍贵的壁画和彩绘雕塑	invaluable murals and painted sculptures
佛经插图	sutra illustrations
绣花图案和丝绸印花	embroidered images and silk prints
可与意大利文艺复兴画作相媲美	comparable to Italian Renaissance paintings
比《蒙娜丽莎的微笑》早一千年	one thousand years earlier than *The Mona Lisa Smile*
非常生动的面部表情	wonderfully animated facial expressions
建筑、雕塑和壁画的综合艺术	an integrated art of architecture, sculpture, and fresco
作品拥有天下无双的美感	creations of an unparalleled aesthetic talent
代表一种独特的艺术成就	represent a unique artistic achievement
描绘不同寻常的文化多样性	portray the unusual cultural diversity
文化十字路口	a cultural crossroads
吸收和重塑外国文化	absorb and remodel foreign cultures
复杂的木板印刷	sophisticated woodblock-printing on paper
世界上现存最早的印刷文本之一	among the world's earliest extant printed texts
发展成熟的出版业	mature publishing industry
飞天洞	Flying Apsaras Cave
藏经洞	the Sutra Cave
到洞窟去朝圣	make pilgrimages to the caves

Vocabulary

1. deterioration / dɪˌtɪrɪəˈreɪʃən / *n.* 恶化;退化
2. conservation / ˌkɑːnsəˈveɪʃən / *n.* (对动植物、自然地区、历史建筑等的)保护;(对自然资源等的)保护,保存,节约
3. discourage / dɪˈskɜːrɪdʒ / *v.* 使泄气,使心灰意冷;(试图)阻挠,阻止
4. mildew / ˈmɪlduː / *n.* 霉;霉菌
5. loom / luːm / *v.* (令人惊恐地)隐约显现;(不希望或不愉快的事情)阴森地逼近
6. panorama / ˌpænəˈræmə / *n.* 全景,全貌;概论,概述
7. retain / rɪˈteɪn / *v.* 保持;保留

文化遗产的保护	**Preservation of Cultural Relics**
敦煌研究院	the Dunhuang Academy
敦煌文物研究所	the Dunhuang Cultural Relics Research Institute
将它置于最高级别的保护之下	put it under top-level protection
将它置于国家法律的保护之下	put it under the protection of national laws
与国际同行合作	cooperate with international counterparts
借鉴国内外先进经验	learn from advanced experiences at home and abroad
从创造到恶化再到保护	from creation to deterioration to conservation
寻宝者	treasure hunters
启动保护计划	launch conservation plans
进行考古探险	undertake archeological expeditions
开展考古调查	conduct archaeological investigations
确定保护区的边界	confirm the boundaries of the conservation area
与缓冲区重叠	overlap with the buffer zone
将(经文)手稿运至各自国家的博物馆	cart off the manuscripts to museums in their respective countries
散落在全球各地	be scattered over the globe
阻止盗窃中国文化遗产的行为	discourage the act of theft against China's cultural heritage
保护敦煌文献免遭发霉和腐烂	preserve the Dunhuang Manuscripts from mildew and rot
遭遇来自人类和自然的毁灭性威胁	encounter destructive threats from humans and nature
迫在眉睫的旅游扩张	looming potential for touristic expansion
涌入现在的敦煌	stream into present-day Dunhuang
实施计划措施	implement the measures set out in the plan
应对挑战	address the challenges
为子孙后代保护洞窟	conserve and protect the caves for future generations
为子孙后代展示完整的历史信息和历史价值	make its full historical information and value available to future generations
向地球另一端的观众展示奇观	present the wonders to viewers halfway around the world
创造手绘的、全尺寸的复制品	create hand-painted and full-scale replicas
激光扫描	laser scanning
检测毫米级别的差异	detect millimeter-level differences
提供文献记录	provide a documentary record
移动数码展览	mobile digital exhibitions
虚拟现实技术	virtual reality technology

创造身临其境的媒体环境	create immersive media environments
数码摄影和图像处理	digital photography and image processing
三维重建	3D reconstruction
制作一个全景参观	produce a panorama tour
保留这些艺术作品的精神和意义	retain the spirituality and meaning of these works of art
为游客提供近乎真实的体验	provide visitors with a near-authentic experience
加深我们的共识	deepen our collective understanding
保护我们的世界遗产	safeguard our world's heritage

B3. Speaking Activities

Situational Speech

Lectures on China's Buddhist Caves will be held at your university. You are invited to deliver a **5-minute** speech, introducing briefly **the Mogao Caves** to international students. Your speech might cover:

- Its geographic position;
- Its historical significance;
- Its artistic, religious and cultural value.

You may refer to the words and expressions in Part B, but don't confine yourself to them.

Brainstorming

The more than 1,000-year-old Mogao Caves are suffering the effects of changes in temperature and humidity, cliff deterioration, human activities, tourism expansion, etc. In 2019 the grottoes were temporarily closed twice due to heavy rain and grass from the Gobi Desert growing around the grottoes. Scientists are worried that the grottoes are disappearing faster than they expected and they are desperately seeking to protect the ancient remains. What do you think is the **best way to conserve and protect the Mogao Caves**? Please elaborate on your views.

Reading and Sharing

Read the following paragraphs about digitization efforts at the Mogao Caves and share your views.

Paragraph 1

For more than 1,000 years, the murals and statues within the Mogao Caves have represented some of the best of Buddhist art in China. However, the centuries have not been kind, as the elements have taken their toll on some of the delicate artworks within the many grottoes and alcoves at the site. To better preserve this art while also making it accessible to people around the world, scholars at the site have been turning to digital technology to ensure these treasures can be enjoyed for centuries to come.

(Adapted from *globaltimes.cn*)

Paragraph 2

As of 2022, the Dunhuang Academy, a national research institute dedicated to studying the Mogao Caves in Dunhuang, has accomplished quite a great deal, completing digital photography of 278 caves, image processing of 164 caves and 3D reconstruction of 145 painted sculptures and also a total of seven ruins. Additionally, it has produced a panorama-tour program covering 162 caves and digitalized more than 50,000 film negatives of the caves' cultural relics.

(Adapted from *globaltimes.cn*)

Paragraph 3

The results of the digital Dunhuang project, which provides highly accurate photographs and scans of 30 of the caves, have been available to netizens around the world for free since 2016. Such digitalization projects will continue to be carried out and can be expanded to other cultural relics throughout the rest of China. At present, the digital Dunhuang website has been visited by users in 78 countries, including the US, the UK, South Korea and Spain, and earned more than 16.8 million page views.

(Adapted from *globaltimes.cn*)

Ideas for Sharing

- Why is technology playing a crucial role in preserving and protecting cultural relics? Give your reasons with examples.
- Why is technology playing a crucial role in publicizing and sharing cultural relics globally? Give your reasons with examples.

Interpretation

Interpret the paragraphs below into English with the words and expressions you learned in Part B.

Paragraph 1

莫高窟，又名“千佛洞”，位于敦煌市东南25公里处、鸣沙山东麓的断崖上，与河南洛阳龙门石窟、山西大同云冈石窟并称中国三大石窟。洞窟始凿于公元366年前秦时期，后经历代增修，今存洞窟492个，壁画45000平方米，彩塑雕像2415尊。作为世界上现存规模最大的佛教艺术宝库，莫高窟于1987年被联合国教科文组织列为世界文化遗产。

Paragraph 2

莫高窟是隋唐宋时期中国古代文明的绝佳见证,是中国西北地区佛教艺术演变的重要证据,它们提供了生动丰富的资料,描绘了中世纪西部政治、经济、文化、艺术、宗教、民族关系和日常服饰等各个方面,具有无可比拟的历史价值。莫高窟的艺术特点主要表现在建筑、塑像和壁画三者的有机结合上。它不仅是人类稀有的文化宝藏,还是一座名副其实的文物宝库。

Paragraph 3

从20世纪初开始,莫高窟就在不断侵蚀的戈壁沙漠中被开垦出来,但如何保护它们,仍然是一个持续的挑战。除了像沙尘暴和雨水这样的自然威胁,洞穴内精美的壁画还面临着主要由游客(每年数十万人,每天多达6000人)造成的破坏,因为他们的存在给空气增加了二氧化碳和湿度。幸运的是,有关部门正在积极采取措施,如数字技术,以保存和保护这些人类文明的瑰宝,同时让世界各地的人们以及子孙后代都能有机会欣赏到它们。

B4. Culture Highlights

Q: *What does Mogao mean ?*

A: In Chinese, "Mo" means "desert". The Mogao Caves refers to "the caves in high place of the desert". According to the Buddhism term, "Mo" means "no", and the Mogao Caves implies that there is no higher and better caves than the peerless ones.

Q: *What is inside the Mogao Caves ?*

A: On the cliffs of Daquan River and Mingsha Mountain in the East, are 735 caves facing the direction of Sanwei Mountain, the branch of Qilian Mountain in the East. Additionally, there are 2,415 colored sculptures and 45,000 square meters' murals in the cave. More than 50,000 ancient scriptures and documents in the Sutra cave were discovered in modern times.

Q: *Why was the Mogao Caves built on the cliffs ?*

A: According to Buddhism, monasteries and temples need a clean environment, free from the interference of secular life. Therefore, the mountain and forest have always been the sites for Buddhist temples and grottoes. The Mogao Caves is located on the cliffs of Mingsha Mountain formed by river erosion in the west. It is not only far away from secular life, but also because of the existence of Daquan River, which forms a quiet natural scenery. The dryness is more suitable for the preservation of sculptures and murals in the grottoes, and the sedimentary rock is also suitable for excavation.

Q: *Who built the Mogao Caves?*

A: The cave builders are mainly three forces: the cave owner, the benefactor, and the craftsman. The cave owner is the owner of the cave. The benefactor is the one who donated money and helped the cave owner to build the cave. The craftsman is the specific operator of the cave construction. They can be divided by their competency, the sculptor, the painter, the carpenter, etc. However, only the cave owner and benefactor are recorded in the cave. In the caves, you can find the answer in lots of mural paintings of the benefactors and cave owners, including the great clans, eminent monks of Dunhuang, as well as the common people from all walks of life.

Q: *How were the murals in the Mogao Caves painted?*

A: After the caves were dug, the artisans could not draw on the rough sandstone directly. They covered the rocks with Dunhuang soil and invented a composite material with glutinous rice and some herbs. Such mixed soil was sticky and had strong adhesion like concrete. After flattening the cave, the white powder was added to the surface and the preliminary work was done. Later, the painters came through ingenious conception, and started to draw a good manuscript on the wall, and painted with different colors. With the most expensive mineral pigments at that time, some even use gold powder.

Q: *Who discovered the Mogao Caves in modern times?*

A: The Mogao Caves were mostly built in the northern and Southern dynasties and Sui and Tang dynasties. At that time, rulers respected Buddhism and were also obsessed with the construction of grottoes. However, with the collapse of the Tang dynasty (618-907), the excavation gradually subsided. In the Ming and Qing dynasties, because of the historical changes, the Mogao Caves were gradually forgotten and left untouched.

In 1900, a Taoist named Wang Yuanlu had come to the Mogao Caves and settled down for years. When cleaning the grottoes, he found a grotto with many ancient books and scriptures buried inside. He reported his discovery to the local governors. However, nobody really realized their value until the news was known by a British explorer Stein who came to the Mogao Grottoes and bought a large number of these priceless scriptures, which created quite a stir in the archaeology field, and also attracted archaeologists and explorers from France, the United States, Japan and Russia to come here with bringing a large number of scriptures and murals to their home countries. The Mogao Caves is popped out from the desert land and known by the other side of the world.

(Adapted from *chinadiscovery.com*)

B5. Extensive Reading

Passage One

The Mogao Caves

Brief introduction

Located on south-east of the Dunhuang oasis, Gansu province, the Mogao caves, also known as the Thousand-Buddha Caves, are the world's largest, most richly endowed, and longest used treasure house of Buddhist art. They are located at a strategic point along the Silk Road, at the crossroads of trade as well as religious, cultural, and intellectual influences.

According to historical records, the carving of the caves started in 366 and continued for about 1,000 years. The 492 well-preserved cells and cave sanctuaries in Mogao, housing about 45,000 square meters of murals and more than 2,000 painted sculptures, are well-known for their statues and wall paintings. The painted clay figures vary greatly in size, with the largest one being 33 meters high and the smallest only 10 centimeters.

Painted clay sculptures and murals in the Mogao Grottoes have mainly Buddhist themes, but they also include human figures, reflecting various societies and cultures of different times. Besides, they also demonstrate painting styles of different times in layout, figure design, delineation and coloring, as well as the integration of Chinese and Western arts.

In 1900, a total of 4,500 valuable cultural relics dating from 256 to 1002 were found in the Buddhist Sutra Cave, including silk paintings, embroidery and documents in rare languages such as ancient Tibetan and Sanskrit. This is regarded as one of the world's greatest Oriental cultural discoveries. The Mogao Caves were added to the list in December 1987.

Significance

The Mogao Caves, bearing exceptional witness to the civilizations of ancient China during the Sui, Tang and Song dynasties, are important evidence of the evolution of Buddhist art in the northwest region of China, providing an abundance of vivid materials that depict various aspects of medieval politics, economics, culture, arts, religion, ethnic relations, and daily dress in western China, so they are of unmatched historical value. The unique artistic style of Dunhuang art derives not only from the amalgamation of Han Chinese artistic tradition and styles assimilated from ancient

Indian and Gandharan customs, but also from an integration of the arts of the Turks, ancient Tibetans and other Chinese ethnic minorities. The Mogao Caves, an outstanding example of a Buddhist rock art sanctuary, have represented a unique artistic achievement and played a decisive role in artistic exchanges between China, Central Asia and India.

The discovery of the Library Cave at the Mogao Caves in 1990, together with the tens of thousands of manuscripts and relics it contained, has been appraised as the world's most exceptional discovery of ancient oriental culture. This important heritage offers invaluable reference for studying the complex history of ancient China and Central Asia.

Cultural heritage

The Mogao Grottoes show examples of various types of art, such as architecture, painting and statuary. The group of caves at Mogao displays a unique artistic achievement both by the organization of space into 492 caves created on five levels and by the production of more than 2,000 painted sculptures, and approximately 45,000 square meters of murals, among which are many masterpieces of Chinese art. By inheriting the artistic traditions of the central and western regions of China and absorbing the merits of ancient arts from India, Greece and Iran, ancient Chinese artists created Buddhist art works with strong local features. These art works are treasures of human civilization, providing valuable material for studies of the politics, economy, culture, religion, ethnic relations and foreign exchanges of China in olden times. Besides, there are also about 50,000 items of scriptures, documents, paintings and weavings written in several languages spanning the period from the Three Kingdoms Period (220-280) to Northern Song dynasty (690-1127).

Cave 302 of the Sui dynasty includes one of the oldest and most vivid scenes of cultural exchanges along the Silk Road, which displays a camel pulling a cart typical of trade missions of that period. Caves 23 and 156 of the Tang dynasty depict workers in the fields and a line of warriors respectively. Cave 61 of the Song dynasty, the famous landscape of Wutai Mountain, is an early instance of artistic Chinese cartography. It depicted everything, including mountains, rivers, cities, temples, roads and caravans.

Grottoes

So far there are 492 grottoes, with murals and painted clay figures. There are meditation grottoes, Buddha hall grottoes, temple grottoes, vault-roofed grottoes and shadow grottoes. The largest grotto is 40 meters high and 30 meters wide, whereas the smallest is less than one foot high.

Painted Clay Figures

These are the main treasures of the Dunhuang Grottoes. The figures are in different forms, including round figures and relief figures. The tallest is 34.5 meters high, while the smallest is only 2 centimeters. These painted clay figures show such a great variety of themes and subject matter, as well as advanced techniques, that the Mogao Grottoes are generally regarded as the world's leading museum of Buddhist painted clay figures.

Murals

The murals in the Mogao Grottoes display Buddhist sutras, natural scenery, buildings, mountain and water paintings, flower patterns, flying Apsaras (Buddhist fairies) and ancient farming and production scenes. There are 1,045 murals extant, with a total area of 45,000 sq m. They are artistic records of historical changes and customs and traditions from the 4th to the 18th centuries.

Excavated articles

In 1900, about 50,000 cultural relics were found in a sanctum sealed behind the northern wall of Grotto No 16. These articles included Buddhist sutras, documents, embroidery works and paintings from the 4th to the 12th centuries. Apart from ancient Chinese documents, there were also documents in other ancient languages, including Tibetan, Sanskrit and Uygur. The subjects of these documents include religion, literature, contracts, ledgers and official files. This discovery, which attracted world attention, is of great research value for supplementing and emending ancient Chinese documents.

Buddhist culture

The Sui dynasty (518-618) was a golden age for Buddhism in Chinese history. And the Mogao Grottoes experienced their heyday of construction during this dynasty. Born and brought up in a Buddhist nunnery, emperor Yang Jian, founder of the Sui dynasty, was an enthusiastic Buddhist. After he united the whole country, he made Buddhism the national religion. About 5,000 temples were built, thousands of Buddhist sculptures were carved, and there were some 500,000 Buddhist monks and nuns. His son emperor Yang Guang was also keen on Buddhism. He had 1,000 copies of the Fahua Sutra published and established a school of Buddhism.

In this period, a large number of grottoes were carved at Mogao. The most common form of grotto dating from this dynasty is the inverted conical grotto. A typical example is the seven-layer conical tower in Grotto No 303, converted from a central tower pillar. Murals in this period were freed from the limit of foreign arts and demonstrated a liberated dynamic creativity. Generally, they show three major features.

First, murals depicting how Buddhists underwent arduous training and endured humiliation for progress in this life receded, and murals depicting easy ways to become a Buddha and attain Paradise began to occupy prominent positions in the grottoes. Second, Avalokitesvara was no longer an accompanying figure for Sakyamuni Buddha. Instead, she was depicted separately and with more grandeur. The appearance of the separate Avalokitesvara marked progress in China's Buddhism. Third, as secularization of Buddhist art began to emerge, figures in murals in this period were more lifelike.

(Adapted from *chinaculture.org*)

Passage Two

The Digitization Efforts at Mogao Caves

Ji Yuqiao

Carrying the genes and spirit of a nation, cultural relics are irreplaceable resources for a thriving civilization. A huge number of Chinese relics have become more popular over the past 10 years, allowing people from around the world to better understand Chinese culture. To make these cultural relics come alive, the Global Times will feature a number of these "star" artifacts in this series.

As Chinese President Xi Jinping has said, Chinese civilization, together with the colorful civilizations of other countries, should provide mankind with proper spiritual guidance and a strong spiritual impetus.

For our last entry in this series, we arrive at the Mogao Caves in Dunhuang, Northwest China's Gansu Province. Containing 735 caves full of Buddhist art, the Mogao Caves welcomes more than 1 million visitors every year. Currently, Chinese academicians are trying to figure out how to better use digital technology to make the splendid murals, sculptures and buildings at the site available for the world to enjoy while also ensuring they are preserved for generations to come.

For more than 1,000 years, the murals and statues within the Mogao Caves have represented some of the best of Buddhist art in China. However, the centuries have not been kind, as the elements have taken their toll on some of the delicate artworks within the many grottoes and alcoves at the site. To better preserve this art while also making it accessible to people around the world, scholars at the site have been turning to digital technology to ensure these treasures can be enjoyed for centuries to come.

As of 2022, the Dunhuang Academy, a national research institute dedicated to studying the Mogao Caves in Dunhuang, has accomplished quite a great deal, completing digital photography of 278 caves, image processing of 164 caves and 3D reconstruction of 145 painted sculptures and also a total of seven ruins. Additionally, it has produced a panorama-tour program covering 162 caves and digitalized more than 50,000 film negatives of the caves' cultural relics.

In August, Yu Tianxiu, head of the academy's Institute of Cultural Relic Digitalization, discussed these digitalization achievements at the 2022 China Internet Civilization Conference. Chinese academicians attending the conference emphasized that digital technology such as mobile digital exhibitions give those who cannot travel to Dunhuang the opportunity to appreciate these ancient treasures, so they have focused on developing methods to better combine digitalization and the caves.

Ever expanding range

The fruits of the digitalization efforts at the Mogao Caves have been accumulating over the years as the technology has continued to improve and expand to more fields such as publishing and creative cultural products.

Yu said that the caves' earliest digitalization efforts began in the early 1990s. At that time, the biggest debate revolved around what kind of technology should be used to archive the site. Since then the project has evolved greatly, coming to use advanced technology such as laser scanning that can detect millimeter-level differences on the surfaces of statues and other works of art.

The results of the Digital Dunhuang project, which provides highly accurate photographs and scans of 30 of the caves, have been available to netizens around the world for free since 2016. At present, the Digital Dunhuang website has been visited by users in 78 countries, including the US, the UK, South Korea, and Spain, and earned more than 16.8 million page views.

Restoration is a significant part of the digitalization project. Among the many caves at the site, one cave containing an important cache of documents was discovered in 1900. This so-called Library Cave has been one of the most important focuses of the digitalization project being carried out by the Dunhuang Academy and Chinese internet giant Tencent. The every detail of the ancient paintings in the cave and other cultural relics were recreated at a 1:1 millimeter-level accuracy through laser scanning and photo reconstruction technology.

Chinese cultural workers have also been creating digital cultural products based on the art of Dunhuang. The academy recently introduced a virtual figure named Jia Yao as the Mogao Caves' official virtual ambassador.

The figure uses digital technology such as motion capture and AI programming to present an entertaining and lifelike avatar that can introduce the caves to the public.

Promising future

The Trace of Civilization exhibition held at the Beijing Minsheng Art Museum displays high-fidelity digital replicas of the Mogao murals, meeting the needs of people in Beijing who want to appreciate the caves without traveling thousands of kilometers to Dunhuang.

More exhibitions featuring digital replicas are expected in the future. As an experienced expert who has participated in digitalization projects at Beijing's Palace Museum, professor Fei Jun from Central Academy of Fine Arts believed that China is leading the world in this field. Yu noted that digitalization projects will continue to being carried out and can be expanded to other cultural relics throughout the rest of China.

(Adapted from *globaltimes.cn*)

B6. Assignment

Travel Plan

As a professional local guide, you are **planning a 6-day Dunhuang tour for a group of foreign tourists** who intend to catch the highlights there. You need to make a detailed plan which may cover:

- Airport or train station pickup;
- Catering and accommodation arrangement;
- Transportation with comfortable licensed buses;
- Must-go attractions in Dunhuang and along the Silk Road;
- English introductions to the scenic spots;
- Discounted tickets and reservation.

References

Adam Augustyn. (2021). Forbidden City. *Britannica*. Retrieved from https://www.britannica.com/topic/Forbidden-City on April 25, 2023.

Times Mojo Team. (2022).Is It Important to Preserve Historic Buildings? *Times Mojo*. Retrieved from https://www.timesmojo.com/is-it-important-to-preserve-historic-buildings/ on April 25, 2023.

SS Homes. (2022). Old Building Demolition — Pros & Cons of Tearing Down Historic Structures. *SafeAndSanitaryHomes*. Retrieved from https://www.safeandsanitaryhomes.org/old-building-demolition-pros-cons/ on April 25, 2023.

Brenda Lian. (2023). Fun Facts about the Forbidden City. *Travel China Guide*.

Retrieved from https://www. travelchinaguide. com/attraction/beijing/forbidden-city/facts.html on April 25, 2023.

Jeremiah Jenne. (2021). Beijing's Five Architectural Colors and the Symbolism Behind Them. *thebeijinger*. Retrieved from https://www.thebeijinger.com/blog/2018/11/29/beijings-five-architectural-colors-symbolism-behind on April 25, 2023.

Dr. Ying-chen Peng. (2021). The Forbidden City. *smarthistory*. Retrieved from https://smarthistory.org/the-forbidden-city/ on April 25, 2023.

Chris Quan. (2022). Forbidden City: Uncover Its History and Facts You Didn't Know. *China Highlights*. Retrieved from https://www. chinahighlights. com/beijing/forbidden-city/ on April 25, 2023.

Ivana. (2021). The Potala Palace. *China Travel. com*. Retrieved from https://www.chinatravel.com/lhasa/attraction/potala-palace on April 25, 2023.

Sarah Margaret H. The Potala Palace. *Elevated Trips*. Retrieved from https://www.elevatedtrips.com/locations/the-potala-palace/ on April 25, 2023.

Neville Agnew. Mogao Caves. *UNESCO World Heritage Convention*. Retrieved from https://whc.unesco.org/en/list/440 on April 25, 2023.

China Discovery Team. Mogao Caves Facts — 10 Questions about the Mogao Caves. *China Discovery*. https://www. chinadiscovery. com/gansu/dunhuang/mogao-caves/facts.html on April 25, 2023.

Tess Humphrys.(2019). China's Buddhist Caves: The Enduring Art of the Silk Road. *lonely planet*. Retrieved from https://www.lonelyplanet.com/articles/chinas-buddhist-caves on April 25, 2023.

China Discovery Team. (2017). Mogao Caves. *China Culture*. Retrieved from http://en.chinaculture.org/2017-07/18/content_1039563.html on April 25, 2023.

Ji Yuqiao. (2022). Digitization Efforts at Mogao Caves Set the Standard for Protection and Promotion of China's Ancient Culture. *Global Times*. Retrieved from https://www.globaltimes.cn/page/202209/1275236.shtml on April 25, 2023.

Unit 4 Chinese Martial Arts

Part A Shaolin Kung Fu

A1. Introduction

Shaolin Kung Fu

Shaolin Kung Fu, or Shaolin martial arts, is the best-known and most popular style of martial arts in China. It ranks first among the top 3 Chinese kung fu styles (the other two are Wudang and Emei). Featuring a combination of Zen Buddhism and martial arts, Shaolin Kung Fu originated 1,500 years ago at the Shaolin Temple in Mt. Songshan, Henan province.

The history of Shaolin Kung Fu

Historically, Shaolin Kung Fu has gone through three main phases of development.

- Northern Wei dynasty (386-534): Establishment

The Shaolin Temple was founded in 495 by emperor Xiaowen for an Indian monk called Batuo to preach Buddhism on Mt. Songshan. A large number of local martial artists became odd-job men in the temple.

- Sui and Tang dynasties (581-907): Shaolin Monk Soldiers

At the end of the Sui dynasty, the political situation was chaotic, with a scramble underway for the throne. Shaolin Kung Fu was developed and promoted through battles and wars, eventually becoming the leading kung fu school in the central plains of China. Thereafter, the temple was allowed to organize an army of monk soldiers, who served as soldiers in times of war and as monks in peacetime, thus greatly contributing to the development of Shaolin martial arts. The "Hands of 18 Arhats", with a strong Buddhist flavor, have been practiced by Shaolin monks ever since that time. They were later used to create more advanced Shaolin martial arts.

- Ming dynasty (1368-1644): Resisting Foreign Enemies

From 1552 to 1554, Japanese pirates known as wokou invaded the southeastern coast of China. More than 30 patriotic monks from the Shaolin Temple organized a troop and went to the front line, sacrificing their lives in the fight against the enemy.

Later, Shaolin monks participated in the war at least six times and performed immortal feats for the country and people. Since then, Shaolin Kung Fu has further established its authority in Chinese martial arts circles. During this period, Shaolin monks switched from cudgel fighting to fist fighting, so that fist fights were promoted to have the same status as cudgel fights.

In modern times, Shaolin Kung Fu has gained increasing popularity at home and abroad. And the word "Shaolin" has become a symbol of Chinese traditional martial arts.

Classification of different forms of Shaolin Kung Fu

Shaolin Kung Fu is rich in content with lots of different forms, a series of skills and tricks. According to historical records, Shaolin martial arts have 708 forms, including 552 boxing styles and weapon skills, and 156 sets of combat techniques. The basic skills involve daily exercises of stance and conditioning. Some incomplete records show that the forms handed down from ancient times are as follows.

- Boxing

The Shaolin Boxing style is vigorous and powerful, conducive to actual combat. Emphasizing practical skills rather than appearance, boxing mainly embodies the word "strong" and gives priority to attack. There is no restriction on the venue when practicing Shaolin Boxing. You can "practice in the area where a bull lies." In terms of stance and footwork, Shaolin Boxing requires lightning-fast movements, standing like a nail but moving like a swallow. Major boxing styles include Arhat Boxing, Hung Kuen, Shaolin Five Fists, Drunken Boxing, and Animal Imitation Boxing.

- Weapons

There are many weapons in the kung fu system of Shaolin, ranging from a simple wooden cudgel to various swords and spears, and rare weapons (Staffs of Dharma). It is a remarkable fact that in the Temple, priority was given to training in unarmed Kung Fu. In principle, any weapon can be taken from an opponent and used against him. Superior knowledge of unarmed combat includes extensive training in disarming opponents. In the hands of someone who is well-trained, a weapon is simply an extension of the body.

- Qigong

Unlike the "internal" Wudang Kung Fu, Shaolin Kung Fu emphasizes the physical aspect of martial arts, namely the "external" power. Monks used Shaolin Kung Fu to defend the monastery from roving bandits and when necessary from soldiers of competing warlords, but they also used Wudang Kung Fu on a daily basis as a more peaceful form of physical and mental exercise, to keep body and mind both healthy. Therefore, Qigong exercises are also a major category of Shaolin Kung Fu, such as "muscle-changing scripture"(Yijin Jing), "eight pieces of brocade" (Baduanjin) and others.

Ten taboos

People who practice any of the following behaviors cannot learn Shaolin Kung Fu.

- Bad conduct
- Disloyalty or failure to honor parents
- Lack of perseverance
- Lack of accomplishment with pen and sword
- Impure motives
- Tackiness
- Deceitfulness
- Weakness
- Learning without practical use
- Lack of respect

(Adapted from *chinatravel.com*)

A2. Words and Expressions

Vocabulary

1. extrinsic / eksˈtrɪnsɪk / *adj*. 非固有的;非本质的;外在的
2. intrinsic / ɪnˈtrɪnsɪk / *adj*. 固有的;内在的
3. esteem / ɪˈstiːm / *n*. 尊重;敬重
4. rib / rɪb / *n*. 肋骨;排骨;(船或屋顶等的)肋拱
5. armpit / ˈɑː(r)mˌpɪt / *n*. 腋窝
6. coccyx / ˈkɒksɪks / *n*. 尾骨
7. auricle / ˈɔːrɪkl / *n*. 耳廓;心耳

中国功夫的特点	The Features of Chinese Kung Fu
中国文化遗产的珍贵元素	a precious element of Chinese cultural heritage
数百种的打法合集	a collection of hundreds of fighting style
融入哲学理念	incorporate philosophical concept
外家拳	external style
敏捷和体力	agility and physical strength
内家拳	internal styles
修心养性	cultivate the mind and spirit
行气	circulation of qi
内外兼修	the cultivation of extrinsic and intrinsic values
形神合一	achieve harmony between body and mind
刚柔并济	strike an appropriate balance between hardness and softness
卧似一张弓，站似一棵松。	Lie like a bow, and stand like a pine tree.
不动不摇坐如钟，走路一阵风。	Sit like a bell and walk like the wind.
养气立德	nurture qi and cultivate morality
内力与外力的结合	a combination of external and internal forces
以静制动	control mobility with stillness
练武者不尚武。	Resort to force only when there is no alternative.
尚德不尚力。	Hold morals in esteem, rather than force.

Vocabulary

1. rigorous / ˈrɪgərəs / *adj*. 严密的，缜密的；严谨的
2. Buddhism / ˈbʊdɪz(ə)m / *n*. 佛教
3. meditation / medɪˈteɪʃ(ə)n / *n*. 冥想；沉思；深思
4. pagoda / pəˈgəʊdə / *n*. 宝塔
5. roving / ˈroʊvɪŋ / *adj*. 流动的；漂泊的
6. bandit / ˈbændɪ / *n*. 强盗；土匪

少林功夫历史	History of Shaolin Kung Fu
中国功夫的主流	main stream of Chinese Kung Fu
武术最宏大最古老的风格之一	one of the largest and oldest styles of martial arts
以禅宗和武术的结合为特色	feature a combination of Zen Buddhism and martial art

天下功夫出少林	All Kung Fu comes out of Shaolin
少林功夫流芳世界	Shaolin Kung Fu excels in the world
始于 1500 年前的少林寺	originate 1,500 years ago at Shaolin Temple/Monastery
嵩山历史文化的突出代表	the outstanding representative of Songshan history and culture
少林寺塔林	the Pagoda Forest at Shaolin Temple
一所严谨的武术学院	a rigorous martial arts college
少林武僧	Shaolin Kung Fu warrior monks
禅宗佛教	Zen Buddhism
参禅	practice of Zen meditation
印度高僧跋陀	Indian Buddhist monk Buddhabhadra
佛教大师	Buddhist master
宣扬佛法	preach Buddhism
他的第一批中国弟子	his first Chinese disciples
精通武术	well-versed in the martial arts
过着僧侣般的生活	live monastic lives
护寺措施	temple protecting measures
通过战斗和战争得到发展和促进	be developed and promoted through battles and wars
帮助李世民登基	help Li Shimin accede to the throne
组建僧兵	organize an army of monk soldiers
牺牲自己的生命来对抗倭寇	sacrifice their lives in the fight against the Wokou
为国为民立下不朽功勋	perform immortal feats for the country and people
用少林功夫保护寺院不受流寇侵扰	use Shaolin Kung Fu to defend the monastery from roving bandits

Vocabulary

1. swallow / ˈswɑːləʊ / *n.* 燕子
2. Arhat / ˈarhət / *n.* 罗汉;阿罗汉
3. tranquility / træŋˈkwɪlɪtɪ / *n.* 宁静
4. exquisitely/ ˌɛkˈskwɪzɪtli / *adj.* 精巧的;精致的
5. transcendental / trænsenˈdent(ə)l / *adj.* (尤指宗教或精神方面)超验的

少林功夫的特点	**The Features of Shaolin Kung Fu**
在中国武术界树立起自己的权威	establish its authority in Chinese martial arts circle
有丰富的套路	rich in content with lots of different forms
包括拳术、器械和对练套路	include boxing styles and weapon skills, and combat techniques
日常的站立训练	daily exercises of stance
拳术刚健有力	vigorous and powerful
有利于实战	conducive to actual combat
强调实用技能而非花架子	emphasize practical skills rather than appearance
体现"强"字,以攻为主	embody the word "strong" and give priority to attack
练习少林拳时不受场地限制	no restriction on the venue when practicing Shaolin boxing
要求动作快如闪电	require lightning-fast movements
站如钉立,跳似轻飞	stand like a nail but moving like a swallow
训练徒手功夫	train in unarmed Kung fu
任何武器都可以从对手身上夺取并用来对付他	any weapon can be taken from an opponent and used against him
南少林	Southern Shaolin Kung Fu
强调腿部动作、站姿和有力的手部技巧	emphasize legwork, stances, and powerful hand techniques
北少林	Northern Shaolin Kung Fu
强调流动性和杂技动作	emphasize fluidity and acrobatic movements
拿手绝招	claim its own unique
罗汉睡觉	Arhat sleeping
童子拜观音	child worshipping Guanyin
童子拜佛	child worshipping Buddha
朝天蹬	kick up
燕式平衡	balance stand
少林秘诀	the secrets of Shaolin
内功	inner discipline
所有气力凝聚于一只手指	condenses and focuses all one's energy and strength onto one finger
结合精神的纯净和身体的韧性	combine spiritual purity and physical toughness
设计精巧	exquisitely designed
攻防灵活	easy for attack and defense
少林拳法的上上之技	"the best of the best" in Shaolin martial arts
基本功	training in the basics
延续少林的辉煌传统	carry on the splendid tradition of Shaolin

	martial arts
拳禅合一	oneness of movements and Zen Buddhism
静修	quietly practicing Buddhism
静坐蒲团	sit in quietude on a rush cushion
静中凝气	achieve calm and focus energy
空洞无我处生	coming from emptiness or soullessness
动静结合	combine mobility with tranquility
追求超人力量	in the pursuit for superhuman strength
对超凡力量和智慧的渴望	the desire for transcendental strength and wisdom
心拳合一	the integration of mind and fist
化有形为无形	change the tangible into the intangible
无形中制敌	control the enemy in the intangible
跟从内心	for all to be guided by the heart
从有形到无形的战斗	to fight not just from form but from the formless
秀如猫，抖如虎，行如龙，动如闪，声如雷。	Elegant like a cat, yet fierce like a tiger; walk like a dragon, move like lightning, with a voice like thunder.

Vocabulary

1. sheer / ʃɪə / *adj*. 纯粹的；完全的
2. subdue / səbˈduː / *v*. 制服；征服
3. harness / ˈhaːrnɪs / *v*. 控制；利用
4. crane / kreɪn / *n*. 鹤；吊车
5. beak / biːk / *n*. 喙；鸟喙
6. leopard / ˈlepərd / *n*. 豹子；豹

少林五拳	**Shaolin Kung Fu Five**
模仿某些动物的动作	mimic movements of certain animals
五禽戏	Five Animals Exercise
龙的形象	the figure of the Dragon
力量的象征	a symbol of strength and power
控制水、海洋和河流	control water, the seas, and rivers
反映慷慨程度	reflect the extent of generosity
体现勇猛、和谐和繁荣	embody prowess, harmony, and prosperity
象征引导内部能量的能力	symbolize the capacity to channel internal energy

特定的腰部和呼吸技巧	specific waist and breathing techniques
"之"字形	in zig zag
体现内部和外部功夫哲学的结合	exemplify the combining of both internal and external Kung Fu philosophies
动物王国被认为由老虎统治。	The animal kingdom is thought to be governed by the tiger.
代表纯粹的力量和权力	represent sheer strength and power
通过肌肉和骨骼的力量来体现	display power by means of muscle and bone
控制力	strength
最容易识别的虎爪	the most easily identifiable tiger claw
手法和踢法的结合	a combination of hand and kicking technique
制服对手	subdue opponents
以顽强的力量使用身体力量	use physical power with tenacious force
蛇的本性是冷静和矜持。	The nature of snake is calm and reserved.
战斗策略是速度和准确性。	Fighting strategy is speed and precision.
最注重的是驾驭气力	most concentrate on harnessing the qi
蛇形拳没有踢腿技术,也不涉及闭拳。	The snake form does not involve kicking techniques nor closed fists.
利用上半身的部位和张开的双手	make use of upper body parts and open hands
蛇形拳	snake fist
以食指为主要武器	index finger being used as the main weapon
快如闪电	as fast as lightning
精准无比	with utmost precision
鹤	the crane
善于观察和沉思的动物	observant and contemplative animal
蛇一样的速度和精确的品质	the Snake-like qualities of speed and precision
类似于龙的动作	resemble movements of the Dragon
采用圆周运动	adopt circular movements
单腿站立数小时	stand on a single leg for hours
看不出任何疲劳的迹象	without showing any sign of fatigue
以其"啄击技术"而闻名	be known for his "beak striking technique"
手掌呈钩状,所有手指并拢	consist of a hand set in the shape of a hook with all fingers joined together
迅速地攻击对手的软肋	swiftly attack the opponent's soft spots
豹拳	Leopard
豹子拳/半开的拳头	leopard fist / a half-opened fist
前臂击打	forearm strikes
低踢	low kick

有角度的、高速的战术打击	angular, high-speed tactical strike
针对对方身体脆弱部位	target the vulnerable parts of the opponent's body

A3. Speaking Activities

Situational Speech

As the president of Chinese Kung Fu Club in your university, you are invited to present in a one-day Martial Arts Festival to international students. Prepare a **5-minute speech**, briefly introducing **Shaolin Kung Fu**. Your speech might cover:

- The history and style of Shaolin Kung Fu;
- The characteristics of Shaolin Kung Fu;
- The basic techniques of Shaolin Kung Fu;
- The philosophies of Shaolin Kung Fu.

You may refer to the words and expressions in Part A, but don't confine yourself to them.

Interview

When people talk of the martial arts, or Kung Fu, they most immediately think of Bruce Lee (1940-1973), and his great accomplishments in boxing, swordplay, and skill with knives and sticks. With his superb kung fu popularized throughout the world, he became the embodiment of Chinese martial arts. Bruce Lee's kung fu was deeply rooted in traditional Chinese martial arts. As a journalist, you and your colleagues plan to **interview 5 students about their understandings of Bruce Lee and Chinese marital arts.** Your interview questions might include:

- Can you list some movies that Bruce Lee starred in?
- Why did he practice Kung Fu?
- What contributions did he make to Chinese Kung Fu?
- What are the characteristics of Chinese Kung Fu?
- What is the true spirit of Chinese Kung Fu?
- Would you like to practice Kung Fu? Why?
- Others.

Brainstorming

As a country with time-honored and diverse cultural traditions passed down from one generation to another, China has developed a variety of sports. Except for Shaolin Kung Fu, could you name other kinds of Chinese Kung Fu? What do you think is **the best way to develop and promote Chinese Kung Fu**? Please elaborate on your views.

Reading and Sharing

Read the following paragraphs about **values** of Shaolin Kung Fu and share your views.

Paragraph 1

Much of the Shaolin's philosophy and viewpoints are from the tenets of Chan Buddhism, the precursor to Zen Buddhism. Shaolin philosophy is all about achieving harmony between Chan (the religion) and Quan (martial arts). Chan Quan directly translates to "Chan Fist" (or "Zen Fist" in Japanese). The spiritual and martial aspects of Shaolin are not seen as separate, but the Shaolin path to enlightenment. It seems paradoxical to combine combat with Buddhism, which is mostly seen as non-combative. However, with the unifying of these two extremes, the Shaolin achieve a state of balance through years of rigorous training and study.

(Adapted from *ninjaphd.com*)

Paragraph 2

Since the Shaolin Temple is a Buddhist Temple, Shaolin Kung Fu shares the same values as Buddhism. Master Shi Xing Hao has summarized some of the most important of these values into the Tenets of Shaolin Kung Fu. Shaolin students are expected to understand these tenets before they learn to execute a single strike. In order to pass their first Kung Fu level rank test, students are required to recite the tenets from memory. Shaolin Kung Fu, as in Buddhism, ultimately lives in the heart. These tenets emphasize the Buddhist virtues of pure-minded concentration, fairness, and righteousness in all social interactions, including the training hall. These values are taught to Shaolin students because they define the true spirit of Shaolin Kung Fu. Those who do not live by them are not true Shaolin practitioners.

(Adapted from *kungfucleveland.com*)

Ideas for Sharing

- What are the core values of Shaolin Kung Fu?
- How to become a true Shaolin practitioner?

Interpretation

Interpret the paragraphs below into English with the words and expressions you learned in Part A.

Paragraph 1

中国武术的一种常见分类方法是将其分为外式(外家拳)和内式(内家拳)。外家拳侧重于发展人的敏捷和体力,而内在风格侧重于操纵气和培养内在的思想和精神。内家拳的练习者应用了许多道教所信奉的哲学思想。中国武术最流行的内功是太极拳，而外家拳最著名的风格是少林功夫。少林功夫“禅武合一”的精神对中华武术有着非常深远的影响。

Paragraph 2

隋朝末年，政治局势混乱，争夺皇位的斗争频发。少林功夫在战争中得到发展和推广，最终成为中国中原地区的主要功夫流派。此后，寺院获准组织僧兵，平时为僧，战时当兵，这极大地促进了少林武术的发展。从那时起，带有浓厚佛教色彩的“十八罗汉手”就一直为少林寺僧人所练习。

Paragraph 3

少林武术刚健有力，利于实战。招招势势非打即防，没有花架子。在练习少林拳时，不受场地限制，有“拳打卧牛之地”之说，其风格主要体现一个“硬”字，攻防兼备，以攻击为主。拳势不强调外形的美观，只求技击的实用。步法进退灵活、敏捷，有冲拳一条线之说。在身段与步法上，其动作迅如闪电，站如钉立，跳似轻飞。主要的拳种包括罗汉拳、洪拳、少林五拳、醉拳等。

A4. Culture Highlights

Q: *There are hundreds of different styles of Chinese martial arts. How to categorize them ?*

A: One common way of classifying Chinese martial arts is by separating them into external styles (外家拳) and internal styles (内家拳). External styles focus on developing agility and physical strength, while internal styles focus on manipulating qi and cultivating the mind and spirit. Many of the philosophical ideas espoused by Taoism are applied by practitioners of internal martial arts styles. The most popular internal style of Chinese martial art is Tai Chi, also called Taiji while the most famous style associated with the external style is Shaolin Kung Fu. The internal versus external classification is a popular one that has been used since 1669. It remains somewhat controversial, however, with some experts arguing that there is actually no difference between the two due to the fact that every style includes some mix of “internal” and “external” elements.

Another common way to classify Chinese martial arts styles is by geographical region. There are many notable differences between northern and southern China. Not only is this true when it comes to food, the arts, architecture, and language, but it is also true of martial arts. Martial arts from northern China are referred to as “北派” and include well-known schools such as Baguazhang (八卦掌) and Bajiquan (八极拳). Northern styles are known for incorporating high kicks and acrobatic elements. Southern martial arts styles are called “南派” and place more emphasis on arm and full-body movements.

(Adapted *from studycli.org*)

Q: *Although there are a multitude of different styles of Chinese martial arts, some are more popular than others. What are the most common and influential styles?*

A: The five of the most common and influential styles are as followed.

- Shaolin Kung Fu: Shaolin Kung Fu is one of the most popular styles of Chinese martial arts. Considered an "external style," Shaolin Kung Fu was developed by monks at the Shaolin Temple in Henan Province.
- Wing Chun: Wing Chun (咏春) is a southern Chinese kung fu style descended from Shaolin Kung Fu. It has the distinction of having been founded by two women, Ng Mui and Yim Wing-chun.
- Bajiquan: Bajiquan is another popular Chinese martial art. It emerged in the 18th century and was originally called Baziquan, or "rake fist," because of its trademark use of swift downward strikes using partially opened fists.
- Tai Chi: Tai Chi is the most well-known of the "internal" Chinese martial arts styles. While it is most commonly practiced today as a meditative, gentle form of exercise, it also has its roots in the martial arts and was originally developed as a form of self-defense.
- Baguazhang: Like Tai Chi, Baguazhang is considered an "internal style" martial art. Its philosophy draws heavily on Taoist concepts like yin and yang and it even takes its name from the Taoist trigrams, or bagua.

(Adapted from *studycli.org*)

Q: *What are the features of Shaolin Kung Fu?*

A: (1) Short but precise. (2) Box in a line. (3) Casual footwork. (4) Roll in and out. (5) Integration of mind and behavior. (6) Bending but actually not and straight but actually not. (7) Rise high in a tight form and drop in a spreading way. Rise to move with an intention of advance and drop to move with an intention of retreat. (8) Integration of Buddhism and boxing. (9) Focus on defense. (10) Combination of attacking and defending. (11) Numerous tricks. (12) Simple and practical. (13) Vigorous and strong. (14) Numerous acts shrinking back. (15) Numerous kicks. (16) Produce sounds.

(Adapted from *shaolinskungfu.com*)

A5. Extensive Reading

Passage One

The Philosophy of Kung Fu

For most Westerners, Kung Fu refers to a set of combat techniques that originated in China, as well as a type of martial art that is also enveloped in a thick enigmatic and allegorical veil, with an unclear significance. Because of limited exchanges between China and the West over the course of history, little was known about the meaning of Chinese belief systems, which were considered at the time 'exotic'. But let's clarify things.

Conceptual influences

A great majority of Kung Fu styles are practical direct derivations from Taoism and Buddhism, the two main religious and philosophical traditions in China. While each style exhibits a unique inclination towards the specific forms of knowledge these offer, Kung Fu's conceptual stance is generally considered to be the fusion between the two philosophical movements. Not only does the term Kung Fu stand for the effort and dedication that is invested in the mastering of a given skill, but also, it refers to the personal stamina that is revealed in the pursuit of truth, and the experience of non-self.

The concept of "Tao" or "the Way", the core philosophical insight of Taoism, is the basic principle that underlies reality, which, it is believed, can only be grasped through an intuitive process of harmony between the self and the universe. This can be achieved in daily live by means of the adoption of different virtues such as humility, patience, compassion, selflessness, and impartiality, virtues which are also upheld by Buddhist thought and in Kung Fu training.

Aside of Tao, Taoism thinking includes a range of other concepts, such as yin-yang, which have also been incorporated into Kung Fu practice. Describing the dynamic of two interdependent dualities as they sway together in an endless dance of interchanging positions, yin-yang is a noticeably important concept in Tai Chi and Baguazhang Kung Fu styles.

The animals of Kung Fu

From the moment of its inception as a martial art, Kung Fu underwent numerous variations which involved the emergence of several hundreds of different styles, which each carried distinctive approaches to combat and fighting movements. The styles that originated in Southern China were particularly distinct in that their movements not only mimicked those of certain animals, but also featured a particularly visually appealing and striking aesthetic which promoted Taoist holistic philosophy by encouraging harmony between man and his living environment.

It is said that Hua Tuo, the physician of the Han dynasty, introduced the "exercise of the Five Animals" into the Qigong curriculum that existed at the time, which sought to facilitate the flow of qi around the body. The exercise of the five animals bases itself on emblematic postures of five different animals that are native to China: the Tiger, the Deer, the Crane, the Monkey and the Bear.

In Qigong, each of the five animals is linked with one of the five elements, the five yin-yang pair of organs as well as different parts of the body. In different ways, these exercises aimed to, by means of directing qi flow through different internal channels, achieve a desired effect on a specific bodily function. Following this introduction, it did not take long before the qigong animal exercises were translated into concrete Kung Fu forms and adopted by practitioners, often also incorporating other animals into their practice.

However, of all the animal forms that are congregated in Kung Fu today, the "Shaolin Kung Fu five" have persisted over time as the most popular ones. The five Shaolin animals, however, slightly differ from the five animals that are featured in qigong as they consist instead of the Dragon, the Tiger, the Leopard, the Snake and the Crane. All of them, aside of the Dragon, an everlasting spiritual symbol in China, are otherwise existing animals.

- The Dragon

In imperial China, the figure of the Dragon has been a symbol of strength and power for centuries. Dragons are believed to control water, the seas and rivers; and rain, allegorically speaking, reflects the extent of their generosity.

Indeed, in China, dragons are not fear mongering villains who "breathe" fire, but rather, mythological figures that embody prowess, harmony and prosperity. Thus, the dragon symbolizes the capacity to channel internal energy — through specific waist and breathing techniques — into a fierce and powerful counter attack, typically in circular moves or in zig zag with the exertion of claws. As such, the Dragon figure perfectly exemplifies the combining of both internal and external Kung Fu philosophies.

- The Tiger

The animal kingdom, in China, is thought to be governed by the Tiger, who represents sheer strength and power. In Kung Fu, the Tiger is a form which refers to a type of relentlessness that manifests itself in the moment of attack. While adequate breathing is deemed important, the form is purely external. Indeed, the Tiger form displays power by means of muscle and bone strength, chiefly in leg, back and neck muscles.

Through a combination of hand — the tiger claw being the most easily identifiable — and kicking techniques, it seeks to mark the opponent's face, groins, wrists, etc. To subdue opponents quickly, the Tiger form uses physical power with tenacious force and coercion.

- The Snake

The snake is the opposite of the Tiger in many ways. While his nature is calm and reserved, his fighting strategy is speed and precision. It is said that of all the existing animal forms in Kung Fu, the snake form is the one which most concentrates on harnessing the qi.

In contrast with previous style, the Snake form does not involve kicking techniques nor closed fists. Instead, the Snake form only makes use of upper body parts and open hands. The open hand is called the "snake fist", and the index finger is used as the main weapon. As fast as lightning and with utmost precision, the counterattack targets the opponent's vulnerable sports, such as the eyes, the groins, their Adam's apple, etc.

- The Crane

Likely to be the most complex of the five animal forms, is the Crane. Exhibiting the Snake-like qualities of speed and precision, the Crane adopts circular movements, which resemble those of the Dragon. And unlike the Tiger, who displays a rough force, the Crane is an observant and contemplative animal. A certain softness and elegant transpires through his coordinated and balanced combat techniques. These can be identified by their speed, their agility and the physical distance between the two adversaries. The Crane can spend hours standing on a single leg without showing any sign of fatigue and is mostly known for his "beak striking technique", which consists of a hand set in the shape of a hook with all fingers joined together, and swiftly attacks the opponent's soft spots.

- The Leopard

In terms of overall strength and size, the Leopard seconds the Tiger; but in terms of pace, flexibility, and agility, the former surpasses the latter, with a faster outburst, and a wider range of striking techniques. The combat moves typical to the Leopard consist of the notorious for the "Leopard fist" (a half-opened fist), forearm strikes, as well as low kicks. The principal force of the Leopard form is an angular, high-speed tactical strike which targets the vulnerable parts of the opponent's body.

In this article, we have seen how different philosophical and spiritual beliefs native to

Chinese society have left their distinctive conceptual footprints on Kung Fu. In the same way Kung Fu cannot survive being stripped of the conceptual framework it is entangled with, the practice cannot be alienated from the traditional Chinese identity it nurtures and stimulates.

(Adapted from *chinaeducationaltour.com*)

Passage Two

Kung Fu in Western Society

The endurance and perseverance of Chinese martial arts over time has been astounding: for over 2,000 years, martial arts such as Kung Fu have been again and again associated with eminence and social prestige in China. It may come as a surprise, then, that the cultural exchanges between China and the West only really materialized in the last century.

Indeed, for most of history, the relations between both regions were limited to rather sporadic instances of exchange that took place mostly through individuals. What really propelled Chinese martial arts or Kung Fu the Western cultural imagery was, instead, the explosion of pop culture that took place during the 60s and 70s, through movies, literature and even music (hip hop). How can this shift be explained?

Kung Fu in Chinese / Western relations: an overview

The reason for this sudden development is multifaceted as well as entangled with the broader political context which shaped the cultural relationship between China and the West. On the one hand, China had for centuries shown a propensity for cultural isolation, which was reflected in the advocacy of isolationist policies in its dealing with foreign affairs. By contrast, the Western model of both international relations and economics was aggressive and belligerent; beyond the projected value of trade and potential economic exploitation, there was little if any interest in Chinese society and its way of life. Hence, the idea of China that existed in the Western imagination was shaped by the few merchants, missionaries and adventurers who had dared to tread on the silk routes that led to distant China and who came back with astonishing tales of the great and rich empire of the East.

This was for instance the case of the Venetian merchant, Marco Polo, who spent more than twenty years in China during the Yuan dynasty (1271-1368) and became famous because of his writing of a book, *Book of the Marvels of the World* which recorded his travels. This scarce contact meant that Kung Fu never reached Western shores. But this was no accident. As Western powers followed by Japan deployed their policies of economic and cultural imperialism onto Chinese land in the last two hundred years, Kung Fu masters swore to an unwritten consensus to not divulge the skill to non-Chinese individuals, a consensus which perdured well into the 20th century (for instance Bruce Lee, after opening his school to the non-Chinese, was harshly criticized by the Kung-Fu community).

Kung Fu, with its merging of combat martial art with distinct elements of Chinese philosophy, was meant to be a well-preserved secret which could, arguably, provide an efficient weapon and identity to counter Western and Japanese hegemony. This point hints at why many of the most well-known Kung Fu movies are set in the times of Japanese invasion. Later in the 20th century, Kung Fu — through art and popular fiction — became for the first time a medium that served to showcase Chinese identity and culture to the rest of the world. And it was precisely in these domains — and fore mostly in cinema, that Kung Fu carved a name for itself and left an everlasting impact in the Western society.

Why is Chinese Kung Fu popular in Western Society today?

The ascent towards fame of the remarkable martial art master and actor, Bruce Lee's ascent to fame was without doubt, a key development that led to the popularity of Kung Fu in the West.

While Kung Fu had already been featured in Hong Kong cinema since the 1940s, the practice did not hold the attention of the Western public, which instead showed a greater interest in the Japanese martial arts of Karate and Judo. This was in part because of closer ties between Japan and the West, the export of Japanese cinema was substantially larger than its Chinese counterpart. This tendency, in turn, was inverted with the rise of Bruce Lee in Hong Kong and Hollywood cinematic productions.

The practice became eminently popular in Chinese cultural artworks: the number of chuanqi (legendary tales) in Wuxia novels and theatrical plays featuring Kung Fu scenography and storylines exploded, even though those who actually practiced it were typically involved with the military in a way or another. The most distinguished military warriors were often simultaneously the most remarkable Kung Fu masters, and pioneers of new forms and styles.

The reason for his success was manifold. While on the one hand, his fanatical working ethic and unparalleled charisma served him well, the forces that enabled his success to take dumfounding proportions were historical.

Indeed, a dramatic shift in the sensibilities of the Western population, which took place through the post-war baby-boom generation and rebelled against dominant cultural narratives, colonialism and fought for minority as well as human rights, facilitated the ascent and almost foretold the imminent popularity of Bruce Lee's character.

The fact that he embodied a charismatic hero from a disadvantaged social and cultural reality and yet who at the same time fought for the same ideals and virtues that were in vogue at the time, provided an immense source of identification for the Western public who saw him as a hero they could praise and glorify.

Bruce Lee typically appeared in cinema performing ordinary yet also highly moral characters which saw found themselves entrenched in the grim reality of subordination, exploitation and injustice. Just as Lee had struggled personally against prejudices and discriminatory treatment he faced in the U.S., the characters instrumentalize Kung Fu as a tool to physically and symbolically wrestle against oppression and injustice.

In other words, Kung Fu was introduced to international audiences as a practice which could empower the self against social hierarchies and the grinding complexities of modern life.

A spiritual shift?

The protracted popularity of Kung Fu has facilitated the spreading and accessibility of Chinese culture in the West.

In the context of a surge of New Wave spirituality movements seeking to comprehend and deal with the transformations taking place in Western societies, many turned to the well-kept wisdom of traditional Chinese philosophical systems.

Today, China is recognized as global economic, technological and military power which poses a real threat to the long-lasting hegemony of the West. While in terms of soft power, China's global reach is still lagging that of the West, this gap is narrowing by the second.

The early beginnings and ascent of Chinese soft power should always be associated with Kung Fu, which played a critical role in this development, by virtue of its appeal to the rest of the world.

(Adapted from *chinaeducationaltours.com*)

A6. Assignment

Brochure Design

Form **groups of 3 or 4** and **design an English brochure for Shaolin Kung Fu school.** The brochure should:

- Review the history of Shaolin Kung Fu;
- Elaborate the category and characteristics of Shaolin Kung Fu;

- Discuss the cultural impact of Shaolin Kung Fu.

Part B Wudang Kung Fu

B1. Introduction

Wudang Kung Fu

Wudang Kung Fu and Shaolin Kung Fu are the two most representative styles of traditional Chinese martial arts, thus there is a popular saying in China that "Shaolin Kung Fu is the king of the north while Wudang Kung Fu rules the south." Unlike Shaolin Kung Fu, which is referred to as "external" martial art and integrated with Zen Buddhism, Wudang Kung Fu is an "internal" martial art based on the philosophy and canons of Taoism, an indigenous Chinese religion.

Wudang Kung Fu originated from Taoism

Wudang Kung Fu (or Wudang martial arts) draws upon a long history and profound knowledge of Taoism. According to legend, Wudang Kung Fu was established by a famous Taoist named Zhang Sanfeng, who lived during the late Yuan (1279-1368) and early Ming (1368-1644) dynasties. Zhang masterfully combined the essence of *I Ching* and *Tao De Ching* with traditional Shaolin Kung Fu to found Wudang Kung Fu, which mainly includes Tai Chi, Xingyi Quan, and Eight Trigram Palm (Bagua Palm), contributing to health promotion and body-building.

Zhang Sanfeng was a master in martial arts, especially boxing and swordplay. Based on Taoist theories, such as naturalness and humility, he synthesized Taoist internal exercises, regimen guarding skills, martial arts boxing, and military science into one, hence creating Wudang Internal Boxing. The boxing style uses principles of internal exercise, attack, regimen, self-protection, conquering the unyielding by yielding, confronting the active with stillness, attacking an opponent with his own force, and striking only after the enemy has struck.

Wudang Kung Fu, after hundreds of years of innovation and development, has spread among the people and had a long-lasting and profound influence. It now constitutes an important and unique form of Chinese martial arts.

Three main styles

Wudang Kung Fu has three main styles, namely, Tai Chi, Xingyi Quan, and Eight Trigram Palm. These illustrate the major skills of Wudang Kung Fu.

- Tai Chi combines slow, deliberate movements, meditation, and deep breathing.

Today it is chiefly a mind-body exercise to help treat or prevent health problems, as well as to delay aging.

- Baguazhang, literally "Eight Trigram Palm", is named after the trigrams of *I Ching*, an ancient Chinese divination text and one of the key ideological foundations of Taoism. Circle walking is the customary movement of Baguazhang.
- Xingyi Quan, literally "Shape-Will Boxing," is the oldest of the Wudang internal martial arts, concentrating on the mind and shape of the body, rather than physical strength and heavy-handed force. It is primarily composed of five basic fist movements, all executed at short range.

Some documents indicate that Xingyi Quan was created in imitation of the fighting techniques and spirits of 12 animals — such as the tiger, monkey, snake, eagle, horse, and bear — to tap into the natural instincts and fighting abilities those animals possess.

Characteristics of Wudang Kung Fu

- Guided by Taoist ideology

As mentioned above, Wudang Kung Fu was based on Taoist theories. Zhang's Tai Chi Chuan and Wudang Kung Fu were supposedly created according to Taoist ideology, incorporating softness, quietness, emptiness, unification, naturalness, harmony, and so on. All these can be summarized in Tai Chi, yin and yang, the five elements (metal, wood, water, fire, and earth), and the Eight Trigrams. Under the guidance of these philosophical principles, Wudang Kung Fu achieves more effective results.

- Having health as the goal

The initial purpose of Zhang's Wudang Kung Fu was to maintain fitness. Its function of art and attack was derived from the premise of guaranteeing health. Thus, the movements and skills of this kung fu style were designed to improve blood circulation, relax muscles and joints, and cultivate physical and mental health.

- Defense rather than offence

With the original purpose of maintaining fitness, Wudang Kung Fu later became a fighting form of self-defense, with strategies of fending off hard attacks with soft movements, defeating the strong in a yielding way, confronting the active with stillness, beating the fast in a slow manner, and striking out only after an opponent has struck first. It emphasizes defense rather than offense, which is because Taoism promotes peace and harmony, rather than conflict; so Wudang Kung Fu is meant for protection rather than attack.

- Observing martial morality

The disciples of the Wudang School must observe some moral disciplines. For instance, their basic admonishments are:

(1) "Three Pieces of Obedience"— wholeheartedly believing in Taoism, observing 36 pieces of Taoist scripture, and complying with the direction of the Taoist master.

(2) "Five Restrictions"— no killing, no meat or drinking, no lying, no stealing, and no wickedness.

(3) "Ten Prohibitions"— it's forbidden to disobey parents or teachers, to kill or trample livestock or people, to rebel against one's monarch or betray one's country, to be prurient, to slander Taoist scriptures, or to detest or abandon seniors.

(Adapted from *chinatravel.com*)

B2. Words and Expressions

Vocabulary

1. canon / ˈkænən / *n.* 原则;标准
2. synthesize / ˈsɪnθəsaɪz / *vt.* 综合;合成
3. regimen / ˈredʒɪmən / *n.* 养生;养生之道
4. yielding / ˈjiːldɪŋ / *n.* 屈服;让步

武当功夫	**Wudang Kung Fu**
南尊武当,北崇少林	Shaolin Kung Fu is the king of the north while Wudang Kun Fu rules the south
基于道教哲学和教规的内家拳	internal martial arts based on the philosophy and canons of Taoism
汲取了历史悠久、博大精深的道家知识	draw on a long history and profound knowledge of Taoism
将《易经》《道德经》的精髓与传统的少林功夫巧妙地结合起来	masterfully combine the essence of *I Ching* and *Tao De Ching* with traditional Shaolin Kung Fu
融合了道家内功、养生功、武术拳法、军事学等内容	synthesize Taoist internal exercises, regimen guarding skills, martial arts boxing, and military science
包括太极拳、形意拳、八卦掌等	include Tai Chi, Xingyi Quan, and Eight Trigram Palm
有助于促进健康和增强体质	contribute to health promotion and body-building

以屈服征服不屈服	conquer the unyielding by yielding
以静制动,对抗主动	confront the active with stillness
用对手的力量攻击对手	attack an opponent with his own force
敌方出手后才出手	strike only after the enemy has struck
结合缓慢、审慎的动作,冥想和深呼吸	combine slow, deliberate movements, meditation, and deep breathing
心灵一身体的锻炼	mind-body exercise

Vocabulary

1. respiratory / rɪˈspɪrət(ə)ri / *adj*. 呼吸的
2. dodge / dɒdʒ / *v*. 避开;躲开;闪开
3. disturbance / dɪˈstɜː(r)bəns / *n*. 干扰;障碍;紊乱
4. infusion / ɪnˈfjuːʒ(ə)n / *n*. 注入;灌输
5. collateral / kəˈlæt(ə)rəl / *adj*. 附属的;附加的;附带的
6. choreography / ˌkɒriˈɒgrəfi / *n*. 编舞艺术

太极	**Tai Chi**
软手	lithe hands
绵拳	cotton circles
柔术	gentle art
突然发力	sudden attack
柔似水,力无边	gentle but powerful
神经系统	neural system
呼吸系统	respiratory system
消化系统	digestive system
心脑血管系统	coronary, brain, and circulatory system
防病治病	disease prevention
中国哲学术语	Chinese philosophical term
八卦	Eight Trigrams
太极图说	Taiji Diagram
连环圆活	smooth and round
乾坤	Heaven and Earth
蹿蹦跳跃,闪展腾挪	move, jump, dodge, and unfold
潜气内转	interior circles of energy
流动的韵律	flowing rhythm

优雅宁静	a sense of elegance and quietude
静气中的变化	changes in tranquility
端正身体	straighten the body
合目收气	close the eyes and keep energy in check
两手下垂	let the hands naturally down
万念全除	expel all worry and disturbance
阴阳二气互为包裹，俯仰变化。	Yin and yang interchange, infuse and change.
拳势如大海，滔滔而不绝。	The momentum of Tai Chi is like the ocean, surging forward without cease.
缓慢、专注地锻炼	perform in a slow, focused manner
伴有深呼吸	be accompanied by deep breathing
非竞争性、自定节奏的系统	noncompetitive, self-paced system
低强度运动	low-impact exercise
对肌肉和关节的压力最小	put minimal stress on muscles and joints
对所有年龄和健康水平的人都是安全的	safe for all ages and fitness levels
刚柔并济	infusion of the hard and the soft
轻揉匀缓	even and slow
行云流水	like floating clouds and flowing rivers
经络学说	theory of main and collateral channels
内外结合	combination of the interior and the exterior
外练身手	improve physical health
内练心气	achieve evenness in breathing and calmness in mind
中国文化特性	the identity of Chinese culture
中国传统养生观念	traditional Chinese life-nourishing views
起源于气功	descend from Qigong
中国古代学科	ancient Chinese discipline
根植于中医	roots in traditional Chinese medicine
冥想的身体运动	meditative body movements
自卫	self-defense
重复韵律动作	repeat rhythmic choreography
将武术和冥想融合	fuse both martial arts and meditation

Vocabulary

1. combo / ˈkɒmbəʊ / *n*. 混合物
2. alert / əˈlɜː(r)t / *adj*. 警觉的;警惕的;戒备的
3. arthritis / aːrˈθraɪtɪs / *n*. 关节炎
4. digestive / daɪˈdʒestɪv / *adj*. 消化的;和消化有关的
5. endorphin/ enˈdɔːrfin / *n*. 内啡肽
6. agility / əˈdʒiliti: / *n*. 敏捷
7. stamina / ˈstæmɪnə / *n*. 耐力;耐性;持久力

太极的益处	**Benefits of Tai Chi**
提高四肢、头脑的协调性	improve your overall coordination between your hands, feet, and head
肌肉协调	muscle coordination
改善体态	optimize your posture
锻炼头部	practice head movement
保护自己免受反攻	protect yourself from counterattacks
避免身体接触	escape from physical contact
训练拳击组合	train Boxing Combos
增强肌肉记忆	improve muscle memory
更持久、更准确的头脑联系	build a more durable and accurate brain-body connection
获得信心	gain confidence
改善步法	improve your footwork
更好地感知对手	give you a better sense of your opponent
结合策略保护自己	combine your strategies to defend yourself
格斗不会受伤	practice fighting without getting hurt
让人更加警觉	make one more alert
训练全身	full body training
灵活格斗	learn to fight intelligently
无需器械	no boxing equipment is needed
摆脱压力	get rid of stress
减肥	lose weight
延缓衰老	delay aging and prolong life
高血压	high blood pressure
关节炎	arthritis
消化紊乱	digestive disorders

抑郁症	depression
缓解压力和焦虑	relieve stress and anxiety
平静你的心灵	calm your mind
提高注意力	improve focus
触发内啡肽的释放	trigger the release of endorphin
提高认知能力	boost cognitive ability
提高灵活性和敏捷性	increase flexibility and agility
提高平衡和协调能力	improve balance and coordination skill
增强力量和耐力	enhance strength and stamina

Vocabulary

1. substantiality / səbˌstænʃɪˈælɪtɪ / *n.* (有)实质;(有)实体;坚固
2. cessation / seˈseɪʃ(ə)n / *n.* 停止;终止;中断
3. descend / dɪˈsend / *v.* 下降;下来;降临
4. ascend / əˈsend / *v.* 上升;升高;登高
5. blaze / bleɪz / *v.* 闪耀;熊熊燃烧

阴阳	**Yin and Yang**
自然和心灵的统一结构	coherent fabric of nature and mind
体现在所有的存在中	exhibit in all existence
宇宙和人类兴衰之间的整合	integration between the waxing and waning of the cosmic and human realms
一个协调的过程	a process of harmonization
确保万物的持续、动态平衡	ensure a constant, dynamic balance of all things
阴的最高形式是极冷。	Yin in its highest form is freezing.
阳的最高形式是极热。	Yang in its highest form is boiling.
形成统一世界观的启发式机制	heuristic mechanism for formulating a coherent view of the world
否定	negativeness
被动	passiveness
柔和	gentleness
脆弱	insubstantiality
肯定	positiveness
主动	activeness
坚固	firmness

结实	substantiality
一分为二	separate oneness into two
对立统一	unity of opposites
相生相克	reinforce or counteract each other
互补	complement
连续不断的相互补充的作用力	mutually complementary forces that act continuously, without cessation
坚韧但不僵硬	firm yet not hard
柔中带刚	firmness concealed in softness
协调法则	the Law of Harmony
武术修养	cultivation of the martial art
五行	wuxing/five phases
水代表浸润。	Water is said to soak and descend.
火代表燃烧。	Fire is said to blaze and ascend.
木代表弯曲或舒张。	Wood is said to curve or be straight.
金代表遵从或改变。	Metal is said to obey and change.
土代表播种和收获。	Earth is said to take seeds and give crops.

B3. Speaking Activities

Situational Speech

The International Sports Club is about to hold a seminar on Chinese martial arts. You are invited to deliver a **5-minute** speech on **Wudang Kung Fu** to club members. Your speech might cover:

- The history of Wudang Kung Fu;
- The features of Wudang Kung Fu;
- The benefits you may gain by practicing Wudang Kung Fu.

You may refer to the words and expressions in Part B, but don't confine yourself to them.

Interview

Tai Chi is a discipline that involves the mind, breath, and movement to create a calm, natural balance of energy that can be used in work, recreation or self-defense. Your community is about to hold a lecture on Tai Chi. As a volunteer of your community, you and your partners plan to interview 5 residents about their understanding of Tai Chi. Your interview questions might include:

- Have you ever practiced Tai Chi? Why or why not?
- If you practice Tai Chi, what do you expect from it?
- Is Tai Chi only suitable for the elderly?
- Are you going to promote Tai Chi abroad? Why?
- Others.

Brainstorming

Look at the picture (4-1) on the right side.

- What is the symbol called?
- What does the white part and black part symbolize respectively?
- What philosophical idea does the symbol convey?

pic. 4-1

Reading and Sharing

Tai Chi is a practice that involves a series of slow gentle movements and physical postures, a meditative state of mind, and controlled breathing. Tai Chi originated as an ancient martial art in China. Over the years, it has become more focused on health promotion and rehabilitation. Read the following paragraphs about benefits of Tai Chi and share your views.

Paragraph 1

A 2019 review of 9 studies (656 participants) looked at the use of Tai Chi in the early stages of dementia in older adults (average age of 78). The short-term effect of Tai Chi on the overall cognition of people with mild cognitive impairment was found to be beneficial and similar to that seen with other types of exercise. The results of the studies suggested that Tai Chi done three times a week for 30 to 60 minutes per session for at least 3 months had a positive impact on some cognitive functions.

(Adapted from *nccih.nih.gov*)

Paragraph 2

A 2019 review evaluated 10 studies with 959 participants who had low-back pain. The duration of the Tai Chi interventions ranged from 2 to 28 weeks, with sessions done two to six times weekly and the majority lasting from 40 to 60 minutes. Because the studies used different Tai Chi interventions and assessment methods, the authors drew a cautious conclusion that Tai Chi alone or in addition to physical therapy may decrease pain intensity and improve everyday function (such as the ability to carry groceries, climb stairs, walk, and bathe and dress oneself).

(Adapted from *nccih.nih.gov*)

Ideas for Sharing

- What health benefits of Tai Chi can be found from the above paragraphs?
- Can you list other benefits of practicing Tai Chi?
- What do you think is the best way to promote the international communication of Tai Chi culture?

Debate

Mastery of 24 basic Tai Chi moves is now required for students to graduate from high school in east China's Fujian Province, according to the latest statement from the province's education administration, triggering heated debate. Tai Chi is listed as a mandatory sport in the high school physical education test, which makes up around 10 percent of the total grade, said the Fujian education department, reported Xinhua News Agency. As one of the many branches of Chinese Wushu, the broad term applied to the country's various forms of martial arts, Tai Chi is known for its slow moves that are part of defense training. It's also practiced for its health benefits. Accompanied by regulated deep breathing, it allows the body to achieve a state of relaxation and harmony. While supporters welcome the change as a way to promote traditional Chinese martial arts and help junior students to relieve academic pressure, others think Tai Chi is too mild a physical activity for active teenagers.

(Adapted from *CGTN.com*)

Topic for Debate

Tai Chi class should be made compulsory for college students.

Interpretation

Interpret the paragraphs below into English with the words and expressions you learned in Part B.

Paragraph 1

武当功夫和少林功夫是中国传统武术中最具代表性的两种风格,因此在中国有一句流行语:“南尊武当,北崇少林”。与受禅宗思想影响的“外家拳”——少林功夫不同,武当功夫是基于中国本土宗教——道教的哲学和教规发展的“内家拳”。据说,武当功夫是由元末明初武当道士张三丰创立。张三丰将《易经》和《道德经》的精髓与传统的少林功夫巧妙融为一体,创造了具有养生健身价值,以太极拳、形意拳和八卦掌为主体的武当功夫。

Paragraph 2

在中国武术中,有一种被称为“太极拳”的功夫受到人们的普遍喜爱,至今仍然是中国人强身健体的重要方式之一。它本来是一种武术,由于具有护身和健体的双重功能,所以很快发展成为人们锻炼身体的方式。这套功夫还具有调节人的神经系统、呼吸系统、消化系统以及心脑血管系统的作用，所以它又有防病治病的功能。

Paragraph 3

太极拳在发展过程中，吸收了中医的经络学说和道教的导引之术。太极拳是内外结合，外练身手，内练心气。在打太极拳的过程中，需特别注意气的吐纳，即从口中吐出浊气，又将新鲜空气从鼻中纳入，吐故纳新，保持身体中的新鲜能量。人们往往喜欢在空气清新的早晨打太极，一套拳术打下来，通体透灵，身心好像在清新空气中洗涤过一般，万念全除。

B4. Culture Highlights

Q: *Qigong, pronounced "chi gong," was developed in China thousands of years ago. It involves using exercises to optimize energy within the body, mind, and spirit, with the goal of improving and maintaining health and well-being. Is Qigong the same as Tai Chi?*
A: Tai chi originated as an ancient martial art, but over the years it has become more focused on health promotion and rehabilitation. When Tai Chi is performed for health, it is considered a form of Qigong and involves integrated physical postures, focused attention, and controlled breathing. Tai Chi is one of the hundreds of forms of Qigong exercises that was developed in China. Other forms of Qigong include Baduanjin, Liuzijue, Hu Yue Xian, Yijin Jing, and medical Qigong.
(Adapted from *nccih.nih.gov*)

Q: *Tai Chi is circular in shape, including the yin and the yang, and shadow boxing was created exactly on the basis of this theory. What is shadow boxing?*
A: This martial art training method involves throwing punches into the air while pretending to be an imaginary opponent. Boxers usually use this technique to prepare their muscles before engaging in more vigorous boxing exercises. In addition to getting the muscles ready for another activity, this exercise helps the fighter maintain a sense of rhythm and plans to face a particular opponent. In order to be prepared to face their future opponents, fighters may find it helpful to visualize. This gives them an idea of what they need to fix and what they do not. Shadow boxing drills can be done anywhere and at any time. Punching bags, a pair of boxing gloves, and headgear are not necessary for this endurance workout. Having the coach observe your boxing is recommended for the best results. Or, do it surrounded by mirrors so that you can check your movement with a critical eye.
(Adapted from *punchingbagsguide.com*)

Q: *Who can do Tai Chi? How to get started with Tai Chi?*

A: Tai Chi is low impact and puts minimal stress on muscles and joints, making it generally safe for all ages and fitness levels. In fact, because Tai Chi is a low-impact exercise, it may be especially suitable if you're an older adult who otherwise may not exercise.

You may also find Tai Chi appealing because it's inexpensive and requires no special equipment. You can do Tai Chi anywhere, including indoors or outside. And you can do tai chi alone or in a group class.

Although Tai Chi is generally safe, women who are pregnant or people with joint problems, back pain, fractures, severe osteoporosis or a hernia should consult their health care provider before trying Tai Chi. Modification or avoidance of certain postures may be recommended.

Although you can rent or buy videos and books about Tai Chi, consider seeking guidance from a qualified Tai Chi instructor to gain the full benefits and learn proper techniques.

You can find Tai Chi classes in many communities today. To find a class near you, contact local fitness centers, health clubs and senior centers. Tai Chi instructors don't have to be licensed or attend a standard training program. It's a good idea to ask about an instructor's training and experience, and get recommendations if possible.

A Tai Chi instructor can teach you specific positions and breathing techniques. An instructor can also teach you how to practice Tai Chi safely, especially if you have injuries, chronic conditions, or balance or coordination problems. Although Tai Chi is slow and gentle, and generally doesn't have negative side effects, it may be possible to get injured if you don't use the proper techniques.

After learning Tai Chi, you may eventually feel confident enough to do Tai Chi on your own. But if you enjoy the social aspects of a class, consider continuing with group Tai Chi classes.

(Adapted from *mayoclinic.org*)

B5. Extensive Reading

Passage One

Explore Chinese Kung Fu in Wudang Mountain

Wudang Mountain and Tai Chi

Wudang Mountain has long been a cherished Taoist Mountain in China, and now also a famed scenic area to explore the Taoist culture as well as enjoy the beautiful natural scenery. Tai Chi, short for Tai Chi Chuan is China's precious intangible cultural heritage. It focuses on Chinese Confucianism, great harmony of Taoism and Concepts of yin-yang. More than a kind of Chinese martial arts, it is also a good way to create an overall well-being and improve physical health. Featuring in its agility, tardiness, inflexibility as well as yielding at the same time, Tai Chi has spread worldwide and been practiced by many exercisers. Wudang Mountain is believed to be birthplace of Tai Chi.

Origin and development of Tai Chi

It is said that the Taoist holy man Mr. Zhang Sanfeng set up Wudang Sect in Wudang Mountain in the early Ming dynasty (1368) and recruited followers from different places. After years of the study of Taoism, he made a great contribution to promoting Taoist theory. Besides, he created several Martial arts with using fist only, Tai Chi included. One legend tells that when Zhang Sanfeng practiced in a cave, he found a magpie and snake fighting. The magpie took the initiative attack and the snake just avoided hitting. When the magpie was exhausted, the snake gave a deadly strike. Illuminated by the snake, Zhang Sanfeng created Tai Chi which is famous for conquering the unyielding with the yielding and coping with all motions by remaining motionless. Because of his Kungfu accomplishments and Taoist attainments, Zhang Sanfeng enjoys a long-standing reputation. The emperor Zhu Di has invited him to the Forbidden City to propagate Taoism in spite of his refusal.

Afterwards, Tai Chi was come down in Wudang Mountain. On the basis of Zhang Sanfeng's accomplishments, many successive generations continue the traditions and several branches of practice have been evolved over years. Since the founding of People's Republic of China, it has experienced a rapid expansion and the Tai Chi players are popping up all around China. As the birthplace of Tai Chi, Wudang Mountain is still popular place for learning Tai Chi. Many modern style of Tai Chi traced their development to several schools, most influential schools including Chen, Yang, Wu, Wu and Sun.

At present, there are many Scientific Research Departments researching on Tai Chi from the perspective of medicine, physiology, psychology, biochemistry etc. Their research shows that playing Tai Chi is helpful to prevent or cure some chronic diseases, like hypertension, heart disease, arthropathy, intestinal tract disease etc.

Tai Chi 13 Form (Tai Chi Shi San Shi)

As the name implies, Tai Chi 13 Form means 13 groups of movements (60 postures) with a strong purpose of offense and defense. It was the mother of all Tai Chi forms and created by Zhang Sanfeng. People praised it as the treasure of Chinese martial arts and the essence of Tai Chi. The 13 groups of movements were created according to Eight Extra-Meridians which connect with five internal organs. The 13 Form contains eight basic movements and five steps and the two are integrated with each other closely. The eight hand movements were derived from Eight Trigrams, which can be interpreted as heaven, earth, water, fire, wind, thunder, lake, and mountain. It can be divided into two parts — four primary hands (warding off, pulling back, pressing, and pushing) and four corner hands (pulling down, splitting, elbowing, and shouldering). The five steps refer to five footwork sills, namely advancing forward, retreating backward, stepping to the left side after faking right, stepping to the right side after faking left, and settling at the center.

For thousands of years, the Wudang Taoism has always been a key school of Chinese Taoism, and has the same religious doctrine and dogmata with Chinese Taoism. This religion put emphasis on the faithful filial piety ethics and the harmonious combination of three religions, namely the Taoism, Confucianism, and Buddhism. Besides, Wudang Mountain is preferred for its Wudang martial arts. The famous Tai Chi also called shadowboxing, Eight Diagrams Palm, Xingyi Quan, etc. were originated there. Therefore, so many martial arts likers visit Mount Wudang from different countries and regions to feel its charm and the benefits to their bodies and minds.

Brief explanation of 13 form of Tai Chi

- Beginning Phase: sinking shoulders and dropping elbows.
- Hugging a ball — relaxing chest and arching back.
- Single pushing — breathing into belly.
- Exploring — pointing up the head lightly.
- Holding — relaxing waist and hip.
- Flapping — differentiating between the empty and full, namely yin and yang.
- Loading — coordination of upper and lower parts of body.
- Separating — using the mind instead of force.
- Surging — harmony between internal and external.

- Dissolving — connecting the mind and the breathe.
- Push with both hands — find stillness within movement.
- Pressing down — movement and stillness present at once.
- Finishing phase — continuity and evenness through the form.

(Adapted from *chinadiscovery.com*)

Passage Two

Yin-yang

Yin-yang is one of the dominant concepts shared by different schools throughout the history of Chinese philosophy. Just as with many other Chinese philosophical notions, the influences of yin-yang are easy to observe, but its conceptual meanings are hard to define. Despite the differences in the interpretation, application, and appropriation of yin-yang, three basic themes underlie nearly all deployments of the concept in Chinese philosophy: (1) yin-yang as the coherent fabric of nature and mind, exhibited in all existence, (2) yin-yang as jiao (interaction) between the waxing and waning of the cosmic and human realms, and (3) yin-yang as a process of harmonization ensuring a constant, dynamic balance of all things.

As the Zhuangzi (Chuang-tzu) claims, "Yin in its highest form is freezing while yang in its highest form is boiling. The chilliness comes from heaven while the warmness comes from the earth. The interaction of these two establishes he (harmony), so it gives birth to things. Perhaps this is the law of everything yet there is no form being seen". In none of these conceptions of yin-yang is there a valuational hierarchy, as if yin could be abstracted from yang (or vice versa), regarded as superior or considered metaphysically separated and distinct. Instead, yin-yang is emblematic of valuational equality rooted in the unified, dynamic, and harmonized structure of the cosmos. As such, it has served as a heuristic mechanism for formulating a coherent view of the world throughout Chinese intellectual and religious history.

Origins of the terms yin and yang

The earliest Chinese characters for yin and yang are found in inscriptions made on "oracle bones" (skeletal remains of various animals used in ancient Chinese divination practices at least as early as the 14th century BCE). In these inscriptions, yin and yang simply are descriptions of natural phenomena such as weather conditions, especially the movement of the sun. There is sunlight during the day (yang) and a lack of sunlight at night (yin). According to the earliest comprehensive dictionary of Chinese characters (ca. 100), Xu Shen's *Shuowen Jiezi* (*Explaining Single-component Graphs and Analyzing Compound Characters*), yin refers to "a closed door, darkness and the south bank of a river and the north side of a mountain." Yang refers to "height, brightness and the south side of a mountain." These meanings of yin and yang originated in the daily life experience of the early Chinese. Peasants depended on sunlight for lighting and their daily life routines. When the sun came out, they would go to the field to work; when the sun went down, they would return home to rest. This sun-based daily pattern evidently led to a conceptual claim: yang is movement (dong) and yin is rest (jing). In their earliest usages, yin and yang existed independently and were not connected. The first written record of using these two characters together appears in a verse from the *Shijing* (*Book of Songs*): "Viewing the scenery at a hill, looking for yin-yang." This indicates that yang is the sunny side and yin is the shady side of hill. This effect of the sun exists at the same time over the hill.

The yin-yang school

According to Sima Tan (Ssu-ma Tan, c. 110 BCE), there existed a school of teaching during the "Spring and Autumn" (770 BCE-481 BCE) and "Warring States" (403 BCE-221 BCE) periods that bore the name of yin-yang. He lists this yin-yang school alongside five others (Confucian, Mohist, Legalist, Fatalist, and Daoist) and defines its theory as "the investigation of the shu [art] of yin and yang." According to him, this school focused on omens of luck and explored the patterns of the four seasons. In other words, the yin-yang school was concerned with methods of divination or astronomy (disciplines that were not distinct from one another in early China, as elsewhere in the ancient world) and the calendrical arts (which entailed study of the four seasons, eight locations, twelve du [measures] and twenty-four shijie [time periods]). Just as the Confucians (rujia) arose from the ranks of rushi ("scholar-gentlemen") who excelled at ritual and music, those of the yingyang school came from the fangshi ("recipe-gentlemen") who specialized in various numerological disciplines known as shushu ("number-arts"). These shushu included tianwen (astronomy), lipu (calendar-keeping), wuxing ("five phases" correlative theory), zhuguai (tortoise-shell divination), zazha (fortune-telling) and xingfa (face-reading). The Han dynasty chronicle Shiji (Records of the Historian) lists Zou Yan (305 BCE-240 BCE) as a representative of the yin-yang school who possessed a profound knowledge of the theory of yin-yang and wrote about a hundred thousand words on it. However, none of his works have survived.

By the Han dynasty (202 BCE-220 CE), yin-yang was associated with wuxing ("five phases") correlative cosmology. According to the "Great Plan" chapter of the *Shujing* (*Classic of Documents*), wuxing refers to material substances that have certain functional attributes: water is said to soak and descend; fire is said to blaze and ascend; wood is said to curve or be straight; metal is said to obey and change; earth is said to take seeds and give crops. Wuxing is used as a set of numerological classifiers and explains the configuration of change on various scales. The so-called yin-yang wuxing teaching — an "early Chinese attempt in the direction of working out metaphysics and a cosmology"— was a fusion of these two conceptual schemes applied to astronomy and the mantic arts.

(Adapted from *iep.utm.edu*)

B6. Assignment

Brochure Design

Form students into groups of 3 or 4 and design an English Brochure on Tai Chi. You need to include:

- The history and features of Wudang Kung Fu;
- The relationship between Wudang Kung Fu and Tai Chi;
- The benefits of practicing Tai Chi.

References

Editors of CGTN (2018). Chinese Students Required to Master Tai Chi to Graduate High School. *CGTN*. Retrieved from http://news.cgtn.com/news/3d3d414d7a496a4d30457a6333566d54/share_p.html on Nov. 22nd, 2022.

Editors of China Educational Tours (2022). The Philosophy of Kung Fu. *China Educational Tour*. Retrieved from https://www.chinaeducationaltours.com/guide/culture-chinese-kungfu philosophy.htm on June 22nd, 2022.

Editors of Kunfucleverland. (2022). Tenents of Shaolin Kung Fu. *Kunfuclever Cand*. Retrieved from http://www.kungfucleveland.com/about/tenents-of-kung-fu/ on June 21, 2022.

Editors of Ninjaphd (2022). Shaolin. *Ninjaphd*. Retrieved from https://www.ninjaphd.com/shaolin/ on June 23rd, 2022.

Editors of Punching Bags Guide (2022). What Are the Benefits of Shadow Boxing? 14 Reasons to Do It!. *Punching Bags Guide*. Retrieved from https://punchingbagsguide.com/shadow-boxing-benefits/ on Nov. 22nd, 2022.

Editors of Saholinskungu. (2022). Shaolin Kung Fu. *Shaolin Kung Fu*. Retrieved from https://www.shaolinskungfu.com/KungFu/Shaolin-Kung-Fu-20.html on June 22nd, 2022.

Editors of China discovery (2022). Wudang Tai Chi Experience. *China Discovery*. Retrieved from https://www. chinadiscovery. com/hubei/wudang-tai-chi-experience. html on July 26th, 2022.

Wendy Rose Gould. (2021). What Is Tai Chi? The Different Forms and Many Benefits. *Verywellmind*. Retrieved from https://www. verywellmind. com/what-is-tai-chi-5073074 on Nov. 23rd, 2022.

Renjun Gu, Yujia Gao, Chunbing Zhang, et, al. (2022). Effect of Tai Chi on Cognitive Function among Older Adults with Cognitive Impairment: A Systematic Review and Meta-Analysis. *National Library of Medicine*. Retrieved from https://www.ncbi.nlm. nih.gov/pmc/articles/PMC8360724/ on Nov. 21st, 2022.

Sally Guo. (2022). Shaolin Kung Fu. *China Travel*. Retrieved from https://www. chinatravel.com/culture/kungfu/shaolin-kung-fu on Nov. 25th, 2022.

Leon Long. (2023). Kung Fu in Western Society. *China Educational Tours*. Retrieved from https://www. chinaeducationaltours. com/guide/culture-chinese-kungfu-in-western-society. htm on January 1st, 2023.

Anne Meredith. (2022). The Who, What and Why of Chinese Martial Arts. *Studycli. org*. Retrieved from https://studycli.org/chinese-culture/chinese-martial-arts/ on July 1st, 2023.

Rousseau Robert. (2018). Kung Fu History and Style. *liveabout. com*. Retrieved from https://www.liveabout.com/history-and-style-guide-kung-fu-2308273 on June 23rd, 2022.

Dana Sparks. (2018). Mayo Mindfulness: Tai Chi Is a Gentle Way to Fight Stress. *Mayoclinic*. Retrieved from https://newsnetwork. mayoclinic. org/discussion/mayo-mindfulness-tai-chi-is-a-gentle-way-to-fight-stress/ on Nov. 22nd, 2022.

Hannah Wabe. (2022). Differences Between Tai Chi and Qi Gong. *circledna. com*. Retrieved from https://circledna. com/differences-between-taichi-and-qigong/ on Nov. 21st, 2022.

Robin R. Wang. (2022). Yinyang. *Internet Encyclopedia Philosophy*. Retrieved from https://iep.utm.edu/yinyang/ on Nov. 23rd, 2022.

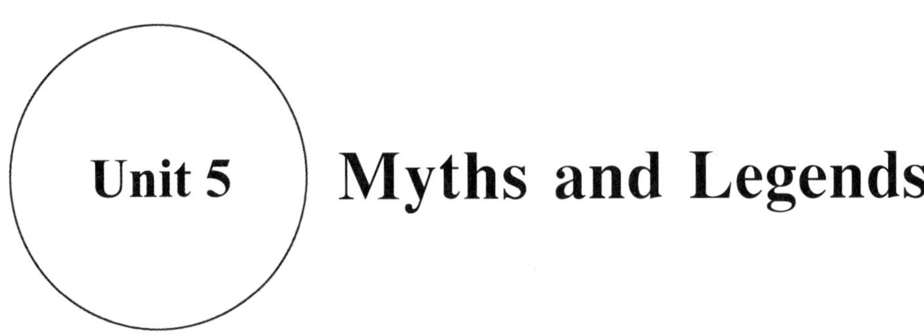

Unit 5 Myths and Legends

Part A Creation Myths

A1. Introduction

Pan Gu & Nüwa

Pan Gu — creator of the world

In Chinese mythology, Pan Gu was the first living creature and the creator of the world. Among his acts of creation were the separation of the earth and sky, the placement of the stars and planets in the heavens, and the shaping of the earth's surface.

At the beginning of time, the universe consisted only of dark chaos, in the form of a cosmic egg. Within the egg lay a sleeping giant named Pan Gu. One day Pan Gu awoke and stretched, causing the egg to split open. After Pan Gu emerged, the light, pure parts of the egg became the sky, while the heavy parts formed the earth. This separation of the earth and sky marked the beginning of yin and yang, the two opposing forces of the universe.

Already gigantic in size, Pan Gu grew 10 feet taller each day. This went on for 18,000 years, and as Pan Gu became taller, he pushed the earth and sky farther apart and shaped them with his tools until they reached their present position and appearance. Exhausted by his work, Pan Gu finally fell asleep and died.

When Pan Gu died, parts of his body were transformed into different features of the world. According to some stories, his head, arms, feet, and stomach became great mountains that help to anchor the world and mark its boundaries. Other stories say that Pan Gu's breath was transformed into wind and clouds; his voice became thunder; and his eyes became the sun and moon. Pan Gu's blood formed rivers and seas; his veins turned into roads and paths; his sweat became rain and dew; his bones and teeth turned into rock and metal; his flesh changed into soil; the hair on his head became the stars; and the hair on his body turned into vegetation.

Some myths say that humans developed from fleas and parasites that fell from Pan Gu's body and beard. Other stories, however, tell how Pan Gu created humans by shaping them from clay and leaving them in the sun to dry. When a sudden rain began to fall, Pan Gu hastily wrapped up the clay figures, damaging some in the process, which explains why some humans are crippled or disabled.

Although a giant, Pan Gu is usually portrayed in Chinese art as a little person clothed in a bearskin or leaves, holding a hammer and chisel or the cosmic egg of creation. Sometimes he is shown working with his tools to create the world, accompanied by four supernatural creatures: a unicorn, tortoise, phoenix, and dragon. Though primarily a figure in Taoist belief, he also appears sometimes in Chinese Buddhist mythology.

Nüwa — creator of mankind

In Chinese mythology, Nüwa is the first being with the ability to procreate and is the creator of all mankind. Ancient Chinese society was fiercely matriarchal, so Nüwa, being the mother of all humans, was considered a very important deity. She has a hand in a number of stories but is most commonly associated with China's creation myth and for saving humanity by mending a hole in the sky after a great flood. Today, Nüwa is still a popular deity and is usually prayed to by women who need divine assistance with marital affairs or fertility issues.

There are two widely told versions of China's creation story. The most commonly told one is where Nüwa crafts humanity from river clay.

After Pan Gu emerged from his mythical egg and created the physical universe, the earth separated from the heavens and became a beautiful place full of lush, green vegetation, vast rivers, tall mountains, and all sorts of animals. One day, Nüwa decided to go for a walk in the woods among the mountains and animals. As she walked along, she was suddenly overcome with loneliness. Even though everything around her was strikingly beautiful, Nüwa had no one to keep her company. She decided to pause along the banks of a river and began to make figures out of clay from the mud.

At first, she began to make easy shapes like chickens and sheep, and though they amused her, she soon became bored with them. Gazing into the river and seeing her reflection, she was struck with inspiration. Why not make clay figures that looked like her? She began to shape the mud into figures with faces, arms, hands, and legs. To her delight, they began to dance and talk with her when she put them on the ground. She decided to name them humans.

Nüwa was so excited by her creation that she made clay figures until her hands hurt. She took the end of a rope, dipped it in the mud, and began to swing it around her head forming blobs of sticky mud around her.

In an alternative creation myth, a cataclysmic flood wiped out all of mankind except for Nüwa and her brother, Fuxi, who happened to escape into a boat at just the right moment. After the floodwaters died down, they discovered that they were the last humans left on Earth. Although they realized that they should procreate to continue the survival of the human race, they were deeply conflicted about the idea since they were siblings. Fuxi and Nüwa, decided to ask for heaven's guidance. After praying, they concluded that they needed to undergo a divination test that could indicate whether they were destined to be husband and wife.

Fuxi and Nüwa ascended two different mountains and lit two fires. They decided that if the smoke blew straight up that they would not get married. But, if the smoke trails intertwined with one another, it was a sign that they should continue the human race. The smoke from their fires twisted and curled in with one another so Fuxi and Nüwa became husband and wife and repopulated the earth.

Nüwa — mending the pillars of heaven

The world of the first beings was very different from ours now. The earth was just in its infancy and was only separated from the sky by four very large pillars.

One day, Gong Gong, the god of water, and the god of fire, Zhu Rong became locked in a massive battle that would determine the ruler of heaven. Wildfires raged and floods plagued the countryside. Gong Gong, who was motivated by evil, ultimately lost the fight. Gong Gong was so angered that he bashed his head against Buzhou mountain — one of the four pillars holding up the heavens. The earth began to tremble and the pillar collapsed and ripped a hole in the sky.

At this point, the earth was completely in tatters from Zhu Rong and Gong Gong's epic battle. Fires had scorched the earth, water was pouring incessantly from the hole in the sky, and the heavens no longer covered the earth. Seeing how her children were suffering, Nüwa immediately sprang to action. She went to the sky turtle, Ao, and begged him to grant her a miracle to save her children. The turtle obliged and used a sword she had given him to cut off his own four legs.

Nüwa then gathered five colored stones and melted them together to fix the hole in the sky. She used Ao's legs to replace the four broken pillars all the while holding up the sky with her back while rain poured down upon her. The ancient Chinese historian Sima Qian, recorded the following account of Nüwa's heroic deed: The pillars of Heaven were broken and the corners of the earth gave way. Hereupon Nüwa melted stones of the five colours to repair the heavens, and cut off the feet of the tortoise to set upright the four extremities of the earth. Gathering the ashes of reeds she stopped the flooding waters, and thus rescued the land.

One version of the story says that after she was done, she was so tired that she laid down to rest and died from exhaustion. Another version says that while she was working, she discovered there wasn't enough stone to fix the sky, so she sacrificed herself to use her body to fill the last bits. Either way, order was restored to earth and humanity was able to live peacefully once again.

Although she did her best, Nüwa couldn't get the sky and earth to align exactly the way it had before. The earth became permanently tilted and that's why it's said that all of the rivers in China run in a southeastern direction.

(Adapted from *mythencyclopedia.com* & *mythopedia.com*)

A2. Words and Expressions

Vocabulary

1. theological / ˌθiːəˈlɒdʒɪk(ə)l / *adj*. 神学(上)的;神学性质的
2. eon / ˈiːən/ *n*. 极漫长的时间;千万年
3. patrilineal / pætriˈlɪniəl / *adj*. 父子相传的;父系的
4. matrilineal / mætriˈlɪniəl / *adj*. 母系的;基于母系的
5. anthropology / ˌænθrəˈpɒlədʒi / *n*. 人类学

创世神话的意义	**The Significance of Creation Myths**
亿万年	eons of years
神话学	mythology
原始观念	primitive ideas
组织原则	an organizing principle
父系社会	patrilineal society
母系社会	matrilineal society
整体观念	holistic concept
理解未知	make sense of the unknown
文明的开端	the dawn of civilization
智力的贫弱	intellectual impotence
人类的起源	the origin of humanity
民族的由来	the origin of ethnic groups

人类起源神话	mythology of human origin
流传千年的故事	stories that have survived millennia
低下的生产能力	low production capacity
贫乏的生活经验	poor life experience
哲学和神学的阐述	philosophical and theological elaboration
文化中的自我认同	the self-identity of the culture
记录在石板、卷轴上	recorded on tablets and scrolls
作为文化文献的一部分	incorporated as part of a cultural literature
宇宙创造的现代科学观	the modern scientific view of the creation of universe
人类在世界中定位的基础	a basis for the orientation of human beings within the world
将神圣创造的语言融入叙事	incorporate the language of divine creation into the narrative
为正式神话的形成奠定基础	lay the foundations for a well-formed mythology
强化普遍理解的真理的手段	a means of reinforcing commonly understood truths
文化形成和社会秩序的重要方面	important facets of cultural formation and societal ordering
对自然和自然世界的高度关注	a heavy focus on nature and the natural world
宇宙从混乱或无道德状态中建立秩序	the ordering of the cosmos from a state of chaos or amorphousness
涵盖文学、史学、人类学、社会学、心理学甚至科学	touch on literature, history, anthropology, sociology, psychology, and even science

Vocabulary

1. coalesce / ˌkoʊəˈles / *v*. 合并,联合;使(元素)结合
2. void / vɔɪd / *n*. 空白,空虚
3. primordial / praɪˈmɔːrdiəl / *adj*. 原始的;根本的
4. disproportionate / ˌdɪsprəˈpɔːrʃənət / *adj*. 不成比例的
5. dwarfism / ˈdwɔːfɪzəm / *n*. 侏儒症;矮小
6. writhe / raɪð / *v*. 翻滚;蠕动; 扭曲;扭动
7. canyon / ˈkænjən / *n*.(两边为峭壁、谷底通常有溪流的)峡谷
8. ravine / rəˈviːn / *n*. 沟壑,山涧;峡谷
9. Neolithic / ˌniːəˈlɪθɪk / *adj*. 新石器时代的

盘古开天辟地	**Creator of the World — Pan Gu**
巨蛋	a(n) enormous / great / giant egg
合并而成的第一个生命	the first thing to be coalesced into being
漂浮在虚无中	float in nothingness
创造大地和天空	the creation of the land and sky
宇宙的混沌虚无	the void of chaos / the chaotic void of the universe
原始状态	a primordial state
宇宙的二元性	the cosmic dualities
不断相互争斗	constantly fight against one another
不断相互吸引	be constantly attracted to one another
阴阳——两个截然相反完美平衡的元素	yin and yang — two opposite elements in perfect balance
长相丑陋	an unattractive human face
额头上有圆角	with rounded horns on the forehead
(胳膊和腿)被毛发覆盖	(arms and legs) covered in hair
原始的衣服	primitive clothing
被限制在狭小空间	be confined in a very tight space
扭曲翻滚	twist and writhe
打破蛋壳	break the shell of the egg
进入虚空	emerge into the void
创造世界和天空的所有物体	create all the features of the world and the sky
裂开的蛋	the cracked egg
天体	the heavenly bodies
(轻盈的蛋白)漂浮变成云朵和星星	(the light egg whites) float up and become the clouds and stars
(浓稠的蛋黄)下沉变成陆地	(the dense yolk) sink down and become the lands
(两半蛋壳)变成太阳和月亮	(the two halves of the shell) become the sun and the moon
让天空远离陆地	push the sky away from the land
与宇宙一起生长	to grow with the universe
(四肢)变成支撑天空的四大支柱	(limbs) become the four pillars that hold up the sky
(脊柱)形成巨大的山脉	(spine) form a great mountain range
(牙齿和骨骼)变成金属和宝石	(teeth and bones) become metal and gems
(气息)变成云朵	(breath) become the clouds
(血管)变成了巨大的峡谷和沟壑	(veins) become great canyons and ravines
(血液)变成河流	(blood) become the rivers
(汗液)变成雨水	(sweat) become the rain
(声音)成为雷声	(voice) be preserved as thunder

(浓密毛发中的跳蚤)变成各种动物	(the fleas that lived in his thick hair) be transformed and become the animals
居住在人类诞生之前的土地上	inhabit the land before humans were created
(头发)变成了森林 / 灌木 / 树木	(hair) become the forests / bushes / trees
向上漂移	drift upward
(眼睛)从身体飘走,变成了太阳和月亮	(eyes) float away from his body and become the sun and the moon
追溯到	date back to
早期青铜时代	early Bronze Age
新石器时代	Neolithic period

Vocabulary

1. serpent / ˈsɜːrpənt / *n.* 蛇(尤指大蛇或毒蛇)
2. calamity / kəˈlæməti / *n.* 灾难,灾祸
3. procreative / ˈprəʊkriˌeɪtɪv / *adj.* 生殖的;有生殖力的
4. laborious / ləˈbɔːriəs / *adj.* 耗时费力的,辛苦的
5. aristocrat / əˈrɪstəkræt / *n.* 贵族,贵族成员
6. matriarchal / ˌmeɪtriˈɑːkl / *adj.* 母系氏族的;女家长的
7. patriarchal / ˌpeɪtriˈɑːk(ə)l / *adj.* 父权制的,男性主宰统治的

女娲造人	**Creator of Human — Nüwa**
人类的创造者	Creator of Mankind / Human
动物和人类的创造者和保护者	a creator and protector of animals and people
神话人物	a mythological character
在大灾难之后创造和繁衍人类	create and reproduce people after a great calamity
中国第一位创世之神	the first creative Chinese deity
在中国文化中受到高度重视	be highly regarded in Chinese culture
人头蛇身	a snake body and a human head
半人半蛇(龙)	half people, half snake / serpent
执行各种角色	perform various roles
繁衍角色	a procreative role
四处游荡/闲逛	roam around / wander about
感到孤独	feel lonely / be overcome with loneliness
消除孤独感	dispel one's loneliness
创造一个和她相似的人	create a being in her likeness

河底的黄色黏土	yellow clay from the riverbed
捏一个人形	mold a figure
艰苦的过程	a laborious process
把绳子浸入湿黏土中	dip a rope in the wet clay
摆动绳子	swing the rope around
黏土滴	drops of clay
手工制作而成的人	handmade figurines / handcrafted people
富有的贵族	wealthy aristocrats
可怜的普通人	poor common folk
将它们分为男性和女性	separate them into male and female
创造自己的后代	create their own offspring
中国古代母系社会	ancient Chinese matriarchal society
父权制	a patriarchal system
泼水节	Water-Splashing Festival
致敬女娲的牺牲	pay a tribute to the sacrifices of Nüwa
苗族的传统女神	the traditional divine goddess of the Miao people

Vocabulary

1. deluge / ˈdeljuːdʒ / *n*. 暴雨,洪水
2. extinguish / ɪkˈstɪŋgwɪʃ / *v*. 熄灭;消灭
3. ferocious / fəˈroʊʃəs / *adj*. 凶猛的,残暴的
4. predatory / ˈpredət(ə)ri / *adj*. (动物)捕食性的,食肉的
5. blameless / ˈbleɪmləs / *adj*. 清白的;无可责备的
6. tear / ter / *n*. 裂口,破洞
7. tilt / tɪlt / *v*. (使)倾斜,(使)倾侧

女娲补天	**The Myth of Nüwa Patching Up / Mending the Heavens**
洪水神话	a deluge myth
共工,水神,强大的龙神	Gong Gong, the Water God, a powerful dragon-deity
相柳,一条九人头的巨型毒蛇	Xiang Liu, a giant poisonous snake with nine human heads
造成巨大破坏和可怕的洪水	cause great destruction and terrible floods
祝融,火神	Zhu Rong, the Fire God
挑战某人进行决斗	challenge sb. to a duel
通过武力一决胜负	settle sth. with a fight

真正撼动世界	literally rock the world
从天上坠落到大地	fall from the Heaven and crash down to the Earth
蒙受屈辱	be wrought with humiliation
不周山，支撑天空的八根支柱之一	Buzhou Mountain / Mount Buzhou, one of the eight pillars that held up the sky
神山	a mythical peak
新疆南部的昆仑山	the Kunlun range in southern Xinjiang
天空撕裂	a tear in the Heavens
（支柱）崩塌	(the pillar) collapse
（半边天）塌下来	(half the sky) fall in
（大地）裂开	(the earth) crack open
（森林）付之一炬	(forests) go up in flames
（洪水）从地下涌出	(flood waters) sprout from beneath the earth
（龙、蛇和猛兽）跳出来冲向人群	(dragons, snakes and fierce animals) leap out at the people
被淹死，被烧死（伤），被吃掉	be drowned, burned and devoured
火势失控	(fire) blaze out of control
熄灭	extinguish
洪水肆虐，泛滥成灾	(water) flood in great expanses
猛兽和猛禽	ferocious animals and predatory birds
无辜的人	blameless people
掠走年长体弱者	snatch the elderly and the weak
修复伤害	fix the damage
巨龟	a giant turtle
砍下，剁下	chop off
替代损坏的支柱	replace the damaged pillar
熔炼	smelt
五色石	Five-Colored Stones (one color for each element)
恢复和平	restore peace
（洪水）退去	(flood) recede
（支柱）竖起	(pillar) erect
纠正所有的错误	right all the wrongs
（天）向西北倾斜	(the Heavens) tilt to the northwest
（太阳和月亮）从东向西划过天空	(the Sun and the Moon) move across the sky from east to west

A3. Speaking Activities

Situational Speech

Your university is about to hold a seminar on Chinese mythology. You are invited to deliver **a 5-minute speech** on the seminar, introducing briefly **the Creation Myths** in Chinese culture to international students. Your speech might cover:

- The myth of Pan Gu creating the world;
- The myth of Nüwa creating humans;
- The myth of Nüwa repairing the heavens;
- Other creation myths.

You may refer to the words and expressions in Part A, but don't confine yourself to them.

Reading and Sharing

Read the following paragraphs about similarities and differences in creation myths around the world and share your views.

Paragraph 1

Creation stories have different supreme beings that were the ones that created all that followed. In the biblical myth, there was only one supreme being, unlike some of the others. God was the only one who existed, and from him came all of the creations. In the Greek myth, there were many different Supreme beings that created many different things on earth. The Greek mythology was unlike the others because it was the only one to strongly use many different creatures and stories of how different things came to be on earth. Some of the main supreme beings that we can see are Chaos, Uranus, Mother Earth, the Titans, and Prometheus. In the Chinese creation myth, there are only two supreme beings Pan Gu and Nüwa. "The first living thing was Pan Gu. He evolved inside a gigantic cosmic egg which contained all the elements of the universe totally intermixed together". In the last creation myth based on Ugandan writings, there was only one Supreme Being Kabezya-Mpungu. He was the highest god, and there was little known about him.

(Adapted from *blablawriting.net*)

Paragraph 2

Creation myths often share a number of features. They often are considered sacred accounts and can be found in nearly all known religious traditions. They are all stories with a plot and characters who are either deities, human-like figures, or animals, who often speak and transform easily. They are often set in a dim and nonspecific past, what historian of religion Mircea Eliade termed in illo tempore ("at that time"). Also, all creation myths speak to deeply meaningful questions held by the society that shares them, revealing of their central worldview and the framework for the self-identity of the culture and individual in a universal context.

(Adapted from *crystalinks.com*)

Brainstorming

Young Chinese people are increasingly favoring Hanfu, clothes once worn by ancient Han Chinese, as an expression of cultural identity and fashion. Some of them even dress up as legendary figures from ancient China, including Mulan, a young maiden disguising herself as a male warrior to take her ailing father's place in the army. **If you were to cosplay in a Hanfu, who would you like to portray**?

(Adapted from *scmp.com*)

Discussion

Chinese President Xi Jinping strongly advocates protecting the country's cultural heritage and has repeatedly called on the people to cherish, honor, and deepen the knowledge of Chinese civilization and strengthen cultural self-confidence. Wearing Hanfu for cosplay is one way to showcase Chinese history and legends. Please work with your teammates and come up with **more strategies to keep our history and legends alive**?

(Adapted from *cgtn.com*)

Interpretation

Interpret the paragraphs below into English with the words and expressions you learned in Part A.

Paragraph 1

创世神话是人类幼年时期用幻想的形式对自然、宇宙所做的稚拙的解释和描述，反映出原始古代人对天地宇宙和人类由来的原始观念。中国古代的创世神话，以盘古故事最为著名。创世神话主要有两个方面：解释和描述天地开辟，包括世界和万物的形成；说明人类的起源，包括民族的由来等。关于天地开辟的神话，各民族的早期几乎普遍存在。原始人由于生产能力的低下和智力的贫弱，对于自然宇宙的由来是不可理解的。只有以他们贫乏的生活经验为基础，进行想象和揣测。于是，便产生出这种创世神话。

Paragraph 2

女娲是中国上古神话中的创世女神，传说女娲用泥土仿照自己创造了人，创造了人类社会，她用手在池边挖了些泥土与水混合，照着自己的影子捏了起来，捏成了一个小小的东西，模样与女娲差不多，也有五官七窍，双手两脚，捏好后往地上一放，居然活了起来。女娲一见，满心欢喜，接着又捏了许多，她想让世界到处都有她亲手造出来的东西，于是，就顺手从附近折下一条藤蔓，伸入泥潭，沾上泥浆向地上挥洒，结果点点泥浆变成一个个小东西,她把这些小东西叫作人。

Paragraph 3

很久以前,天和地还没有分开,宇宙混沌一片。有个叫盘古的巨人,在这个混沌的宇宙之中,他睡了一万八千年。有一天,盘古突然醒了。他见周围一片漆黑,就抡起大斧头,朝眼前的黑暗猛劈过去。只听一声巨响,一片黑暗的东西渐渐分散开了。缓缓上升的东西,变成了天;慢慢下降的东西,变成了地。天和地分开以后,盘古怕它们还会合在一起,于是他头顶着天,脚蹬着地。这样不知过了多少年,天和地逐渐成形,盘古也累得倒下了。盘古倒下后,他的身体发生了极大的变化。他呼出的气息,变成了风和云;他发出的声音,化作了雷声;他的双眼变成了太阳和月亮;他的四肢,变成了大地上的东、西、南、北四极;他的肌肤,变成了辽阔的大地;他的血液,变成了奔流不息的江河。

A4. Culture Highlights

Q: *What are the similarities between Chinese creation myths and those in the West?*

A: The Chinese creation myths have **many similarities** with those in the West, such as the state of the pre-creation world, the way in which man was created and its implied meaning.

At the beginning of the creation, whether in the Chinese myths, the Bible, or Greek myths, **the world was chaotic and invisible.** In the Bible, "The earth was formless, darkness was over the surface of the deep." In Chinese ancient times, as history recorded, heaven and earth were in chaos as egg white and yolk. Then from the void came all the natural things and elements which are necessary in the world, such as light, day, night, sky, land, sea, etc.

From the creation myths of China and the West, we can see that **their creation work is orderly and the world is constructed in a certain order.** In Genesis, God first created light to divide day and night, then he created heaven and earth and all living things, and finally created Adam — the representative of human being. China's creation myths also follow a certain order. Firstly, Pan Gu "opening up the heavens and opening up the earth". Secondly, Pan Gu's body changed into thunderbolt, the sun and the moon, mountains, rivers and so on. After all this, it came to the myth of Nüwa creating human. Only after all the natural elements were prepared, the creation of animals and humankind could later take place. It implied that all living creatures including human cannot live without nature.

Besides, whether it is the God or Chinese deities, they all have supreme power and can do everything. But **they all used dust or mud on the ground**, which seems to imply a preliminary reflection on the fact that human beings come from the earth and finally will return to it after death.

(Adapted from *ukessays.com*)

Q: *What are the differences between Chinese creation myths and those in the West?*
A: In addition to the similarities between the creation myths in China and in the West, there are also many differences.
First, the Greek creation system constructs a reasonable pedigree origin through a clear reproductive relationship of sexes. It is the combination of sexes that produced all things in the world. The earth gave birth to the sky, mountains and sea; the earth and the sky gave birth to the Titan God, and the Titan God gave birth to the gods and all things. the status and functions of each God in Greek myths are clear. Erebus — the God of darkness, Nyx — the God of night, Eros — the God of love, Gaea — the God of Earth and Tartarus. However, most of the gods in Chinese creation myths accomplish a creation work by themselves.
Second, in the Bible, God is the only one with supreme power, and there is a contractual relationship between him and human. In ancient Greek myths, the position of God was also supreme, and Zeus even once wanted to destroy human beings. However, the creators of Chinese myths not only have Pan Gu, but also Nüwa. They have a harmonious relationship with nature and human beings. Pan Gu devoted his body to create the world. Then Nüwa also made man out of clay like a mother.
The differences of creation myths in different regions reflect diverse cultures, while the similarities imply the common recognition to the world. The creation myths not only explain the beginning of the world, but also perfectly reflect the daily lives of people, their cultural values and personal perspective on how they view their surroundings.
(Adapted from *ukessays.com*)

Q: *What are the major views of creation in China?*
A: There are five major views of creation in China:
The first, and most consistent historically, is that no myth exists. This is not to say there were none existing at all, only that there is no evidence showing an attempt to explain the world's origin.
The second view is very indirect. It is merely based on a question of a dialog in an earlier reference. The idea in the question implies that the heavens and the earth separated from one another.

The third view is the one perpetuated by Taoism by the nature of its philosophy. It appears "relatively" late in Chinese history. In it, Tao is described as the ultimate force behind the creation. With tao, nothingness gave rise to existence, existence gave rise to yin and yang, and yin and yang gave rise to everything. Due to the ambiguous nature of this myth, it could be compatible with the first myth (and therefore say nothing). But it could, like its antithesis, be explained in a way to better fit the modern scientific view of the creation of universe.

The fourth view is the relatively late myth of Pan Gu. This was an explanation offered by Taoist monks hundreds of years after Laozi; probably around 200. In this story, the universe begins as a cosmic egg. A god named Pan Gu, born inside the egg, broke it into two halves: The upper half became the sky; the lower half became the earth. As the god grew taller, the sky and the earth grew thicker and were separated further. Finally, the god died and his body parts became different parts of the earth.

The fifth view would be tribal accounts that vary widely and not necessarily connect to a system of belief.

(Adapted from *crystalinks.com*)

A5. Extensive Reading

Passage One

Creation Myths — Nature and Significance

Creation myth, also called cosmogonic myth, philosophical and theological elaboration of the primal myth of creation within a religious community. The term myth here refers to the imaginative expression in narrative form of what is experienced or apprehended as basic reality (see also myth). The term creation refers to the beginning of things, whether by the will and act of a transcendent being, by emanation from some ultimate source, or in any other way.

The myth of creation is the symbolic narrative of the beginning of the world as understood by a particular community. The later doctrines of creation are interpretations of this myth in light of the subsequent history and needs of the community. Thus, for example, all theology and speculation concerning creation in the Christian community are based on the myth of creation in the biblical book of Genesis and of the new creation in Jesus Christ. Doctrines of creation are based on the myth of creation, which expresses and embodies all of the fertile possibilities for thinking about this subject within a particular religious community.

Myths are narratives that express the basic valuations of a religious community. Myths of creation refer to the process through which the world is centered and given a definite form within the whole of reality. They also serve as a basis for the orientation of human beings within the world. This centering and orientation specify humanity's place in the universe and the regard that humans must have for other humans, nature, and the entire nonhuman world; they set the stylistic tone that tends to determine all other gestures, actions, and structures in the culture. The cosmogonic (origin of the world) myth is the myth par excellence. In this sense, the myth is akin to philosophy, but, unlike philosophy, it is constituted by a system of symbols; and because it is the basis for any subsequent cultural thought, it contains rational and nonrational forms. There is an order and structure to the myth, but this order and structure is not to be confused with rational, philosophical order and structure. The myth possesses its own distinctive kind of order.

Myths of creation have another distinctive character in that they provide both the model for nonmythic expression in the culture and the model for other cultural myths. In this sense, one must distinguish between cosmogonic myths and myths of the origin of cultural techniques and artifacts. Insofar as the cosmogonic myth tells the story of the creation of the world, other myths that narrate the story of a specific technique or the discovery of a particular area of cultural life take their models from the stylistic structure of the cosmogonic myth. These latter myths may be etiological (i. e., explaining origins); but the cosmogonic myth is never simply etiological, for it deals with the ultimate origin of all things.

The cosmogonic myth thus has a pervasive structure: its expression in the form of philosophical and theological thought is only one dimension of its function as a model for cultural life. Though the cosmogonic myth does not necessarily lead to ritual expression, ritual is often the dramatic presentation of the myth. Such dramatization is performed to emphasize the permanence and efficacy of the central themes of the myth, which integrates and undergirds the structure of meaning and value in the culture. The ritual dramatization of the myth is the beginning of liturgy, for the religious community in its central liturgy attempts to re-create the time of the beginning.

From this ritual dramatization, the notion of time is established within the religious community. To be sure, in most communities there is the notion of a sacred and a profane time. The prestige of the cosmogonic myth establishes sacred or real time. It is this time that is most efficacious for the life of the community. Dramatization of sacred time enables the community to participate in a time that has a different quality than ordinary time, which tends to be neutral. All significant temporal events are spoken of in the language of the cosmogonic myth, for only by referring them to this primordial model will they have significance.

In like manner, artistic expression in archaic or "primitive" societies, often related to ritual presentation, is modelled on the structure of the cosmogonic myth. The masks, dances, and gestures are, in one way or another, aspects of the structure of the cosmogonic myth. This meaning may also extend to the tools that people use in the making of artistic designs and to the precise technique they employ in the craft.

Mention has been made above of the fact that the cosmogonic myth situates humankind in a place, in space. This centering is at once symbolic and empirical: symbolic because through symbols it defines the spatiality of human beings in ontological terms (of being) and empirical because it orients them in a definite landscape. Indeed, the names given to the flora and fauna and to the topography are a part of the orientation of humans in a space. The subsequent development of language within a human community is an extension of the language of the cosmogonic myth.

The initial ordering of the world through the cosmogonic myth serves as the primordial structure of culture and the articulation of the embryonic forms and styles of cultural life out of which various and differing forms of culture emerge. The recollection and celebration of the myth enable the religious community to think of and participate in the fundamentally real time, space, and mode of orientation that enables them to define their cultural life in a specific manner.

(Adapted from *britannica.com*)

Passage Two

Creation Myths in World History

Ever since the dawn of civilization, we humans have pondered where everything, including life, came from. It has also been the case of why and how we and things around came to being. With the passage of time, there have been quite a number of creation stories from different cultures and civilizations. Often times, those creation stories also help to orient human beings in the world, giving them a sense of their place in the world and the regard that they must have for humans and nature.

Creation myth of Chinese

In this creation myth, the universe began as a chaotic soup without any structure. In this universe lay a black egg that housed a gargantuan being known as Pan Gu — a hairy giant with two horns and two tusks. The giant Pan Gu is believed to have slept in the egg for more than 18,000 years. All the while that Pan Gu slept, the universe was kept in perfect balance — i.e., equal amounts of darkness (yin) and light (yang). Upon waking up from his deep sleep, Pan Gu proceeded to escape from the egg. By so doing, he broke the force that kept the universe in perfect balance. The top half of the egg shell, which represented yang, turned into the sky; while the bottom half, which represented yin, became the earth. Standing in the broken shell, Pan Gu started to push the top part of shell farther away in order to keep yin and yang apart. As he pushes the sky up, he is believed to have grown taller — about ten feet. Aiding him in this task were four celestial creatures — the Qilin, the Phoenix, the Dragon, and the Turtle. He would do this for close to 18,000 years before dying. When Pan Gu died, parts of his body were transformed into different features of the world. Pan Gu's breath was transformed into wind and clouds; his voice became thunder; and his eyes became the sun and moon. Pan Gu's blood formed rivers and seas; his veins turned into roads and paths; his sweat became rain and dew; his bones and teeth turned into rock and metal; his flesh changed into soil; the hair on his head became the stars; and the hair on his body turned into vegetation.

Heliopolis creation story — ancient Egypt

According to the ancient Egyptians, the universe started with a primordial ocean known as Nun. At the center of Nun was a giant pyramid called benben. Deep within benben, came forth Atum, the creator deity. As the physical embodiment of the sun, Atum created life in an asexual manner. He also created the first Egyptian deities — Shu (air) and Tefnut (water/moisture). Together with his children, Atum was able to hold back the destructive forces of chaos and keep the universe in balance. Atum was also supported by Ma'at, the ancient Egyptian goddess of truth and order. The union between Shu and Tefnut brought forth Geb (earth) and Nut (sky). Due to the immense love shared between Geb and Nut, the two deities remained inseparable. Atum then instructed Shu to separate Geb (the earth) from Nut (the sky). But just before Shu could carry out the task, Geb and Nut gave birth to famous Egyptian deities such as Osiris, Isis, Seth, and Nephthys.

Babylonian creation myth

The ancient Babylonians believed that in the beginning two primordial gods — Aspu and Tiamet — existed. Prior to that, the universe was a vast void of nothingness, land and sky had yet formed. Tiamet and Aspu mated and gave birth to a new crop of gods. It is believed that Tiamet grew enormous amount of hatred toward the new gods. Tiamet set out to destroy them. However, just before Tiamet could carry out his plan, the gods found out and proceeded to stop him. The gods threw a strong, powerful net over Tiamet. Once trapped in the net, the gods beat Tiamet to pulp and crack his skull. Tiamet's body was then dismembered; half of the body was used to create the sky while the other half was used to create human beings, plants, animals, and the creatures that occupy the land today.

Creation of mankind according to the ancient Greeks

In ancient Greece, the predominant creation story was the one that involved the Greek Titan Prometheus, the Titan who created man. In the beginning, the world was endlessly empty and full of a being known as Nyx — the deity of darkness. The goddess Nyx is believed to have laid a golden egg. After sitting on the egg for eons of years, the egg hatched, producing the deity of love Eros. The broken shells of the egg became the sky and the earth. The earth was called Gaia, also known as the goddess of the earth. On the other hand, the sky was called Uranus. The goddess Gaia and the god Uranus mated, bringing forth a new generation of gods known as the titans, Hekatonkheires, Cyclopes, etc. Those Greek Titans included the likes of Oceanus, Crius, Iapetus, Tethys, Phoebe, and Kronus. Kronus, who early on had overthrown his father Uranus, then went on to give birth (with Rhea) to another generation of gods, which included the likes of Hera, Hades, Poseidon, Hestia, Demeter, and Zeus. Similar to the fate that Uranus suffered, Kronus and his siblings were overthrown by his children who were led by Zeus (the King of the Olympians). After the battle with the Titans, Zeus commanded Prometheus and his brother Epimethius to go down to earth and create the first humans. Epimethius created animals. Prometheus grew so fond of his creation — mankind — that he stole fire from the home of the gods and gifted it to mankind. This act of his incurred the wrath of Zeus who bound Prometheus to a stone and allowed an eagle to peck his liver for an eternity.

(Adapted from *worldhistoryedu.com* & *mythencyclopedia.com*)

A6. Assignment

Poster Design

Form **groups of 3 or 4** and **design a poster featuring the creation myths in world history.** You need to:

- Discuss what creation myths should be included;
- Design the layout of the creation myths of different cultures;
- Showcase the symbolic figures of different creation myths;
- Share the poster with your classmates.

Part B Chinese Myths and Legends

B1. Introduction

Ancient Myths and Legends in Chinese Idioms

Chinese idioms, or *chengyu*, can be a proverb, a common saying, an idiomatic phrase or a group of words that convey a figurative meaning beyond the words themselves. Chinese Chengyu mostly came from ancient myths, stories or historical facts. Here are several idioms originated from ancient Chinese myths and folklore legends.

Jingwei filling the sea

According to the ancient work *Shan Hai Jing* (*Classic of the Mountains and Seas*), the youngest and most favored daughter of the Yan emperor was named Nüwa (女娃, meaning "little girl"). The Sun God would go to the East Sea to direct the rising of the sun early in the morning every day and he wouldn't return home till sunset. Nüwa eagerly hoped that her father would take her to the sun-rising place at the East Sea for a look. One day, Nüwa was rowing a small boat by herself toward the East Sea sun-rising spot. Unfortunately, a sea storm came and mountain-like waves capsized the small boat. Nüwa lost her life to the merciless sea.

After she died, Nüwa turned into a bird with red claws and a white beak, vowing to fill up the sea. She would hold stones and tree branches with her beak and throw them into the sea, crying the sound of "jingwei, jingwei...", as if encouraging herself. She kept filling up the sea year after year without stop.

Later, the story of "Jingwei Filling the Sea" became one of the most important Chinese myths. It's widely considered as a symbol of dogged determination and perseverance in the face of seemingly impossible odds.

Kua Fu chasing the sun

In ancient times, there lived a group of mighty giants deep in the forests in the north and Kua Fu was their leader. At that time, the world was desolate and uncultured, infested with vipers and beasts. Kua Fu kept hanging the ferocious snakes he caught on ears for decoration, or grabbed them in hands waving proudly. In a year when the weather was extraordinarily hot, the plants were scorched, the rivers were dried and people were suffering from the intense heat of the sun. Kua Fu swore to catch the sun and tame it to serve for all.

The sun moved fleetingly in the sky, while Kua Fu chased it like wind on the ground.

When he shook off the dusts in his shoes, the dusts became a hill; he used three stones to support his boiler when he was cooking, and the stones later became three mountains. He caught up with the sun finally after nine days and nights. However, the sun was so scorching that he felt thirsty and tired and went to the Yellow River and the Wei River to quench his thirst. But the water from these two rivers was not sufficient to satisfy him and he decided to go to the Great Lake to drink its water. Before he got there he died of thirst on the way.

Before his death, Kua Fu cast his walking stick away, and the place it fell off immediately grew a huge lush peach forest. The forest was flourishing all year round, which provides shades and peaches for the passersby and hard-working people to quench thirst.

The story reflects the strong wish of the ancient Chinese people to overcome drought. Although Kua Fu sacrificed himself, his undying spirit keeps inspiring the Chinese people. The legend of Kua Fu Chasing the Sun was recorded in many ancient books in China. In some places of our country, there are even mountains named "Kuafu Mountain" so as to commemorate him.

Sui drilling wood to make a fire

In the ancient time, people did not know the existence of fire; let alone how to make use of it. When the night came, it was as black as pitch and the cries of the beasts lingered on. People had to stick together, cold and frightened. Since there was no fire, they had to eat raw food, as a result of which they got ill easily and lived a short life.

Fuxi, sympathetic towards people who were suffering, wanted to introduce fire to them. Therefore, he created a thunderstorm in the forest during which the trees were struck by the lightning and started to burn. Very soon, a big fire started in the forest. Greatly frightened by the thunder and the fire, people fled away in all directions.

Later the rain stopped and it grew dark. The ground became wet and cold, forcing the dispersed people to gather again. They were very afraid of the burning trees. At this time, a young man found that the regular cries of beasts were gone. He bravely went to the fireside and suddenly felt it so warm to get close to the fire. People gradually gathered towards the fire. Soon, attracted by the pleasant smell nearby from the burnt animals, they tried some toasted meat and found that they had never tasted such delicious food. It was in that way people discovered the wonderful use of fire. They picked up branches and set them on fire in order to keep it alive. But one day, the fire went out when branches were burned up. Thrown back into darkness and coldness, people felt a pain more acute than before.

Seeing all this in heaven, Fuxi went into the dream of the young man who discovered the use of fire and told him, "In the far west, there was a country called Sui Ming where you could find fire and bring it back." When the young man awakened, he recalled the words of the god in his dream and determined to find fire in the country of Sui Ming. Having undergone many hardships, the young man finally arrived in Sui Ming. Yet to his great disappointment, the place was enveloped in complete darkness, having no light from the sun or the moon, let alone any sign of the existence of fire. The young man had to take a rest under a tree named "Sui Wood".

While sitting under the tree, the young man suddenly sensed flashes in front of him, which lightened the surrounding areas. The young man stood up at once and started to locate its source. Then he found some big birds pecking for worms in the tree with their short and hard beck. Whenever they pecked, sparks would appear on the bark. A method of getting fire suddenly occurred to the young man at the sight of that. He immediately broke some branches of the Sui Wood and used a small branch to drill a bigger one. Sparks really appeared but it did not make a fire. The young man did not lose heart and keep drilling with different branches. Finally, smoke came out and a fire was started. The young man was so excited that tears rolled down his face.

After the young man returned home, he brought with him the fire that would never go out, that is, the method of drilling wood to make a fire. Hence, people did not have to live in coldness and fear. To express their gratitude to the young man, people elected him as their leader and addressed him "Sui" which meant the person who brought the fire.

Yu Gong moved away mountains

In ancient times, there was an old man called Yu Gong who was nearly ninety years old. Right in front of his house stood two high mountains, the Taihang Mountain and the Wangwu Mountain. Since they blocked traffic and caused much inconvenience, Yu Gong decided to move them away. So he called his family together to discuss this issue. His wife expressed her worries and doubts, but everyone else was convinced that they could move the mountains to the sea as long as they worked hard together.

A man named Zhi Sou tried to stop them, saying, "How silly you are! Being old and weak, how can you move the high mountains?" "You're wrong," Yu Gong sighed and said. "Look, my sons can continue my work after my death. Generations after generations and there is no end, but the mountains can't grow higher. Why can't I move them away?"

Yu Gong and his family continued their work unwaveringly, and their story moved the heavenly god. So he sent down two gods and they moved the two mountains away. Later, "Yu Gong Moved Away Mountains" was coined as a saying to show that as long as one devotes himself and works hard enough, nothing is impossible.

The eight immortals cross the sea

"The Eight Immortals Cross the Sea" is one of the wonderful stories about the Eight Immortals. Its vivid record is found in the *Journey to the East* written by Wu Yuantai of the Ming dynasty. This book describes how the Eight Immortals were always ready to defend the weak and helpless, punish evildoers and encourage the good. One day, they went to the Donghai Sea together and saw gigantic turbulent tides and waves. Lü Dongbin suggested that each of them throw one thing into the water in order to show their "magical power" and cross it. All the other immortals agreed with him. They threw their magic articles onto the sea, and then, standing on them, crossed the sea, braving the wind and the waves. Afterwards, people have compared this anecdote to the way that one creates miracles with one's special ability.

(Adapted from *chinahighlights.com*, *visitbeijing.com.cn*, *chinaculture.org.*, *ewccenter.com.* & *daoinfo.org*)

B2. Words and Expressions

Vocabulary

1. supernatural / ˌsuːpə(r)ˈnætʃərəl / *n.* 超自然物;超自然力量
2. cowherd / ˈkaʊhɜːd / *n.* 牧牛者
3. weave / wiːv / *v.* 织;(用……)编成
4. idealism / aɪˈdɪəˌlɪz(ə)m / *n.* 理想主义;唯心主义
5. aesthetic / iːsˈθetɪk / *adj.* 审美的;有审美观点的
6. disparity / dɪˈspærəti / *n.* 差异

中国神话故事	**Chinese Myths and Legends**
《楚辞》	*Songs of Chu*
《搜神记》	*In Search of the Supernatural*
《西游记》	*Journey to the West*
《山海经》	*Classic of Mountains and Seas*
《聊斋志异》	*Strange Tales from a Chinese Studio*
《封神演义》	*Investiture of the Gods*
嫦娥奔月	Chang'e Flying to the Moon
后羿射日	Hou Yi Shooting the Suns
牛郎织女	the Cowherd and the Weaving Maid
八仙过海	the Eight Immortals crossing the sea

哪吒闹海	Nezha Conquers the Dragon King
夸父逐日	Kua Fu chasing the sun
精卫填海	Jingwei filling up the sea
愚公移山	Yu Gong removing mountains
神农尝百草	Shennong tasting herbs
梁山伯与祝英台	Butterfly Lovers
唯心主义的弊端	disadvantages of idealism
真实的历史记录	actual factual recordings of history
内容丰富,类型多样	rich in content and various in type
包含不同的文化元素	encompass different cultural elements
现实意义与艺术色彩	realistic significance and artistic color
世代相承的美学观念	aesthetic concepts that are inherited from generation to generation
最早的文化传承形式	the earliest form of inherited culture
与普通叙述的巨大差异	great disparities from the common narrative
世界秩序与规则的开始	the beginning of world order and rules
远古的浪漫与神秘氛围	the romantic and mysterious atmosphere of ancient times
神话幻想的现实制约性	the realistic constraints of mythical fantasy
数千年的人类生产经验	thousands of years of human production experience
对美好生活的向往和追求	the longing and pursuit for a better life
不能与封建迷信混为一谈	cannot be confused with feudal superstition
人类历史上最早的文化记忆	the earliest cultural memory in human history
历史经验与人类的价值判断	historical experience and the value judgment of the human race
事物的自然化或历史化版本	a euhemerized or a historicized version of things
关注激动人心、动人心弦的故事	focus on exciting and mind-blowing stories
人类最早的幻想性口头文学作品	the earliest fantasy oral literary works of humanity
原始人类的认识和愿望的理想化	idealization of the understanding and desires of primitive humans
构成中国民间宗教的重要组成部分	form a large part of the Chinese folk religion
中国传统文化不可或缺的组成部分	an indispensable component of traditional Chinese culture
一种包括口述、历史遗迹、风俗和文学的文化传统	a great cultural tradition involving oral accounts, historical relics, customs and literature

Vocabulary

1. hereditary / həˈredət(ə)ri / *adj*. 遗传的;遗传性的;世袭的
2. unrelenting / ʌnrɪˈlentɪŋ / *adj*. 持续的;不缓和的
3. unremitting / ʌnrɪˈmɪtɪŋ / *adj*. 不停的;不懈的;持续不断的
4. incarnate / ɪnˈkɑː(r)nət / *v*. 将(概念或品质)具体化;使人格化
5. align / əˈlaɪn / *v*. 排列整齐;使对齐
6. rejuvenation / rɪˌdʒuːvəˈneɪʃn / *n*. 更新;复苏

中国神话故事的当代价值	**Modern Values of Chinese Myths**
传家宝	hereditary treasures
代代相传	pass down from generation to generation
民族团结	national unity
坚守梦想	hold fast to their dreams
鲜明的中国特色	a distinctive Chinese characteristic
积极的文化信仰	a positive cultural faith
不屈不挠的精神	unrelenting spirit
群体意识的反映	a reflection of group consciousness
文化与智慧的载体	carrier of culture and wisdom
对目标的不懈追求	the unremitting quest for a goal
为人类的利益而战	fight for the benefit of mankind
脚踏实地的创造者	down-to-earth creators
中华文化和民族的命脉	the lifeblood of the Chinese culture and nation
体现了集体追梦的精神	embody a spirit of collective dream chasing
每个民族的优秀文化传统	the excellent cultural traditions of each ethnic group
人类构建信仰的重要载体	important carriers for humans to construct their beliefs
展现中国特色和文化自信	showcase Chinese characteristics and cultural confidence
化身众多的文化祖先和英雄	incarnate numerous cultural ancestors and heroes
中华民族当之无愧的文化始祖	a worthy cultural ancestor of the Chinese nation
人类用来自我调节的神圣叙事	holy narratives that human beings use for self-regulation
鼓励各民族共同努力的文化力量	the cultural power encouraging all ethnic groups to work together
为塑造民族特有的文化祖先形象	serve to build the image of cultural ancestors

	unique to the nation
所有民族都珍视的坚不可摧的梦想	an indestructible dream cherished by all ethnicity
深刻影响人们的价值观和精神信仰	profoundly influence people's values and spiritual beliefs
激励中国人民创造和创新的内在力量	the inner power inspiring the Chinese people to create and innovate
揭示性别概念与社会形态之间的关系	uncover relations between gender concepts and social forms
建设繁荣、民主、文明、和谐的中华民族	build a prosperous, democratic, civilized and harmonious Chinese nation
与新时代坚持的社会主义核心价值观高度一致	highly align with core socialist values upheld in the new era
中国人在自己的文化基础上丰富和发展了神	divine creators enriched and developed by the Chinese based on their own culture
融合进取精神、民族精神和对家庭和国家的奉献精神	integrate an enterprising attitude, national spirit and devotion to family and country
一个国家和民族发展中的基础性、深层次和持久性力量	a basic, profound and lasting power in the development of a nation and an ethnic group
对中华民族的伟大复兴产生积极而深远的影响	exert positive, far-reaching impacts on the great rejuvenation of the Chinese nation

Vocabulary

1. capsize / ˈkæpsaɪz / *v.* 倾覆(特指船);翻覆;弄翻
2. merciless / ˈmɜːsɪləs / *adj.* 残忍的,无慈悲心的
3. claw / klɔː / *n.* (动物的)爪,爪子
4. beak / biːk / *n.* 鸟嘴,喙
5. dogged / ˈdɒgɪd / *adj.* 顽强的,坚持不懈的

精卫填海	**The Myth of Jingwei Filling the Sea**
《山海经》	*Classic of the Mountains and Seas*
划着小船	row a small boat
东海日出点	the East Sea sun-rising spot
海上风暴	a sea storm
像山一样高的波浪	mountain-like waves
(船)倾覆	(boat) be capsized

在无情的大海中失去生命	lose one's life to the merciless sea
一只有红色爪子和白色喙的鸟	a bird with red claws and a white beak
用喙衔住石头和树枝	hold stones and tree branches with her beak
把小石子扔进海里	throw pebbles into the sea
顽强的决心和毅力	dogged determination and perseverance
看似不可逾越的困难	seemingly impossible odds

Vocabulary

1. desolate / ˈdesələt / *adj*. 荒无人烟的,荒凉的
2. uncultured / ˌʌnˈkʌltʃəd / *adj*. [农]未耕作的
3. infest / ɪnˈfest / *v*. 骚扰;寄生于;大批出没;大批滋生
4. viper / ˈvaɪpə(r) / *n*. 毒蛇
5. lush / lʌʃ / *adj*. 茂盛的,郁郁葱葱的
6. luxuriant / lʌgˈʒʊriənt / *adj*. 繁茂的,浓密的
7. undying / ʌnˈdaɪɪŋ / *adj*. 永恒的,不朽的

夸父逐日	**Kua Fu Chasing the Sun**
中国最早的著名寓言之一	one of the earliest famous fables in China
一群巨人	a group of mighty giants
荒无人烟的土地	desolate and uncultured land
毒蛇和野兽到处出没	infest with vipers and beasts
把凶猛的蛇挂在耳朵上做装饰	hang the ferocious snakes on ears for decoration
异常炎热的天气	extraordinarily hot weather
烧焦	scorch
太阳的酷热	the intense heat of the sun
发誓要做某事	swear to do sth
捕捉和驯服太阳	catch and tame the sun
像风一样奔跑	run like wind
追上太阳	overtake the sun
飞快地移动	move fleetingly
解渴	to quench one's thirst
一口气把水喝完	drink the water in one breath
耗尽气力	run out of energy
手杖	walking stick
一大片郁郁葱葱的桃林	a huge lush peach forest

枝叶茂密果实累累	luxuriant foliage and rich fruits
歇脚的地方	a resting place
为过路人提供阴凉	provide shades for the passersby
战胜干旱的强烈愿望	the strong wish to overcome drought
不朽的精神	undying spirit

Vocabulary

1. disperse / dɪˈspɜːrs / *v.* 分散;疏散,驱散
2. beckon / ˈbekən / *v.* (招手)示意,召唤
3. ignite / ɪɡˈnaɪt / *v.* 点燃;燃烧
4. chisel / ˈtʃɪz(ə)l / *v.* 雕,刻,凿
5. artificial / ˌɑːtɪˈfɪʃl / *adj.* 人造的,人工的

钻木取火	**Sui Drilling Wood to Make a Fire**
漆黑的	as black as pitch
野兽的叫声久久不散	the cries of the beasts linger on
吃生食	eat raw food
容易生病,寿命短	get ill easily and live a short life
同情的	sympathetic
在森林里制造一场雷雨	create a thunderstorm in the forest
被闪电击中	be struck by the lightning
自然火	natural fire
四散奔逃	flee away in all directions
分散的人	the dispersed people
向人群招手	beckon the crowd
带来明亮和温暖	bring brightness and warmness
来自被烧焦的动物的宜人气味	the pleasant smell from the burnt animals
烤肉	toasted meat
驱散野兽	disperse wild animals
发现火的奇妙用途	discover the wonderful use of fire
让火继续燃烧	keep the fire alive
阻止火苗熄灭	prevent the fire from going out
被扔回黑暗和寒冷	be thrown back into darkness and coldness
比以前更剧烈的痛苦	a pain more acute than before
钻木生火的方法	the method of drilling wood to make a fire

两块石头的碰撞会产生火花	the collision of two stones would produce sparks
点燃枯萎的树叶和草	ignite withered leaves and grass
凿石取火	chisel stones and take fire
人工火的发明	the invention of artificial fire
人类文明的象征	the symbol of human civilization

Vocabulary

1. level / ˈlev(ə)l / *v.* 使平整;推倒,夷平
2. detour / ˈdiːtʊə(r) / *n.* 绕行,迂回
3. progeny / ˈprɑːdʒəni / *n.* 子孙;后裔
4. patriarchy / ˈpeɪtriɑːki / *n.* 父权制;父系社会
5. unwaveringly / ʌnˈweɪvərɪŋli / *adv.* 毫不动摇地
6. reclaim / rɪˈkleɪm / *v.* 要求归还;利用,改造(荒地)

愚公移山	**Yu Gong Moved Away Mountains**
太行山	the Taihang Mountain
王屋山	the Wangwu Mountain
交通堵塞	blocked traffic
带来诸多不便	cause much inconvenience
绕道而行	make big detour
夷平山脉	level the mountains
开荒垦殖	reclaim wasteland for farming
表达担忧和怀疑	express one's worries and doubts
确信;相信	be convinced
子孙,后裔	progeny
父权制;家长统治	patriarchy
努力辛劳	work with backbreaking effort
毫不动摇地	unwaveringly
感动天神	move the heavenly god
消失得无影无踪	disappear without a trace
辽阔的平原	a vast plain
一条平坦的路通向远方	a level road leading to a long distance away
强大的动力	strong motivation
职业道德	work ethic
人定胜天。	Man's will conquers nature.

一切皆有可能。	Nothing is impossible.

Vocabulary

1. tenet / ˈtenɪt / *n*. 原则，信条
2. gigantic / dʒaɪˈgæntɪk / *adj*. 巨大的，庞大的
3. turbulent / ˈtɜːbjələnt / *adj*.（水）湍急的
4. brave / breɪv / *v*. 勇敢面对

八仙过海	**The Eight Immortals Cross the Sea**
道教故事	a Daoist anecdote
一群传说中的道士	a group of legendary Taoists
神仙	god-like immortal beings, or *xian*
通过虔诚和善行实现长生不老	to achieve immortality through devotion and good works
道教的核心原则	a central tenet of Taoism
超越世俗生活的束缚	to transcend the bonds of mortal life
化身为凡人	reincarnate into a mortal form
王母娘娘的“蟠桃宴”	“Peach of Immortality Gathering” hosted by the Queen Mother
腾云驾雾	ride on clouds
不同的法器	different magical instruments
东海	the Donghai Sea / the Eastern Sea
渤海	the Bohai Sea
滔天巨浪	gigantic turbulent tides and waves
乘风破浪	brave the wind and the waves
八仙桌	the Eight Immortals table
明代吴元台的《东游记》	*Journey to the East* written by Wu Yuantai of the Ming dynasty
保护弱小	defend the weak and helpless
惩恶扬善	punish evildoers and encourage the good
内在美德	inherent virtues
赐福于人	bestow / confer blessings on people
起死回生	bring the dead back to life
各显神通	create miracles with one's special ability

B3. Speaking Activities

Story Telling

An international school will hold a culture festival. You are invited to share some ancient **mythological stories and legends** and idioms to a group of young international school pupils. You might tell:

- The myth of Jingwei filling the sea;
- The myth of Kua Fu chasing the sun;
- The story of Sui drilling wood to make a fire;
- The legend of Yu Gong moving away the mountains;
- The story of the eight immortals crossing the sea.

You may refer to the words and expressions in Part B, but don't confine yourself to them. Try to make your story interesting and appealing.

Pair Work

An idiom is a phrase, or a combination of words, that has developed a figurative meaning through frequency of use. Idioms are a staple in many different languages, and are often shared across languages. They can be useful and even fun to use. Most idioms have symbolic meanings and are originated from some mythological stories or folklore legends.

Now work in pairs to complete the following table with the information about the origins of the idioms as well as their symbolic meaning. You may refer to B1 in Part B or search online for more information.

Idiom	Origin	Symbolic Meaning
Jingwei filling the sea		
Kua Fu chasing the sun		
Sui drilling wood to make a fire		
Yu Gong moved away mountains		

Continued

Idiom	Origin	Symbolic Meaning
The eight immortals cross the sea		

Brainstorming

Which idioms above impress you most and why? Please use your life experience or stories to elaborate on it.

Reading and Sharing

A Modern Story of an Old Tale: Yu Gong Moves the Mountains

Mao Xianglin, a village committee in Southwest China's Chongqing Municipality, spent seven years building a road out of the mountains and over the cliffs.

Located in Chongqing's Wushan County, Xiazhuang Village is surrounded by high mountains and cliffs. Twenty-three years ago, the only way out of the village was an ancient road with countless bends, taking villagers at least four days to go out of the village to the town center. Among nearly 400 villagers, half of them had never gone out of the mountains in their lifetime, leading to the poverty and backwardness of this village.

In 1997, Mao, the 38-year-old CPC branch secretary at that time, decided to construct an eight-kilometer road in the mountains with more than 100 villagers. On a winter day, they started to write a new chapter on"Yu Gong Moves the Mountain", a traditional Chinese tale of determination and courage. Together with Mao, villagers worked day and night to make the road, eating and sleeping in the caves. Mao hadn't gone home for three months. Surrounded by steep road walls, it was hard to find a place to stand as the road is far more difficult than imagined to build. Regardless, Mao and the villagers never gave up and changed the fate of an outdated village. Besides building the road, Mao also helped villagers get out of poverty by providing fruit planting training. Now, he has a bigger dream: to develop rural tourism in Xiazhuang and double the area's income.

(Adapted from *People's Daily*)

Ideas for sharing

- Why is Mao called a modern version of Yu Gong?
- What are the valuable virtues college students can learn from Yu Gong?

Interpretation

Interpret the paragraphs below into English with the words and expressions you learned in Part B.

Paragraph 1

盘古开天地、女娲造人、夸父逐日、精卫填海……一个个脍炙人口的故事以其磅礴的气度和恢宏的格局久久激荡人心。哪吒闹海、八仙过海、柳毅传书……一个个耳熟能详的传说体现了古人的智慧与旨趣,又兼备现实意义与艺术色彩。

Paragraph 2

随着神话的流传与后世的加工,神话故事作为文学艺术中的一种创作题材,逐渐成为中国传统文化不可或缺的组成部分。如嫦娥奔月的故事,后羿与嫦娥天各一方的结局打破了传统的大团圆模式,给文学创作提供了更多的可能性并拓展了更广阔的想象空间。而由故事衍生的蟾宫折桂的意象经久不衰,体现远古的浪漫与神秘氛围。在后世文人的书写中,故事里原本的“蟾蜍”变为了“玉兔”,呈现了世代相承的美学观念,凸显美的价值。

Paragraph 3

很久以前,愚公家的门口有两座山,一座山叫太行,另一座山叫王屋。愚公每天进出家里都要绕很远的路。有一天,愚公对家人说:“我们一起把挡在门口的两座大山移开,好不好?”儿子和孙子一听,都点头赞成。第二天,愚公和他的儿子孙子一起到山边开始挖。有一个名叫智叟的邻居嘲笑他们说:“就算到你死掉的那一天,也不可能把大山移开的!”愚公听了笑笑说:“我虽然很老,我还有儿子;儿子还会生孙子,孙子还会再生儿子,我们的子子孙孙可以一直搬下去,总有一天我们会把这两座山搬走的!”智叟只好走开了。后来,天神听说了这件事,派了两个神仙去把王屋山与太行山背走,放到别的地方去,不再挡在愚公家门口了。愚公移山表现了中国古代劳动人民的信心和毅力,说明了要克服困难就必须坚持不懈的道理。

B4. Culture Highlights

Q: *What is cultivation or Xiuxing in Chinese mythology? Is it true that everything has the possibility to become immortal through cultivation?*

A: Cultivation is a Taoism religion term, which includes two practical phases, *Xiuzhen* and *Xiuxian*. *Xiuzhen* is to practice one's mind and spirit, find the true self and pursue the final truth of the universe. *Xiuxian* is the process of pursuing immortality, usually after the *Xiuzhen* process.

In mythology, cultivation is a person or a creature obtaining immortality and mystical power in certain auspicious places, through physical practices (such as breathing exercises), taking elixirs from special alchemy, or doing good deeds.
In Chinese mythology, everything in the universe has the possibility to gain supernatural power and become immortals.

- **Human.** Those who have made great contributions to human kind, or who had completed orthodox cultivations, would have the chances to fly up to the sky and transform into immortals, such as many Prehistoric Kings.
- **Animal.** Besides mythical creatures, some ordinary animals, such as snakes and foxes, can turn into human or celestial beings, if they went through arduous cultivations, and did extremely contributive activities (like having saved people's lives), or ran into a lucky opportunity.
- **Plants.** Plants have their own wills, and those growing blessed mystical places can absorb nimbus, and obtain different superpowers.

However, after having gained supernatural power, every immortal should behave with high moral standards; otherwise, they would lose everything. Therefore, they usually focus on further practicing in beautiful wonderlands, travelling around the world, and helping humans when it's necessary.
(Adapted from *chinafetching.com*)

Q: *What are the top 10 mythical creatures in Chinese mythology?*
A: Here is a list of the top 10 mythical beasts in Chinese mythology:

- *Loong*, or Chinese dragons are very common legendary creatures in Chinese folklore. It traditionally stands for mighty and auspicious powers, particularly control over water and rainfall. It is also a symbol of good fortune and sign of intense power; hence the emperor of China usually used it as a symbol of his imperial power.
- *Pixiu* can swallow everything without letting anything out, so it is a symbol of bringing wealth from all directions. It can also drive evils away and bring in good luck. In ancient China it is also believed to be a kind of "Fierce Beast" and used as a term for brave troops.
- In Chinese myth *Baize* is a kind of snow white creature living in Kunlun Mountains and is able to speak human language. It can comprehend the nature of all living things. This mythical creature is rarely spotted unless the nation is governed by a wise king.

- *Kui* is a one-legged ox beast in Chinese mythology. It was born in the Liubo Mountain on East China Sea and looks like a cow with grey body. When the storm is yet to come, its body will shine like sunlight and its roar like thunder. The Yellow emperor used its fur to make drum and the drumbeat could be heard five hundred li away.
- *Feng Huang*, or Phoenix, is one of the four famous Chinese mythical creatures. It symbolizes sun, warmth, summer and harvest. It is said to be born of fire and is considered the emperor of all birds. A pair of male and female *Feng Huang* together is the symbol of everlasting love. It is also the emblem of the Empress of China.
- *Qilin* is a mythical Chinese creature known in lots of East Asian cultures, and is believed to emerge when a wise sage or an illustrious king arrives or passes away. It can breathe fire to punish the wicked.
- *Xiezhi* is described as somewhat like a unicorn and a dragon which has high intelligence and can judge between right and wrong and wipe out the wicked by biting or goring them.
- *Hou* looks like a lion with 2 long ears and can roars very loudly. It is said to be the son of Dragon King. Sitting high on a carved column, this creature transmits the voice from the heaven and reflects the messages from the people.
- *Bifang* is a mythical bird. It looks like a crane which owns red marking, white beak, and has only one foot. This creature does not eat grains but flames. Its appearance is a signal of big fire.
- *Taotie* is a mysterious monster in Chinese culture. The monster was very greedy and would eat anything within its sight and even ate its own body, so its image is just a big head and a big mouth without body. Thc *Taotie* ate too much and died as a result, and then it became a symbol of greedy people.

(Adapted from *chinawhisper.com*)

B5. Extensive Reading

Passage One

Must-Read Books of Chinese Mythology

Giving a general overview Chinese mythology and folkloric tradition is nearly impossible because Chinese culture is simply too vast, too complicated, with too many little offshoots and alternating viewpoints all fighting for prominence. Each mythological system comes with its own unique highlights and fascinating characters and stories, making each and every system indispensable, because no matter how much groups throughout China's history have tried to clamp down on other traditions, religions, or mythologies, ultimately cultures and stories cannot be destroyed so long as they genuinely hold the fondness and interest of the people. I will introduce some landmark works of literature that have helped various traditions and tales maintain popularity and longevity.

Journey to the West

If there is one work of Chinese mythology you should know, then it absolutely has to be *Journey to the West*. This is the work of Chinese mythology and literature. Published anonymously in the 1590s of Ming dynasty China (but attributed these days to the scholar Wu Cheng'en), it is one of China's Four Great Classical Novels.

The story is very simple: a Buddhist monk, Xuanzang, makes a long and arduous journey to India in order to receive valuable Buddhist scriptures so he can bring them back to China, translate them, and spread Buddhism. This is, in fact, historical: It is based on the real historical figure of Xuanzang, who did exactly this during the 7th century.

But what the story adds is mythology, and everything becomes much, much more exciting. In the world of *Journey to the West*, gods and Buddhas are very involved in the affairs of humans — as are demons and monsters. So, to help protect Xuanzang on the dangerous journey to the west (roll credits!), the bodhisattva Guanyin sends him three disciples to protect him — monks are peaceful and do not know much about fighting, after all.

And only now do we really get to the protagonist of the story — Sun Wukong, the Monkey King. The first seven chapters (of 100 chapters total, and 1,800 pages in the English translation — whew) focus entirely on Sun Wukong's backstory, where he progresses from a monkey born out of a stone egg, to learning immortality and Daoist magical techniques, to his meteoric rise as a formidable, untameable, mischievous, destructive, immensely powerful immortal being. He causes great chaos in the Heavens, challenging all the gods, and at last he is subdued by Buddha and is trapped under the weight of an entire mountain. The monk Xuanzang rescues him by the decree of the bodhisattva Guanyin, and the story then progresses in a very serial, formulaic fashion describing 81 adventures (or tribulations) that Sun Wukong, his master, and his fellow disciples face on their journey to India, usually with Sun Wukong as the hero in fights against various demons, spirits, devils, and monsters that attempt to capture, eat, and/or kill them.

Journey to the West is at once humorous adventure story, satire of Ming dynasty society, folk religion tale, and moralistic allegory. It is steeped in a mixture of Daoism, Buddhism, and Confucianism, reflecting the man religions that flourished in China during the 16th century. The characters are colorful, powerful, and always entertaining, and it paints a fascinating picture of a world where the gods of three religions coexist in harmony, where the world is a lawless place where demons and monsters roam free outside the safety of civilization, where fantastical spells, beings, and events are always going on right under your nose.

Investiture of the Gods

Investiture of the Gods, also known as *Fengshen Bang*, *Fengshen Yanyi*, or *Creation of the Gods*, is like *Journey to the West* a 16th-century novel and perhaps second only to *Journey to the West* in fame as a novel of the gods and demons genre. Also set historically, but far more back than *Journey to the West*, this novel is set during the fall of the Shang dynasty around 1000 BCE.

This story, full of heroes, gods, immortals, spirits, and demons, tells of the overthrowing of King Zhou by Ji Fa. It mixes history with mythology, making King Zhou's concubine Daji a fox spirit, and having battles call upon supernatural beings to assist them. In the grand, sweeping struggles that occur, heroes are forged, and when the fall, they are inducted to Heaven as gods, thus the title of the novel.

Though more firmly Daoist in its mythology than *Journey to the West*, this novel likewise acknowledges the influence of all the religions of China (even though none of them had begun yet at the time the story is set). Ultimately, there are no true heroes or villains in *Investiture of the Gods*, one point which makes it very interesting and a different take from many other mythological novels of gods and demons. Some felt loyalty to their king, and others felt duty to Heaven; and in the end, everyone, god or demon, is simply following the will of Heaven.

Classic of Mountains and Seas

The Classic of Mountains and Seas, or *Shan Hai Jing*, is an ancient text that may have been written around the Warring States period and the start of the Han dynasty, around 400 BCE-200 BCE. This book is quite different from the previous two we've covered: rather than being a work of fiction, a story, it is instead a geography, a guide to the various flora and fauna of China.

One would think a geographic guide would be dull, but it is not at all: the text is full of incredibly strange and impossible creatures. A fish like a chicken with three tails, four heads, and six feet that stabilizes one's mind; a snake with one head and two bodies that is an omen of oncoming drought; and so on. Interspersed with these fantastical descriptions are also incredibly mundane descriptions of various mountains, wood, minerals, and other normal geographic content, and even the mythological aspects, and the sometimes short myths that accompany a particularly interesting creature or monster, are told in a very matter-of-fact, dry manner.

If you want to read this text, treat it as the reference material it is: I don't mean that you should believe its contents are true, but that it is a slow read, and like most reference material, read a page or so at a time, or skip to what sounds interesting. The wonder in reading it is that it almost feels like discovering these fantastical creatures for yourself, hidden among the mundanity of the real world. And isn't a little bit of wonder what we all want to find?

Strange Tales from a Chinese Studio

Now, let's fast-forward a millennium to 1740 — finally, our first actual publication date! Written by Pu Songling, a Qing dynasty scholar and writer, the *Liaozhai zhiyi* is a collection of almost five hundred mini stories of fantastical, supernatural happenings. All original and devised by Pu Songling, but heavily steeped in folklore — full to the brim with fox spirits, demons, resentful ghosts, eccentric Daoists, and mysterious creatures.

Strange Tales from a Chinese Studio is in the genre of zhiguai xiaoshuo, meaning "tales of the strange." Each tale is usually only a couple pages long, some even only a paragraph in length. Some are jokes, or silly little happenings, while others have a moralistic tone to them. Many of the tales subtly criticize or satirize society, particularly the bureaucracy that overwhelmed the Qing dynasty. Like Classic of Mountains and Seas, the stories are told quite matter-of-factly. Unlike the first two novels I have covered, *Journey to the West* and *Investiture of the Gods*, the setting of the stories here are much more down to earth, with the characters often being simple farmers, merchants, scholars, and other civilians going about their day-to-day business before being thrown into a strange situation: a seductive girl knocking at the door, a gruesome ghost in the middle of the night, a Daoist on the street promising miracles.

Strange Tales from a Chinese Studio captures the horror, humour, love, loss, mundanity, wonder, all in one novel and hundreds of little stories, and present Chinese folklore in its true, natural setting: among the common people, among the lives of people simply going about their day.

(Adapted from *newhanfu.com*)

Passage Two

Interesting Facts About Chinese Mythology

China is one mythical place that is rich in history and some of the most intriguing cultural and societal beliefs, but even more astonishing of what Chinese cultures have to offer is the Chinese Mythology. Some of the most interesting stories about historical beings, unicorns, dragons, and even gods and goddesses often have roots in Chinese Mythology. So, this article takes you through everything you need to know about Chinese mythology and why they are an important part of Chinese culture. Let's jump right to it!

Mythological Chinese meaning

Chinese mythology can be defined as mythology passed down through oral or written/recorded literature in specific areas of the world, but in this case, recorded in China. Notably, China boasts rich cultures and traditions, which is why it doesn't come as a surprise to learn that China has quite a bit to offer in terms of mythology.

It's important to note that Chinese mythology encompasses different cultural elements as well as varied myths from different regions and even cultural traditions. A huge chunk of Chinese mythology is, however, focused on exciting and mind-blowing stories around fantastic people and magical beings. There is also the use of magical powers to a rather large extent, and especially around creatures/beings and events taking place in different exotic and mythical places at different times.

And just like other mythologies from around the world, Chinese mythology has been believed widely in the past as actual factual recordings of history. Alongside Chinese folklore, the mythologies all form a large part of the Chinese folk religion.

It's important to note, however, that many of the stories around the events and the characters of the distant past tend to have what is called a double tradition — this is the tradition that presents more of a euhemerized or a historicized version of things, and one that comes off as more of a mythological version of things. Most of the myths in Chinese mythology tend to involve creation stories and the universe's cosmology, along with the different deities and inhabitants from the past days. Some of these mythological stories also involve creation myths, as well as the origin of people, cultures, and things, and even the origin of the Chinese state. And while most of these myths are seen in the actual present chronology of prehistoric times, a number of them involve specific culture heroes that taught people different things or were an ancestor of a certain dynasty family or ethnic group.

The other notable thing about Chinese mythology is the fact that most of the time, Chinese mythology is tied to some ritual acts like ceremonies, dances, and even sacrifices.

Chinese mythology history

As mentioned above, Chinese mythology is more or less a collection of cultural history, religious traditions, and folktales that have been passed down generations for centuries in either written or oral forms. But never stopped to think about the history of Chinese mythology.

Well, for the most part, Chinese mythology stems from general concerns around morality and societal issues, and they inform individuals about their cultures and values; and there are some factual recordings pointing to the source of these stories.

A huge chunk of the Chinese myths is said to originate from around the 12th century BCE, and for over 1000 years, they were transmitted orally before the first recordings of these myths in books like *Shan Hai Jing* and *Shui Jing Zhu*. These are the early works that are pretty much the sources of the Chinese myths that are shared today. The book *Shan Hai Jing* or the *Mountain and Sea Scroll* lay out different details about myths, religion, and witchcraft across Ancient China while also going into great detail on matters like the records of China's geography, including seas, mountains. The book also covers things like medicine, history, customs, as well as the ethnicities of ancient times. It is, therefore, known as China's early encyclopedia. Then you have the *Shui Jing Zhu* or the *Commentaries on the Water Scroll* that has geographical and historical records, as well as records of legends.

The other book is the *Hei'an Zhuan* or *the Epic of Darkness* that is a collection of legends in their epic form as preserved by the Han. There are other documents and also philosophical canons like the *Shiji*, *Shangshu*, *Lushi Chunqiu*, and *Liji* that details legends, heroes, and Chinese cultures.

Most of the Chinese mythology, along with the main belief systems, stem from Buddhism, Taoism, and Confucianism. It's evident that the elements of the pre-existing mythology have been adapted into teachings and these belief systems. An example is a Taoist belief that spiritual paradise would be incorporated into mythology as a place where the deities and immortals dwell. Then you have the different myths that tend to glorify the benevolent rulers of the past — the 3 August Ones and 5 emperors — and these became an important part of the political philosophies for Confucianism.

(Adapted from *sonofchina.com*)

B6. Assignment

Idiom Sharing

There are many idioms originated from Chinese mythology or folklore legends in addition to the ones listed in Part B. Form **groups of 3 or 4** and share other idioms originated from mythology and their stories. You need to:

- Identify idioms originated from mythology or folklore legends;
- Illustrate their origins, meanings and significance of these idioms in English;
- Share the idioms and the stories with your classmates.

References

Amanda Penn. (2019). Creation Myths: How They're Similar Around the World. *Shortform*. Retrieved from https://www.shortform.com/blog/creation-myth/ on June 27th, 2022.

Callison Hopkins. (2022). The Importance of Myth and Legend in China. *Study*. Retrieved from https://study.com/academy/lesson/chinese-legends-myths.html on July 5th, 2022.

Charles H. Long. (2016). Creation Myths — Nature and Significance. *Britannica*. Retrieved from https://www.britannica.com/topic/creation-myth on June 30th, 2022.

Dani Rhys. (2020). Nüwa — The Great Mother of Humans. *Symbolsage*. Retrieved from https://symbolsage.com/Nüwa-chinese-mythology/ on June 29th, 2022.

Editors of CGTN. (2022). What Is China Doing to Pass on Its Traditional Culture? *CGTN.com*. Retrieved from https://www.cgtn.com/how-china-works/feature/What-is-China-doing-to-pass-on-its-traditional-culture.html on July 1st, 2022.

Editors of Consumer Guide "Meaning of Taoism". (2007). The Taoist Story of Creation. *howstuffworks*. Retrieved from https://people.howstuffworks.com/meaning-of-taoism.html on June 22th, 2022.

Editors of Damien at Hope. (2022). Creation Myths: From Chaos, Ex nihilo, Earth-Diver, Emergence, World Egg, and World Parent. *Slife.org*. Retrieved from https://slife.org/creation-myth/ on June 23th, 2022.

Editors of newworldencyclopedia.org. (2017). Chinese Mythology. *New World Encyclopedia*. Retrieved from https://www.newworldencyclopedia.org/entry/Chinese_mythology on July 9th, 2022.

Editors of newhanfu. com. (2022). 6 Must-Read Books of Chinese Mythology. *Newhanfu.com*. Retrieved from https://www. newhanfu. com/39163. html on July 10th, 2022.

Editors of People's daily. (2023). A Modern Story of an Old Tale: Yu Gong Moves the Mountains. *People's Daily*. Retrieved from https://peoplesdaily. pdnews. cn/china/a-modern-story-of-an-old-tale-yugong-moves-the-mountains-184681.html on Feb. 5, 2023.

Editors of South China Morning Post. (2023). Cultural Power not a Suit and Tie: Hanfu Traditional Fashion Revival Strengthens, Even as China's Economy Slows. *scmp. com*. Retrieved from https://www. scmp. com/news/people-culture/trending-china/article/3190171/cultural-power-not-suit-and-tie-hanfu on Feb. 5, 2023.

Editors of worldhistoryedu.com. (2022). 13 Creation Myths in World History. *World History Edu*. Retrieved from https://www.worldhistoryedu.com/creation-myths-from-around-the-world on June 20th, 2022.

Ellie Crystal. (2019). Chinese Creation Myths. *Crystalinks. com*. Retrieved from https://www.crystalinks.com/chinacreation.html on June 25th, 2022.

Mandy Tie. (2020). The 7 Most Fascinating Chinese Myths and Legends. *Culture trip*. Retrieved from https://theculturetrip. com/asia/china/articles/7-fascinating-chinese-myths-and-legends on July 4th, 2022.

Mike Greenberg. (2020). Pan Gu: The Giant Who Created the Earth. *Mythology Source*. Retrieved from https://mythologysource. com/pangu-chinese-giant/ on June 26th, 2022.

Mike Greenberg. (2023). Who Are China's Eight Immortals? *Mythology Source*. Retrieved from https://mythologysource. com/chinas-eight-immortals/ on Feb. 5, 2023.

Myth of Jingwei Filling the Sea. (2023). *Made in China*. Retrieved from https://resources. made-in-china. com/article/culture-life/KQtnkOsGOmIi/Myth-of-Jingwei-Filling-the-Sea/on Feb. 5, 2023.

Kua Fu Chasing the Sun. (2023). *Beijing Tourism*. Retrieved from https://english. visitbeijing. com. cn/article/47ON6Q1bHQg #: ~: text = Kua% 20Fu% 20Chasing% 20the% 20Sun% 20is% 20one% 20of, the% 20north% 20and% 20Kua% 20Fu% 20was% 20their%20leader on Feb. 5, 2023.

Wang Xianzhao. (2018). Chinese Mythology Mirrors Nation's Unrelenting Spirit. *CSST*. Retrieved from http://www.csstoday.com/Item/6129.aspx on July 5th, 2022.

Yelang. (2021). 9 Interesting Facts About Chinese Mythology-Open Your Eyes. *Son of China*. Retrieved from https://sonofchina.com/what-is-chinese-mythology-all-about on July 7th, 2022.

Sui Drilling Wood to Make a Fire. (2023). *Chinaculture.org*. Retrieved from http://en.chinaculture.org/2014-12/30/content_589802.htm on Feb. 5, 2023.